One-Skein Wonders
for Babies

One-Skein Wonders for Babies

Edited by
Judith Durant

Photography by Geneve Hoffman

Storey Publishing

The mission of Storey Publishing is to serve our customers by
publishing practical information that encourages
personal independence in harmony with the environment.

Edited by Melinda A. Slaving and Gwen Steege
Art direction and book design by Mary Winkelman Velgos
Text production by Michaela Jebb
Indexed by Christine R. Lindemer, Boston Road Communications
Tech edit by Edie Eckman

Cover and interior photography by © Geneve Hoffman Photography, except pages 1, 9,
    49, 107, 123, 135, 169, 181, 201, 217, and 251 by Mary Winkelman Velgos
Set design by Geneve Hoffman
Wardrobe styling by Wendy Freedman
Illustrations by Alison Kolesar, 192, 221, 243, 246, and glossary; Ilona Sherratt, pattern
    schematics; Mary Winkelman Velgos, inside cover
Charts by Edie Eckman

Storey Publishing
210 MASS MoCA Way
North Adams, MA 01247
www.storey.com

Printed in China by Toppan Leefung Printing Ltd.
10 9 8 7 6 5 4 3 2 1

Library of Congress Cataloging-in-Publication Data
One-skein wonders for babies / edited by Judith Durant.
     pages cm
  ISBN 978-1-61212-480-3 (pbk. : alk. paper)
  ISBN 978-1-61212-481-0 (ebook) 1. Knitting—Patterns. 2. Infants' clothing. I. Durant, Judith, 1955–
TT825.O544 2015
746.43'20432—dc23
                            2015010744

CONTENTS

Little Toys ... 217

Little Miscellany ... 251

INTRODUCTION

Welcome to the seventh book in our One-Skein Wonders series! This edition focuses on little ones, and what a joy it is to share these delightful projects with you. Whether you want to knit for a newborn, a toddler, a young child, or even a mother, you'll find something here. We've arranged the projects into categories, including tops, bottoms, bootees, hats, blankets, toys, and more.

Birthday Baby by Melissa Morgan-Oakes (page 46) is a lovely sweater and hat ensemble for a newborn. And Sleeveless Baby Tees by Gail Gelin (page 50) are both practical and cute. Baby Gansey Crossover Coat by Deborah Hess (page 94) will place your three-to-six-month-old on a list of most fashionable babies. If you like good-old practical things, check out the Old-School Baby Soaker by Diana Foster (page 112). Keep heads of many sizes warm and stylish with the collection of more than two-dozen hats, including the Cutie Pie Baby Hat by Anita Grahn (146), Hootenanny Hat of Owls by Anna Smegal (page 159), and even an Infant Crown by Marcia J. Sommerkamp (page 158). There are eight blankets to choose from, ranging from the lacy Falling Leaves Baby Blankie by Myrna A. I. Stahman (page 203), to the Four-Squared Stroller Blanket by Liz Nields (page 205) in which squares are connected as you knit, to the vibrant Colorful Carriage Blanket by Gwen Steege (page 208) that's made with a series of hexagons. Our assortment of toys can help provide your little one with many hours of amusement, from making noise with Baby Rattles by Lynn M. Wilson (page 237), to moving the articulated arms of Toot the Bunny by Noël Margaret (page 220), to imagining deep-sea adventures with Lovey the Octopus by Rachel Henry (page 232). To help stay organized, check out the Bath Toy Hammock by Kathy Sasser (page 255). And after all that new moms go through in a day, my Mom's Stress Reducer (page 267) may be just what the doctor ordered.

Knitting for little ones requires some special considerations, and you'll find tips for success and safety scattered throughout the book. And remember: there is no such thing as the one-skein police. If you love a yarn that would be perfect for a project requiring 100 grams but it comes in 50-gram balls, go ahead and buy two!

Knit on,

Judith Durant

Little

ENSEMBLES

Smocked Mittens and Hat

Designed by Terry Liann Morris, The Sailing Knitter

A touch of smocking worked over lace and a matching topknot flower give this hat and mitten set a feminine touch for that special little girl. One skein of yarn makes both the hat and the matching mittens to fit a toddler.

SIZE AND FINISHED MEASUREMENTS

To fit 1–2 years: 14½"/37 cm hat circumference; 5½"/14 cm mitten circumference

YARN

Blue Moon Fiber Arts Socks That Rock light weight, 100% superwash merino wool, 360 yds (329 m)/4.5 oz (128 g), Peaseblossom **[1]**

NEEDLES

Set of four or five US 1 (2.25 mm) double-point needles and US 1 (2.25 mm) circular needle 16"/40 cm long *or size needed to obtain correct gauge*

GAUGE

32 stitches and 44 rows = 4"/10 cm in stockinette stitch

OTHER SUPPLIES

Stitch markers, scrap yarn for holders, yarn needle

SPECIAL ABBREVIATIONS

STW 5 (smocking triple wrap 5)

K5; bring yarn to front, slip last 5 stitches knitted back to left needle, bring yarn to back, slip 5 stitches back to right needle, slightly tighten yarn to pull the 5 stitches into the space of 3 stitches; one wrap completed. Repeat wrap two more times. Bring yarn behind 5 stitches to continue.

s2kp

Slip 2, knit 1, pass the 2 slipped stitches over the knit stitch.

Pattern Essentials

SMOCKED LACE

(begin with multiple of 12 stitches)

Round 1: *K1, yo, k2, p2, s2kp, p2, k2, yo; repeat from * to end of round.

Round 2: *K4, p2, k1, p2, k3; repeat from * to end of round.

Round 3: *K1, yo, p1, k2, p1, s2kp, p1, k2, p1, yo; repeat from * to end of round.

Round 4: *K1, p2, k2, p1, k1, p1, k2, p2; repeat from * to end of round.

Round 5: *K1, yo, p2, k2, s2kp, k2, p2, yo; repeat from * to end of round.

Round 6: *K2, p2, STW 5, p2, k1; repeat from * to end of round.

Round 7: *K1, p3, ssk, k1, k2tog, p3; repeat from * to end of round.

Round 8: *k1, p3, s2kp, p3; repeat from * to end of round.

KNITTING THE HAT

- On circular needle, cast on 228 stitches. Place marker and join to knit in the round, being careful not to twist the stitches.

- Following the chart on page 13 or line-by-line instructions above right, work Rounds 1 through 8 of Smocked Lace pattern. You will have 190 stitches after Round 7 and 152 stitches after Round 8.

- **Decrease Round:** *P2tog, p7, p2tog, p8; repeat from * to end of round. *You now have* 136 stitches.

- **Next Round:** *K1, p1; repeat from * to end of round.

- Repeat this round until ribbing measures 1¼"/3 cm.

- Work in stockinette stitch (knit every round) until hat measures 5"/12.5 cm from cast-on edge.

Decreasing for the Crown

Note: Change to double-point needles when necessary as stitch count decreases.

- **Round 1:** *K15, k2tog, repeat from * to end of round. *You now have* 128 stitches.

- **Round 2:** Knit.

- **Round 3:** *K14, k2tog, repeat from * to end of round. *You now have* 120 stitches.

- **Round 4:** Knit.

- Continue in this manner, knitting one fewer stitch before the decreases each time and knitting one round even between the decrease rounds, until you have 56 stitches.

- Work decrease round every round until you have 16 stitches.

- **Next Round:** *K2tog; repeat from * to end of round. *You now have* 8 stitches.

- **Last Round:** *K2tog; repeat from * to end of round. *You now have* 4 stitches.

- Place 4 stitches on one double-point needle and work I-cord (see page 277) for 1¾"/4.5 cm. Cut yarn leaving an 8"/20.5 cm tail. Thread tail on yarn needle and draw through 4 stitches. Pull up snug and fasten off.

The Flower Topper

- Cast on 60 stitches. Divide evenly onto double-point needles and join into a round, being careful not to twist the stitches. Work Rounds 1–8 of Smocked Lace pattern. *You now have* 40 stitches.
- Round 1: *K2tog; repeat from * to end of round. *You now have* 20 stitches.
- Round 2: Knit.
- Round 3: *K2tog; repeat from * to end of round. *You now have* 10 stitches.
- Round 4: *K2tog; repeat from * to end of round. *You now have* 5 stitches.
- Cut yarn leaving a 10"/25.5 cm tail. Thread tail onto yarn needle and draw through 5 stitches. Do not gather together snugly, do not fasten off.

Finishing

- Insert I-cord through the center hole of the flower. Pull yarn tail on flower tightly around base of I-cord. Using yarn tail, place several stitches to secure flower to tail, then take tail to inside of hat and tack the flower petals to hat ½"/13 mm from center. Tie an overhand knot in the I-cord. Weave in all ends. Block.

KNITTING THE MITTENS (make 2)

- Loosely cast on 72 stitches. Divide evenly onto double-point needles and join into a round, being careful not to twist the stitches. Work Rounds 1 through 8 of Smocked Lace pattern. You will have 60 stitches at the end of Round 7 and 48 stitches at the end of Round 8.
- Decrease Round: *P2tog, p10; repeat from * to end of round. *You now have* 44 stitches.
- Next Round: *K1, p1; repeat from * to end of round.
- Repeat this round until ribbing measures 1¼"/3 cm.

The Thumb Gusset

- Round 1: M1R, knit to end of round. *You now have* 45 stitches.
- Round 2: K22, pm, k1, pm, knit to end of round.
- Round 3: Knit.
- Round 4: Knit to marker, sm, M1R, k1, M1L, sm, knit to end of round. *You now have* 47 stitches.
- Rounds 5 and 6: Knit.
- Repeat rounds 4 through 6 six more times. *You now have* 15 stitches between the markers and 59 stitches total.
- Next Round: Knit to marker, remove marker, place 15 thumb gusset stitches on scrap yarn to hold; remove marker, tug yarn tightly across the gap and knit to end of round. *You now have* 44 stitches on the needles.

- **Next Round:** K22, M1R in the gap, knit to end of round. *You now have 45 stitches.*
- Work in stockinette stitch (knit every round) until stockinette area measures 3"/7.5 cm.

Decreasing for Top

- **Round 1:** K2tog, knit to end of round. *You now have 44 sts.*
- **Round 2:** *K9, k2tog; repeat from * to end of round. *You now have 40 stitches.*
- **Round 3:** Knit.
- **Round 4:** *K8, k2tog; repeat from * to end of round. *You now have 36 stitches.*
- **Round 5:** Knit.
- **Round 6:** *K7, k2tog; repeat from * to end of round. *You now have 32 stitches.*
- **Round 7:** Knit.
- **Round 8:** *K6, k2tog; repeat from * to end of round. *You now have 28 stitches.*
- **Round 9:** *K5, k2tog; repeat from * to end of round. *You now have 24 stitches.*
- **Round 10:** *K4, k2tog; repeat from * to end of round. *You now have 20 stitches.*
- **Round 11:** *K3, k2tog; repeat from * to end of round. *You now have 16 stitches.*
- **Round 12:** *K2, k2tog; repeat from * to end of round. *You now have 12 stitches.*
- **Round 13:** *K1, k2tog; repeat from * to end of round. *You now have 8 stitches.*
- **Round 14:** *K2tog; repeat from * to end of round. *You now have 4 stitches.*
- Cut yarn leaving an 8"/20.5 cm tail. Thread tail onto yarn needle and draw through 4 stitches. Pull up snug and fasten off.

The Thumb

- **Set-Up Round:** Distribute 15 held stitches evenly onto 3 double-point needles. Join yarn at thumb/hand gap

and k15, M1R in gap. You now have 16 stitches. Join to knit in the round.

- **Rounds 1–8:** Knit.
- **Round 9:** (K3, k2tog) twice, k4, k2tog. *You now have 13 stitches.*
- **Round 10:** Knit.
- **Round 11:** (K2, k2tog) twice, k3, k2tog. *You now have 10 stitches.*
- **Round 12:** (K1, k2tog) twice, k2, k2tog. *You now have 7 stitches.*
- **Round 13:** (K2tog) twice, k1, k2tog. *You now have 4 stitches.*
- Finish as for top. Weave in ends.

Smocked Lace

12-stitch repeat

☐ knit

▪ purl

○ yo

s2kp

ssk

k2tog

STW 5 (see page 10)

Spring Showers

Designed by Alice Curtis

Cool blue ruffles bedewed with beads flow from the cuff of these unabashedly girly little socks and matching hat. They'll be the perfect complement to a pretty spring frock. Both hat and socks are knit flat and seamed.

SIZE AND FINISHED MEASUREMENTS

To fit 6–9 months: 17"/43 cm hat circumference, 6½"/16.5 cm hat height; 4¾"/12 cm foot circumference, 4¾"/12 cm foot length

Note: Hat is loose fitting

YARN

Madelinetosh Tosh Sock, 100% superwash merino wool, 395 yds (361 m)/3.5 oz (100 g), Bloomsbury **❶**

NEEDLES

US 0 (2.0 mm) and US 1 (2.25 mm) straight needles *or size needed to obtain correct gauge*

GAUGE

34 stitches and 44 rows = 4"/10 cm in stockinette stitch on US 0 needles (socks)

30 stitches and 40 rows = 4"/10 cm in stockinette stitch on US 1 needles (hat)

OTHER SUPPLIES

24 g size 6/0 Czech aqua glass beads, big eye beading needle, US 14 (0.75 mm) steel crochet hook, stitch holders or scrap yarn, stitch markers, straight pins, US F/5 (3.75 mm) crochet hook

SPECIAL ABBREVIATIONS

PB (place bead)
    Slip the stitch just knitted back to the left needle, pick up a bead with the small crochet hook, catch the stitch with the hook, and slide the bead off the hook and onto the stitch. Slip the stitch back to the right needle.

ssp (slip, slip, purl)
    Slip 1 knitwise, slip 1 knitwise, slide 2 stitches back to left needle and purl them together through the back loops.

Pattern Essentials

BEADED FERN LACE
(multiple of 9 + 4 stitches)

Row 1 (RS): Slip 1 purlwise with yarn on WS, k2, PB, yo, k2, ssk, PB, k2tog, k2, yo, *k1, PB, yo, k2, ssk, PB, k2tog, k2, yo; repeat from * to last 2 stitches, k2.

Row 2: Slip 1 purlwise with yarn on WS, purl to end of row.

Row 3: Slip 1 purlwise with yarn on WS, k1, PB, yo, k2, ssk, k2tog, k2, yo, *k1, PB, yo, k2, ssk, k2tog, k2, yo; repeat from * to last 3 stitches, ending k1, PB, k2.

Row 4: Slip 1 purlwise with yarn on WS, purl to end of row.

Repeat Rows 1–4 for pattern.

KNITTING THE LEFT SOCK

- Using a big eye beading needle, string 8 beads onto the yarn. Holding beads on yarn tail, use larger needle and the long-tail cast on method (see page 279) to cast on 7 stitches, *push a bead up snug to the needle, cast on 11 stitches; repeat from * 6 times, push up a bead, cast on 8. *You now have* 92 stitches.

The Ruffle

- Row 1 (RS): Slip 1, knit 5, ssk, k2tog, *k7, ssk, k2tog; repeat from * 6 times, k5. *You now have* 76 stitches.

- Row 2: Slip 1, knit to end of row.

- Work rows 1 through 4 of Beaded Fern Lace 4 times, then decrease as follows.

- Row 1: Slip 1, k1 (k2tog) 36 times, k2. *You now have* 40 stitches.

- Row 2: Slip 1, purl to end of row.

- Row 3: Change to smaller needles, slip 1, knit to end of row.

The Ribbed Cuff

- Begin ribbing on WS of ruffle. This is the new RS.

- Row 1 (RS): Slip 1, p2, *k2, p2; repeat from * 9 times, k1.

- Row 2: Slip 1, k2, *p2, k2; repeat from * 9 times, p1.

- Rows 3–18: Slipping the first stitch of every row, work even in established rib.

The Heel Flap

- Row 1 (RS): Slip 1, k2, place these 3 stitches on scrap yarn to hold; slip 1, k17, turn; place remaining 19 stitches on hold. *You now have* 18 flap stitches.

- Row 2: Slip 1, p17, turn.

- Working the flap stitches only, repeat Rows 1 and 2 eight more times.

Working the Dutch Heel Turn

- Row 1 (RS): Slip 1, k11, ssk, turn, leaving 4 stitches unworked.

- Row 2: Slip 1, p6, p2tog, turn, leaving 4 stitches unworked.

- Row 3: Slip 1, k6, ssk, turn.

- Row 4: Slip 1, p6, p2tog, turn.

- Repeat Rows 3 and 4 until all heel stitches have been worked, ending with a WS row. *You now have* 8 heel stitches.

The Gusset

- Row 1 (RS): Knit to the end of the heel; pick up and knit (see page 281) 9 stitches along the side of the flap, pm; k19 held stitches. *You now have* 36 stitches.

- Row 2: Slip 1, p35; pick up and purl (from the back of the stitch) 9 stitches along the side of the flap, pm; p3 held stitches. *You now have* 48 stitches.

- Row 3: Slip 1, knit to marker, sm k1, ssk, knit to 3 stitches before next marker, k2tog, k1, sm, knit to end of row. *You now have* 46 stitches.

- **Row 4:** Slip 1, purl to end of row.
- Repeat Rows 3 and 4 three more times. *You now have* 40 stitches. Remove markers.

The Foot

- Slipping the first stitch of every row, work even in stockinette stitch until foot measures about 3½"/9 cm from the back of the heel, or about 1¼"/3 cm shorter than desired length.

The Round Toe

- **Row 1 (RS):** Slip 1, k2, k2tog, *k3, k2tog; repeat from * to end of row. *You now have* 32 stitches.
- **Rows 2–4:** Work even in stockinette stitch.
- **Row 5:** Slip 1, k1, k2tog, *k2, k2tog; repeat from * to end of row. *You now have* 24 stitches.
- **Rows 6–8:** Work even in stockinette stitch.
- **Row 9:** Slip 1, k2tog, *k1, k2tog; repeat from * to end of row. *You now have* 16 stitches.
- **Row 10:** Slip 1, purl to last 2 stitches, ssp. *You now have* 15 stitches.
- **Row 11:** Slip 1, *k2tog; repeat from * to end of row. *You now have* 8 stitches.
- **Row 12:** Slip 1, purl to end of row.
- Measure out yarn 5 or 6 times the length of sock and cut. Using a yarn needle, thread through last 8 stitches and pull up tight.

Sewing the Seam

- Fold the sock with wrong sides together. Match up the slipped edge stitches and pin in place. Using the larger crochet hook, with right sides facing, slip stitch each pair of slipped edge stitches together, working from the toe to the top of the cuff. Fasten off. Weave in ends. Block as desired.

KNITTING THE RIGHT SOCK

- Work as for Left Sock to Heel Flap.

The Heel Flap

- **Row 1 (RS):** Slip 1, k18, place these 19 stitches on hold; slip 1, k17, turn; place remaining 3 stitches on hold. *You now have* 18 flap stitches.
- **Row 2:** Slip 1, p17, turn.
- Complete Heel Flap and Heel Turn as for Left Sock.

The Gusset

- **Row 1 (RS):** Knit to the end of the heel; pick up and knit 9 stitches along the side of the flap, pm; k3 held stitches. *You now have* 20 stitches.
- **Row 2:** Slip 1, purl 19; pick up and purl (from the back of the stitch) 9 stitches along the side of the flap, pm; p19 held stitches. *You now have* 48 stitches.
- Continue as for Left Sock until Row 12 of Round Toe is complete.

Sewing the Seam

- Cut yarn leaving a 6"/15 cm tail. Using a yarn needle, thread through last 8 stitches and pull up tight. Weave in end to secure.
- Fold the sock with wrong sides together. Match up the slipped edge stitches and pin in place. Using the larger crochet hook, with right sides facing, slip stitch each pair of slipped edge stitches together, working from the top of the cuff to the toe. Weave in ends.

KNITTING THE HAT

- String 15 beads onto yarn tail. Holding beads on tail of yarn, begin long-tail cast on with larger needles. Cast on 7 stitches, *push a bead up snug to needle, cast on 11 stitches; repeat from * 13 times, push last bead up and cast on 8 stitches. *You now have* 169 stitches.

The Edging

- Row 1 (RS): Slip 1, k5, ssk, k2tog, *k7, ssk, k2tog; repeat from * 13 times, k5. *You now have* 139 stitches.

- Row 2: Slip 1, knit to end of row.

- Work Rows 1 through 4 of Beaded Fern Lace 3 times.

- Next Row: Slip 1, knit to end of row decreasing 3 stitches evenly spaced. *You now have* 136 stitches.

- Slipping the first stitch of every row, work even in stockinette stitch until piece measures 4"/10 cm from edge and ending on a WS row.

Decreasing for the Crown

- Row 1 (RS): Slip 1, k14, k2tog, *pm, k15, k2tog, repeat from * to end of row. *You now have* 128 stitches.

- Row 2: Slip 1, purl to end of row.

- Row 3: Slip 1, *knit to 2 stitches before marker, k2tog, sm, repeat from * to end of row. *You now have* 120 stitches.

- Row 4: Slip 1, purl to end of row.

- Repeat Rows 3 and 4 six more times, ending on RS row. *You now have* 72 stitches.

- Next Row (WS): Slip 1, ssp, purl to marker, *sm, p2tog, purl to next marker, repeat from * ending with purl to end of row. *You now have* 64 stitches.

- Continue decreasing each row as established on each RS and WS rows, working k2tog on RS rows and ssp and p2tog on WS rows, until 8 stitches remain, ending on a RS row.

- Last Row: Slip 1, purl to end of row.

Sewing the Seam

- Measure out yarn about 5 times the length of hat seam and cut. Thread through last 8 stitches and pull up tight. Turn hat so right sides are together and with crochet hook, slip stitch seam together as for sock seam. Fasten off and weave in ends. Block as desired.

Beaded Fern Lace

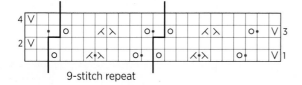

9-stitch repeat

☐ knit

⊡ yo

⦰ k2tog

⦰ ssk

⊡ PB

Ⅴ slip 1 pwise with yarn on WS

Scalloped Ribbing Baby Socks and Cap

Designed by Terry Liann Morris, The Sailing Knitter

Tiny little scalloped edges and a circle of eyelet lace adorn this baby cap with matching socks. Dainty ribbing on the cuffs and foot of the socks help to keep them in place even when baby kicks. Hat and socks are worked in the round.

SIZE AND FINISHED MEASUREMENTS
To fit 0–9 months: 14"/35.5 cm hat circumference; 3½"/9 cm foot length

YARN
Jojoland Melody Superwash, 100% wool, 220 yds (200 m)/1.75 oz (50 g), Morning Abstract (MS40)

NEEDLES
Set of four US 1 (2.25 mm) double-point needles and US 1 (2.25 mm) circular needle 12"/30 cm long *or size needed to obtain correct gauge*

GAUGE
34 stitches and 44 rows = 4"/10 cm in stockinette stitch

OTHER SUPPLIES
Stitch marker, yarn needle, 1 yd/1 m of ¼"/6 mm satin ribbon, sewing needle and coordinating thread

Pattern Essentials

SCALLOPED EDGING
(multiple of 7 stitches)

Round 1: *K6, pass the 5th, 4th, 3rd, 2nd, then 1st over the 6th stitch and off the needle, k1, yo; repeat from * to end of round.

Round 2: *P2, p1 tbl; repeat from * to end of round.

EYELET
(multiple of 2 stitches)

Rounds 1 and 2: Purl.

Round 3: *K2tog, yo; repeat from * to end of round.

Rounds 4 and 5: Purl.

KNITTING THE CAP

- With circular needle, cast on 294 stitches. Place marker and join into a round, being careful not to twist the stitches.
- Work Rounds 1 and 2 of Scalloped Edging pattern. *You now have* 126 stitches.

The Ribbing

- Round 1: *K1, p1; repeat from * to end of round.
- Repeat ribbing as established until piece measures 1"/2.5 cm.
- Work Rounds 1 through 5 of Eyelet pattern.

The Body

- Work stockinette stitch (knit every round) until cap measures 3¾"/9.5 cm from cast-on edge.

Decreasing for the Crown

Note: Change to double-point needles when necessary as stitch count decreases.

- Round 1: *K16, k2tog, repeat from * to end of round. *You now have* 119 stitches.
- Round 2: Knit.
- Round 3: *K15, k2tog, repeat from * to end of round. *You now have* 112 stitches.
- Round 4: Knit.
- Continue in this manner, knitting one less stitch before the decreases each time and knitting one round even between decrease rounds until 49 stitches remain.

- Work decrease round only until 14 stitches remain.
- Last Round: *K2tog; repeat from * to end of round. *You now have* 7 stitches.
- Cut yarn leaving a 10"/25.5 cm tail. Thread tail onto yarn needle and draw through remaining stitches. Pull up snug and fasten off.

Finishing

- Weave in ends. Block. Weave ribbon through eyelets and tie a pretty bow. At back, tack ribbon to hat with a few stitches for safety.

KNITTING THE SOCKS (make 2)

- With double-point needles, cast on 84 stitches. Divide evenly onto 3 needles and join into a round, being careful not to twist the stitches.
- Work Rounds 1 and 2 of Scalloped Edging. *You now have* 36 stitches.

The Ribbing

- Round 1: *K1, p1; repeat from * to end of round.
- Repeat ribbing as established until piece measures 1¾"/4.5 cm.
- Work Rounds 1 through 5 of Eyelet pattern.

The Heel

- **Set-Up Row:** (K1, p1) 8 times, k1, and place these 17 stitches on one needle; evenly divide remaining 19 stitches onto 2 needles and hold for instep. Turn work and work back and forth on 17 heel stitches.

- **Row 1 (WS):** Slip 1 purlwise, p16.

- **Row 2 (RS):** Slip 1 knitwise, *k1, slip 1 purlwise; repeat from * to last 2 stitches, k2.

- Repeat Rows 1 and 2 seven more times, then repeat Row 1 once more.

Turning the Heel

- **Row 1 (RS):** Slip 1 purlwise, k10, ssk, turn, leaving remaining stitches unworked.

- **Row 2 (WS):** Slip 1 purlwise, p5, p2tog, turn.

- **Row 3:** Slip 1 purlwise, k5, ssk, turn.

- Repeat Rows 2 and 3 until 7 stitches remain, ending with Row 2.

- **Next Row (RS):** On needle 1, knit 7 heel stitches, pick up and knit (see page 281) 8 stitches along edge of heel flap, M1R; on needle 2, work 19 instep stitches in established rib pattern onto one needle; on needle 3, M1R, pick up and knit 8 stitches along edge of heel flap, then knit 3 heel stitches onto this last needle. *You now have* 13 stitches on needle 1, 19 stitches on needle 2, and 12 stitches on needle 3.

The Gussets

- **Round 1:** Knit all stitches on needles 1 and 3 and work in rib as established on needle 2.

- **Round 2:** On needle 1, knit to last 3 stitches, k2tog, k1; on needle 2, work in rib as established; on needle 3, k1, ssk, knit to end of round. *You now have* 42 stitches.

- Repeat Rounds 1 and 2 three more times. *You now have* 36 stitches.

The Foot

- Work even in stockinette and rib stitches as established until foot measures 3"/7.5 cm from heel or 1"/2.5 cm less than desired finished length.

Shaping the Toe

- **Round 1:** Knit.

- **Round 2:** On needle 1, knit to last 3 stitches, k2tog, k1; on needle 2, k1, ssk, knit to last 3 stitches, k2tog, k1; on needle 3, k1, ssk, knit to end. *You now have* 32 stitches.

- Repeat Rounds 1 and 2 two more times. *You now have* 24 stitches.

- Work Round 2 only four times. *You now have* 8 stitches.

- Slip 2 stitches from each end of the instep needle to the other 2 needles. Cut yarn leaving a 10"/25.5 cm tail. Hold needles parallel and graft toe stitches together with the Kitchener stitch (see page 278).

Finishing

- Weave in ends. Block. Weave ribbon through eyelets and tie a pretty bow. At back, tack ribbon to sock with a few stitches for safety.

Claredon Baby Vest and Hat

Designed by Karen Marlatt, KDM Creative Knitwear Designs

This lovely textured vest is perfect for your little one and includes a coordinating hat. Pieces are knit flat and seamed.

SIZE AND FINISHED MEASUREMENTS

To fit 0–3 months: 14"/35.5 cm chest circumference; 12"/30.5 cm hat circumference

Note: Stitch pattern is stretchy; sweater and hat have negative ease.

YARN

SweetGeorgia Superwash DK, 100% superwash merino wool, 256 yds (234 m)/4 oz (115 g), Coastal 3

NEEDLES

US 6 (4 mm) straight needles, US 5 (3.75 mm) straight needles, and set of four US 5 (3.75 mm) double-point needles *or size needed to obtain correct gauge*

GAUGE

24 stitches and 30 rows = 4"/10 cm in pattern stitch on larger needles

OTHER SUPPLIES

Stitch marker, yarn needle

Pattern Essentials

PATTERN STITCH
(multiple of 6 stitches)

Rows 1 and 3 (RS): *K4, p2; repeat from * to end of row.

Rows 2 and 4: *K2, p4; repeat from * to end of row.

Rows 5 and 7: *K2, p2, k2; repeat from * to end of row.

Rows 6 and 8: *P2, k2, p2; repeat from * to end of row.

Rows 9 and 11: *P2, k4; repeat from * to end of row.

Rows 10 and 12: *P4, k2; repeat from * to end of row.

Repeat Rows 1–12 for pattern.

KNITTING THE BACK

- With smaller straight needles, cast on 37 stitches.

- Rows 1, 3, 5 and 7: *K1, p1; repeat from * to last stitch, k1.

- Rows 2, 4 and 6: *P1, k1; repeat from * to last stitch, p1.

- Row 8: Work in rib as established for 6 stitches, M1, work 5, M1, work 6, *work 5, M1; repeat from * 2 more times, work to end of row. *You now have* 42 stitches.

- Change to larger needle and work in pattern stitch until piece measures 5"/12.5 cm from cast-on edge.

Shaping the Armholes and Back Neck

- Bind off 3 stitches at beginning of next 2 rows for underarm. *You now have* 36 stitches.

- Continue in pattern as established until piece measures 9"/23 cm from cast-on edge.

- Bind off 8 stitches at the beginning of the next 2 rows. Bind off remaining 20 back neck stitches.

KNITTING THE FRONT

- Work as for back until piece measures 4½"/11.5 cm from cast-on edge, ending with a wrong side row.

Shaping the Front Neck and Armholes

- Row 1 (RS): Work in pattern over 21 stitches, join a second ball of yarn and work to end of row.

- Row 2: Working both sides at once with separate balls of yarn, continue in pattern.

- Row 3 (decrease row): Work in pattern to 3 stitches before neck edge, k2tog, k1; k1, ssk, work in pattern to end of row.

- Continue working shaping at neck edge every other row 9 more times *and at the same time,* work armhole shaping as for back. You have 8 stitches on each shoulder when all shaping is complete. Work even until piece measures same as back. Bind off remaining stitches.

Finishing

- Weave in ends and block to size. Seam shoulders and side seams.

- With smaller double-point needles, RS facing, and beginning at underarm, pick up and knit (see page 281) 48 stitches around armhole edge. Place marker for beginning of round and work k1, p1 rib for 6 rounds. Bind off loosely in pattern. Weave in ends. Repeat for second armhole.

- With smaller double-point needles, RS facing, and beginning at center of the V, pick up and knit 20 stitches from right neck edge, 20 stitches from back neck, and 20 stitches from left neck edge back to center of the V. *Do not join. You now have* 60 *stitches.* Work back and forth in k1, p1 rib for 6 rows. Bind off very loosely in pattern. Weave in ends.

- With right side facing, sew the side of left neck ribbing to the bottom of the right neck ribbing beginning at the center of the V. Then with wrong side facing, and ribbing overlapping at center front, sew the side of right neck ribbing to bottom of the left neck ribbing beginning at the center of the V.

KNITTING THE HAT

Note: Hat is worked flat, then seamed.

- With smaller straight needles cast on 72 stitches.

- Rows 1–7: *K1, p1; repeat from * to end of row.

- Row 8: K12, M1, (k10, M1) five times, k10. *You now have* 78 stitches.

- Change to larger needles and work Rows 1–12 of pattern stitch until piece measures 4"/10 cm from cast-on edge, ending with a WS row.

Decreasing for the Crown

- Row 1 (RS): Purl.

- Row 2: Purl.

- Row 3: *K2tog, k8, ssk, k1; repeat from * to end of row. *You now have* 66 stitches.

- Row 4: Purl.

- Row 5: *K2tog, k6, ssk, k1; repeat from * to end of row. *You now have* 54 stitches.

- Row 6: Purl.

- Row 7: *K2tog, k4, ssk, k1; repeat from * to end of row. *You now have* 42 stitches.

- Row 8: Purl.

- Row 9: *K2tog, k2, ssk, k1; repeat from * to end of row. *You now have* 30 stitches.

- Row 10: Purl.

- Row 11: *K2tog, ssk, k1; repeat from * to end of row. *You now have* 18 stitches.

- Row 12: Purl.

- Row 13: *K2tog, k1; repeat from * to end of row. *You now have* 12 stitches.

- Row 14: Purl.

- **Row 15:** *K2tog; repeat from * to end of row. *You now have* 6 stitches.
- Cut yarn leaving an 8"/20.5 cm tail, draw through remaining 6 stitches twice to secure, sew side seam. Weave in ends.

Pattern Stitch

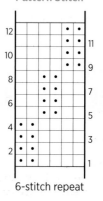

6-stitch repeat

☐ k on RS, p on WS

▣ p on RS, k on WS

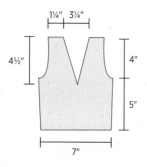

My Beau's Vest and Things

Designed by Tamara Del Sonno

Dress it up with the tie or down with the mini teddy bear. Or go with both accessories. Any way you choose, your little beau will be ready for anything with this vest knitted in a simple knit and purl moss stitch.

Pattern Essentials

DOUBLE SEED STITCH

(even number of stitches)

Rows 1 and 2: *K1, p1; repeat from * to end of row.

Rows 3 and 4: *P1, k1; repeat from * to end of row.

Repeat Rows 1–4 for pattern.

Note: When increasing and decreasing, use an M1 or M1P, ssk, k2tog, ssp or p2tog as necessary to maintain pattern.

ATTACHED I-CORD EDGING

Cast on desired number of I-cord stitches onto a double-point needle. *Slide the stitches to the other end and use a second needle to knit to the last stitch. Slip the last stitch knitwise onto the right needle. Pick up and knit one stitch from the garment edge. Pass the slipped stitch over this stitch. Repeat from * to the end of the edge you're covering. Bind off. If edging a circular piece, sew bind off to cast on.

KNITTING THE VEST

Making the Points

- With larger needle, cast on 6 stitches.

- Row 1 (RS): Work Row 1 of Double Seed Stitch.

- Row 2: P1, increase 1 (see note in Pattern Essentials), work in established pattern to last stitch, increase 1, P1.

- Row 3: K1, increase 1, work in established pattern to last stitch, increase 1, k1.

- Bringing new stitches into pattern, continue to increase 1 stitch each edge every row 7 more times. *You now have* 24 stitches. Place stitches on hold. Repeat to make second vest point but leave stitches on needle.

Joining the Body

- With RS facing, discontinuing stockinette edge stitches, work all point stitches in Double Seed Stitch pattern, turn; using the knitted-on method (see page 279), cast on 12 stitches, pm, cast on 59 stitches, pm, cast on 12 stitches, turn; work held point stitches in pattern. *You now have* 131 stitches.

SIZE AND FINISHED MEASUREMENTS

To fit 0–3 months: 16"/40.5 cm chest circumference

YARN

Noro Taiyo Sock, 50% cotton/17% wool/17% polyamide/16% silk, 460 yds (420 m)/3.5 oz (100 g), 40 Green, Sand ①

NEEDLES

Two US 1 (2.25 mm) double-point needles (for I-cord), US 3 (3.25 mm) straight needles *or size needed to obtain correct gauge*

GAUGE

28 stitches and 40 rows= 4"/10 cm in Double Seed Stitch

OTHER SUPPLIES

Stitch holders or scrap yarn, stitch markers, yarn needle, five ¼"/6 mm buttons, Velcro dots (for bow tie), small amount of toy stuffing and embroidery thread (for bear)

- Next Row (WS): Work left front in pattern as established to marker, sm, p1, work k1, p1 rib to 1 stitch before marker, p1, sm, work pattern as established on right front.

- Next Row (RS): Work right front in pattern as established to marker, sm, slip 1 with yarn in back, work rib as established to 1 stitch before marker, slip 1 with yarn in back, sm, work pattern as established on left front.

- Repeat the last 2 rows until piece measures 5½"/14 cm, ending with a WS row.

Dividing for Fronts and Back

- **Row 1:** Bind off 3 stitches, work in pattern as established to marker. Place next 59 stitches on holder for back, and place the following 36 stitches on separate holder for left front. *You now have* 33 stitches for Right Front.

- **Row 2 (WS):** Bind off 5 stitches for underarm, work in pattern to end of row. *You now have* 28 stitches.

- **Row 3:** K1, decrease 1 (see note in Pattern Essentials, page 25), work in pattern to last 3 stitches, decrease 1, k1. *You now have* 26 stitches.

- **Row 4:** Work even in pattern.

- Continue to decrease 1 st at neck edge every other row 15 more times and *at the same time* decrease 1 at the armhole edge once more. Place remaining 10 stitches on hold for right front shoulder.

The Left Front

- Place 36 left front stitches on needle.

- **Row 1:** With RS facing, attach yarn and bind off 5 stitches for underarm, work in pattern to end of row. *You now have* 31 stitches.

- **Row 2:** Bind off 3 stitches, work in pattern to end of row. *You now have* 28 stitches.

- Shape neck and armholes as for right front.

- Place remaining 10 stitches on hold for left front shoulder.

The Back

- Place 59 held back stitches on needle. Continuing in rib pattern as established, bind off 10 stitches at the beginning of the next 2 rows. *You now have* 39 stitches.

- Continuing in pattern, decrease 1 stitch at the beginning and end of every RS row twice. *You now have* 35 stitches. Work even until piece measures ½"/13 mm less than fronts, ending with a WS row.

- Work 10 stitches in pattern for right shoulder, place next 15 stitches on hold for back neck; leave remaining 10 stitches on needle for left shoulder, turn. Working on right shoulder stitches only, continue in pattern until armhole measures same as front armhole. Use three-needle bind off (see page 282) to join front and back right shoulder.

- With right side facing, join yarn and continue in pattern on left shoulder stitches until armhole measures same as front armhole. Use three-needle bind off to join front and back left shoulder.

The Edging

- With RS facing and beginning at lower right side "seam," work 3-stitch attached I-cord along entire right front to the shoulder seam; work I-cord bind off along 15 back neck stitches; work attached I-cord along left front as follows: work to ½"/1.5 cm below base of V neck shaping, *work 3 rows of I-cord without attaching, work 10 rows of attached I-cord; repeat from * 3 more times (4 buttonholes made), work attached I-cord to lower right side "seam."

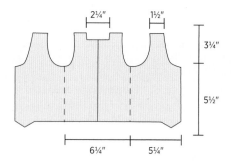

The Pocket

- Cast on 20 stitches.
- **Rows 1, 3, and 6:** K4, (p4, k4) twice.
- **Rows 2, 4, 5 and 7:** P4, (k4, p4) twice.
- **Row 8:** Repeat Row 1.
- Repeat Rows 1 through 8 once, then work Rows 1 through 4 once more. Bind off.

Finishing

- Weave in all ends. Use the photograph as a guide and sew pocket to right front of vest. Sew decorative button to pocket, if desired.

KNITTING THE BOW TIE

- With larger needle, cast on 8 stitches.
- **Row 1:** Slip 1, *p1, k1; repeat from * to last stitch, p1.
- Repeat Row 1 until piece measures 8"/20.5 cm.
- Bind off in pattern.

The Neckband

- With larger needle, cast on 6 stitches.
- **Row 1:** Slip 1, *p1, k1; repeat from * to last stitch, p1.
- Repeat Row 1 until piece measures 12"/30.5 cm.
- Bind off in pattern.

The Binding

- Using smaller needle, cast on 4 stitches.
- **Row 1:** Knit.
- **Row 2:** K1, p2, k1.
- Repeat Rows 1 and 2 until piece measures 1½"/4 cm.
- Bind off.

Finishing

- Weave in ends. Fold tie into zigzag with ends extending just beyond the folds; tack to hold in place. Place tie over neckband and binding over tie. Fold binding over tie and around neckband; stitch in place. Attach Velcro dots on ends of neckband for closure.

KNITTING THE BITTY BEAR BUDDY

- The bear is knitted in two pieces, front and back, and sewn together around the edges with the purl side out.

The Legs and Body (make 2)

- With smaller needle, cast on 6 stitches. Work in reverse stockinette stitch for 1"/2.5 cm. Place stitches on holder. Repeat for second leg but leave stitches on needle.
- Knit leg stitches, cast on 3, knit held leg stitches. *You now have* 15 stitches.
- Work body in stockinette stitch for ¾"/2 cm.

Adding the Arms

- Continuing in reverse stockinette stitch, cast on 8 stitches at the beginning of the next 2 rows. *You now have* 31 stitches. Work 6 more rows, then bind off 10 stitches at the beginning of the next 2 rows. *You now have* 11 stitches. Work 2 rows even.

The Head

- Increase 1 stitch at the beginning of the next 4 rows. *You now have* 15 stitches. Work even in stockinette stitch for 1"/2.5 cm, ending with a purl row.
- **Next Row:** K3, turn, slip 1, p2, turn; bind off until 2 stitches remain on right needle, knit to end, turn; p2, slip 1, turn. Bind off remaining 3 stitches.

Finishing

- Use embroidery thread to stitch simple facial features to one side of head, using photo as a guide. Sew bear together, stuffing with fiberfill before completing seams.

Welcome Home Baby Set

Designed by Pam Sluter

Baby will be handsomely coordinated in this outfit knit in color-shifting yarn. The sweater is knit back and forth from the top down, and the hat is knitted in the round. Both are accented with a simple eyelet trim.

SIZE AND FINISHED MEASUREMENTS
To fit newborn: 18"/45.5 chest circumference; 14"/35.5 cm hat circumference

YARN
Skacel Yarn Collection, Schoppel Wolle Zauberball Crazy, 75% superwash wool/25% nylon, 459 yds (420 m)/3.5 oz (100 g), Color 1564 **(2)**

NEEDLES
US 4 (3.5 mm) circular needle 24"/60 cm long (sweater body) and set of four US 4 (3.5 mm) double-point needles (sleeves), US 3 (3.25 mm) circular needle 24"/60 cm long (front and neck bands) and set of four US 3 (3.25 mm) double-point needles (hat) *or size needed to obtain correct gauge*

GAUGE
24 stitches and 28 rows = 4"/10 cm in stockinette stitch on larger needles
26 stitches and 32 rows = 4"/10 cm in stockinette stitch on smaller needles
23 stitches and 46 rows = 4"/10 cm in garter stitch on larger needles

OTHER SUPPLIES
Stitch markers, stitch holders or scrap yarn, yarn needle, 1"/25 mm button

KNITTING THE SWEATER

- With larger needles, cast on 46 stitches.

- **Set-Up Row (WS):** K2, pm, k12, pm, k18, pm, k12, pm, k2.

- Work raglan increases as follows.

- **Row 1:** Kfb, kfb (sm, kfb, knit to 1 stitch before next marker, kfb) 3 times, sm, (kfb) 2 times. *You now have 56 stitches.*

- **Row 2:** Knit.

- **Row 3:** Kfb, (knit to 1 stitch before marker, kfb, sm, kfb) 4 times, knit to last stitch, kfb.

- Work Rows 2 and 3 once more. *You now have 76 stitches (24 stitches between 2nd and 3rd markers for back).*

- **Next Row:** Cast on 4 stitches, knit to end of row, cast on 4 stitches. *You now have 84 stitches.*

- **Next Row:** (Knit to 1 stitch before marker, kfb, sm, kfb) 4 times, knit to end of row. *You now have 92 stitches.*

- **Next Row:** Knit.

- Repeat the last 2 rows 11 more times. *You now have* 180 stitches (48 stitches between 2nd and 3rd markers for back).

Dividing for Sleeves

- Knit to 1st marker, remove marker; place next 24 sleeve stitches on hold, remove marker; cast on 5 stitches; knit 48 back stitches, remove marker; place next 24 sleeve stitches on hold, remove marker, cast on 5 stitches; knit to end of row. *You now have* 106 stitches.

The Body

- Row 1 (WS): Purl.
- Row 2: Knit.
- Repeat Rows 1 and 2 until piece measures 4½"/11.5 cm from underarm, ending with Row 2.
- Next Row (WS): Knit.
- Next Row: K1, *yo, k2tog; repeat from * to last stitch, k1.
- Next Row: Knit.
- Bind off.

The Sleeves (make 2)

- Place held sleeve stitches onto 2 double-point needles. With 3rd needle, RS facing, and beginning at armhole edge, pick up and knit (see page 281) 3 stitches, pm, pick up and knit 3 stitches. Work sleeves in the round as follows. *You now have* 30 stitches.
- Round 1: Purl.
- Round 2: Knit.
- Repeat Rounds 1 and 2 four more times.
- Next Round: Purl.
- Next Round: *K2tog, yo; repeat from * to end of round.
- Next Round: Purl.
- Bind off.

The Neck Band

- With smaller circular needle, RS facing, and beginning at right neck edge, pick up and knit 10 stitches for right front neck, 12 stitches for right sleeve, 18 stitches for back, 12 stitches for left sleeve, and 10 stitches for left front neck. *You now have* 62 stitches.
- Row 1: *K1, p1; repeat from * to end of row.
- Work in rib as established for 1"/2.5 cm. Bind off in pattern.

The Front Bands

- With smaller circular needle, RS facing, and beginning at lower right front edge, pick up and knit 35 stitches to neck edge. Work garter stitch (knit every row) for ½"/1.5 cm. Bind off. With smaller circular needle, RS facing, and beginning at left front neck edge, pick up and knit 35 stitches to

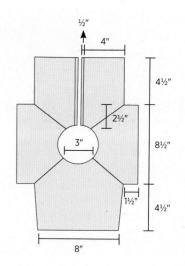

bottom. Work garter stitch (knit every row) for ½"/1.5 cm. Bind off.

Finishing

- With smaller double-point needle, cast on 3 stitches. Work I-cord (see page 277) for 3"/7.5 cm. Bind off, fold to form a loop, and sew to right front neck band. Sew button to left front, opposite button loop.

KNITTING THE HAT

- With smaller double-point needles, cast on 90 stitches. Divide evenly onto 3 double-point needles and join into a round, being careful not to twist the stitches.

- Round 1: Purl.

- Round 2: *K2tog, yo; repeat from * to end of round.

- Round 3: Purl.

- Round 4: Knit.

- Repeat Round 4 until piece measures 4"/10 cm from cast-on edge.

Decreasing for the Crown

- Round 1: *K8, k2tog; repeat from * to end of round. *You now have* 81 stitches.

- Round 2: Knit.

- Round 3: *K7, k2tog; repeat from * to end of round. *You now have* 72 stitches.

- Round 4: Knit.

- Round 5: *K2, k2tog; repeat from * to end of round. *You now have* 54 stitches.

- Round 6: Knit.

- Round 7: *K1, k2tog; repeat from * to end of round. *You now have* 36 stitches.

- Round 8: Knit.

- Round 9: *K2tog; repeat from * to end of round. *You now have* 18 stitches.

- Cut yarn leaving a 12"/30.5 cm tail. Thread tail onto yarn needle and draw through remaining stitches. Pull up snug and fasten off.

Trellis Lace Sweater and Hat

Designed by Uyvonne Bigham

The simple lace pattern used here is lovely to look at. The sweater's garter-stitch trim is slightly scalloped by the lace pattern. The hat frames the face and is secured by a button and strap under the chin. The design is a quick knit and makes a great shower gift.

KNITTING THE SWEATER

Note: Before beginning, wind 2 balls of 1 oz/28.5 g each and set aside.

- With smaller needles, cast on 103 stitches. Beginning with a right side row, work 6 rows of garter stitch. Change to larger needles. Work 16-row Trellis Lace pattern until piece measures 5½"/14 cm, ending with a wrong side row.

Dividing for Fronts and Back

- Row 1 (RS): Continuing in pattern as established, work 26 right front stitches, pm, work 51 back stitches, pm; attach separate ball and work remaining 26 left front stitches.

- Row 2: Work 26 stitches, sm; pick up original yarn, work 51 stitches, sm; attach 3rd ball of yarn and work remaining 26 stitches.

- Working the back and each front with its own ball of yarn, continue in pattern as established until piece measures 8"/20.5 cm, ending with a WS row.

Shaping the Neck

- Continuing in lace pattern as established, bind off 2 stitches at the beginning of the next 2 rows. Bind off 3 stitches at the beginning of the next 2 rows. Bind off 2 stitches at the beginning of the next 4 rows. *You now have 17 stitches for each front and 51 stitches for the back.* Continue even in pattern until piece measures 10"/25.5 cm, ending with a WS row. Bind off each section separately. Sew fronts to back at shoulders.

SIZE AND FINISHED MEASUREMENTS
To fit 6–12 months: 18"/45.5 cm chest circumference; approximately 16"/40.5 cm hat circumference

YARN
Lion Brand Babysoft, 60% acrylic/40% nylon, 459 yds (420 m)/5 oz (141 g), Color 100 White (3)

NEEDLES
US 5 (3.75 mm) and US 6 (4 mm) straight needles *or size needed to obtain correct gauge*

GAUGE
22 stitches and 26 rows = 4"/10 cm in Trellis Lace pattern with larger needles

OTHER SUPPLIES
Stitch markers, stitch holders, seven ⅜"/10 mm buttons, yarn needle

Pattern Essentials

GARTER STITCH

Knit every row.

TRELLIS LACE
(multiple of 10 + 3)

Rows 1, 3, 5, and 7: K1, k2tog *k3, yo, k1, yo, k3, sk2p; repeat from * to last 10 stitches, k3, yo, k1, yo, k3, ssk, k1.

Rows 2 and all even-numbered rows: Purl.

Rows 9, 11, 13, and 15: K2, *yo, k3, sk2p, k3, yo, k1; repeat from * to last stitch, k1.

Row 16: Purl.

Repeat Rows 1–16 for pattern.

The Sleeves (make 2)

- With smaller needles, cast on 33 stitches. Beginning with a right side row, work 5 rows of garter stitch. Knit 1 row, increasing 10 stitches evenly spaced. *You now have* 43 stitches.

- Change to larger needles. Work in Trellis Lace pattern, increasing 1 stitch each side every 4th row 9 times, bringing new stitches into pattern. *You now have* 61 stitches.

- Work even in pattern as established until piece measures 7"/18 cm, ending on a WS row. Bind off.

The Buttonhole Band

- With smaller needle, RS facing, and beginning at bottom edge, pick up and knit (see page 281) 41 stitches along right front edge. Knit 2 rows.

- **Buttonhole Row:** K3, *yo, k2tog, k5; repeat from * 4 more times, knit to end of row.

- Knit 2 rows. Bind off.

The Button Band

- With smaller needle, RS facing, and beginning at neck edge, pick up and knit 41 stitches along left front edge. Knit 5 rows. Bind off.

Finishing

- Sew sleeve seams and sew sleeves to armhole openings. Sew buttons to button band opposite buttonholes. Weave in all ends.

KNITTING THE HAT

- With smaller needles, cast on 63 stitches. Knit 3 rows. Knit 1 row, increasing 10 stitches evenly spaced. *You now have* 73 stitches.

- Change to larger needles. Work Rows 1–16 of lace pattern 1 time, work Rows 1–8 of lace pattern 1 time.

- Bind off 23 stitches, k27; attach new yarn and bind off 23 stitches. *You now have* 27 stitches.

The Top of the Hat

- **Row 1 (WS):** Knit.

- **Row 2:** K1, k2tog, knit to last 3 stitches, k2tog, k1. *You now have* 25 stitches.

- **Rows 3–7:** Knit.

- Repeat Rows 2 through 7 three more times. *You now have* 19 stitches.

- Work in garter stitch until top of hat measures 4"/10 cm. Place remaining stitches on holder.

- Sew sides of hat to sides of hat top.

The Band

- With smaller needle and RS facing, cast on 7 stitches using the cable method (see page 276), knit these 7 stitches; pick up and knit 18 stitches along lower edge; on held stitches, k1, (k2tog) 9 times; pick up and knit 18 stitches along lower edge; turn work and cast on 7 sts using the purl cable method. *You now have* 60 stitches.

- Knit 1 row.

- **Next Row (RS):** Knit to last 8 stitches, yo, k2tog (buttonhole made), k2, yo, k2tog (buttonhole made), k2.

- Knit 3 rows. Bind off.

Finishing

- Weave in all ends. Sew 2 buttons to one end of band, opposite buttonholes.

Trellis Lace

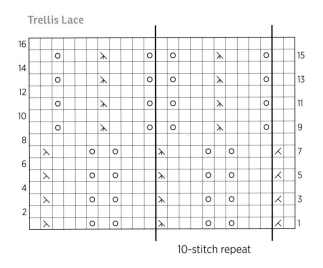

10-stitch repeat

	k on RS, p on WS
o	yo
k2tog
ssk
sk2p

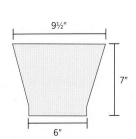

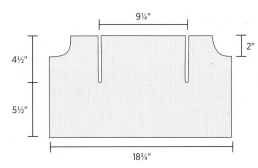

Mushishi Jacket and Cap Set

Designed by Judith Durant

Keep your toddler warm in this handsome ensemble with an easy-to-knit pattern. The buttons on the jacket are decorative, being sewn over snaps, and the fringes on top of the hat are knitted in one continuous piece.

SIZE AND FINISHED MEASUREMENTS
To fit 12–24 months: 22½"/57 cm chest circumference; 14"/35.5 cm hat circumference, unstretched

YARN
Plymouth Yarn Mushishi, 95% wool/5% silk, 491 yds (449 m)/8.8 oz (250 g), Color 05, Oceanic

NEEDLES
US 7 (4.5 mm) straight needles and US 6 (4 mm) circular needle 36"/90 cm long for jacket; US 7 (4.5 mm) circular needle 16"/40 cm long and set of five US 7 (4.5 mm) double-point needles for cap *or size needed to obtain correct gauge*

GAUGE
20 stitches and 24 rows = 4"/10 cm in pattern

OTHER SUPPLIES
Five ½"/13 mm snaps, five ¾"/19 mm buttons, stitch holders, stitch markers, yarn needle, sewing needle and coordinating thread

Pattern Essentials

ANDALUSIAN STITCH
(back and forth; multiple of 2 stitches)

Row 1: Knit.

Row 2: Purl.

Row 3: *K1, p1; repeat from * to end of row.

Row 4: Purl.

Repeat Rows 1–4 for pattern.

ANDALUSIAN STITCH
(in the round; circular on multiple of 2 stitches)

Rounds 1 and 2: Knit.

Round 3: *K1, p1; repeat from * to end of round.

Round 4: Knit.

Repeat Rounds 1–4 for pattern.

KNITTING THE JACKET BACK

- With straight needles, cast on 58 stitches. Establish edge stitches and work k1, p1 rib as follows.

- Row 1: K2, *p1, k1; repeat from * to end of row.

- Row 2: *P1, k1; repeat from * to last 2 stitches, p2.

- Repeat Rows 1 and 2 twice more.

- Maintaining established stockinette edge stitches, work Andalusian stitch until piece measures 10"/25.5 cm, ending with Row 4 of pattern.
- **Next Row:** K20 and place on holder for right shoulder; bind off 18 stitches for back neck; k20 and place on holder for left shoulder.

KNITTING THE JACKET RIGHT FRONT

- Cast on 28 stitches. Work k1, p1 rib with stockinette edge stitches for 6 rows as for back. Work in pattern stitch as for back until piece measures 8"/20.5 cm, ending with a WS row.

Shaping the Neck

- Continue in pattern and bind off 2 stitches at the beginning of every RS row 2 times. *You now have* 24 stitches.
- Decrease 1 stitch at the beginning of every RS row 4 times. *You now have* 20 stitches.
- Work 1 WS row. Continue if necessary until length of piece matches back.

WORKING THE LEFT FRONT

- Cast on 28 stitches. Work k1, p1 rib for 6 rows as follows.
- **Row 1:** *K1, p1; repeat from * to 2 last stitches, k2.
- **Row 2:** P2, *k1, p1; repeat from * to end of row.
- Maintaining established stockinette edge stitches, work in Andalusian pattern stitch as for right front until piece measures 8"/20 cm, ending with a RS row.

Shaping the Neck

- Continue in pattern and bind off 2 stitches at the beginning of every WS row 2 times. *You now have* 24 stitches.
- Decrease 1 stitch at the beginning of every WS row 4 times. *You now have* 20 stitches.
- Continue if necessary until length of piece matches right front.

JOINING THE SHOULDERS AND KNITTING THE SLEEVES

- Join the front and back shoulders together with a three-needle bind off (see page 282).
- Measure down 4"/10 cm from the shoulder seam on both fronts and back and place a marker.

The Right Sleeve

- With right side facing and beginning at the marker on the right back, pick up and knit (see page 281) 40 stitches between the markers. Purl 1 row.
- Maintaining 1 stockinette edge stitch on each end of every row, begin Andalusian pattern stitch and at the same time decrease 1 stitch with ssk at the beginning and k2tog at the end of every 8th row 5 times. *You now have* 30 stitches. Work even in pattern until sleeve measures 7"/18 cm. Work K1, P1 rib for 6 rows. Bind off loosely.

The Left Sleeve

- With right side facing and beginning at the marker on the left front, pick up and knit 40 stitches between the markers. Continue as for right sleeve.
- Beginning at the lower side seams, seam the sides and the under sleeves on both sides with full-stitch mattress stitch (see page 281).

KNITTING THE BUTTON BAND AND COLLAR

Note: The bands and collar are worked in one piece. In order to pick up the stitches along the neck edge onto one circular needle, you'll need to pull a length of cable through the previous stitches to free the needle to make the turns. This is similar to the Magic Loop method of knitting (see page 280).

- With smaller circular needle, right side facing, and beginning at the lower right front, pick up and knit 44 stitches to neck edge; cast on 1 stitch and mark this stitch; pick up and knit 18 stitches to shoulder seam; pick up and knit 18 back neck stitches; pick up and knit 18 stitches along to end of neck edge; cast on 1 stitch and mark this stitch; pick up and knit 44 stitches to lower left front. *You now have* 144 stitches.

- **Row 1:** K44 left front stitches, knit the marked stitch, and shape neck as follows: k48, WT (see page 282); k42, WT; k36, WT; k30, WT; k24, WT; k18, WT; k12, WT; k6, WT; k30 neck stitches, knit the marked stitch, k44 right front stitches.

- **Row 2:** K44, M1R, knit the marked stitch, M1L, k54, M1R, knit the marked stitch, M1L, k44. **You now have** 148 stitches.

- **Row 3:** Knit.

- **Row 4:** K45, M1R, knit the marked stitch, M1L, k56, M1R, knit the marked stitch, M1L, k45. *You now have* 152 stitches.

- **Row 5:** Knit.

- **Row 6:** K46, M1R, knit the marked stitch, M1L, k58, M1R, knit the marked stitch, M1L, k46. *You now have* 156 stitches.

- **Row 7:** Knit.

- **Row 8:** K47, M1R, knit the marked stitch, M1L, k60, M1R, knit the marked stitch, M1L, k47. *You now have* 160 stitches.

- Bind off knitwise on WS.

Finishing

- Weave in ends. Securely sew snaps to button bands. Securely sew buttons over snaps.

KNITTING THE CAP

- With short circular needle, cast on 80 stitches and join into a round, being careful not to twist the stitches.

- Work 6 rows of K1, P1 rib.

- Work in Andalusian Stitch until piece measures 5½"/14 cm from beginning, ending with pattern row 4.

Shaping the Crown

- Round 1: *K8, k2tog; repeat from * to end of round. *You now have 72 stitches.*

- Round 2: Purl.

- Round 3: *K7, k2tog; repeat from * to end of round. *You now have 64 stitches.*

- Round 4: Purl.

- Round 5: *K6, k2tog; repeat from * to end of round. *You now have 56 stitches.*

- Round 6: Purl.

- Round 7: *K5, k2tog; repeat from * to end of round. *You now have 48 stitches.*

- Round 8: Purl.

- Round 9: *K4, k2tog; repeat from * to end of round. *You now have 40 stitches.*

- Round 10: Purl.

- Round 11: *K3, k2tog; repeat from * to end of round. *You now have 32 stitches.*

- Round 12: Purl.

- Round 13 (eyelet round): *K1, k2tog, yo, k1; repeat from * to end of round.

- Round 10: Purl.

- Round 11: Knit.

The Fringe

- *Using the backward loop method (see page 276), cast on 20 stitches, being sure to snug the first stitch up to the next stitch of the round.

- Row 1: K19, k2tog, turn.

- Row 2: Slip 1, k19, turn.

- Row 3: Bind off 18, k2tog, pass the remaining stitch from the bind off over the k2tog and off the needle; slip 1 from right to left needle, pass the second stitch on the right needle over the slipped stitch; slip remaining stitch back to left needle.

- Repeat from * until you've used all stitches and have 16 fringes. Fasten off.

The Drawstring

- Cast on 80 stitches. Knit 2 rows. Bind off.

Finishing

- Weave in all ends. Thread the drawstring in and out of the eyelets. Pull up tight and tie.

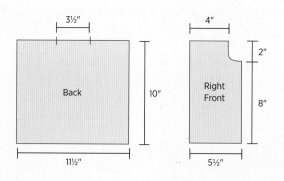

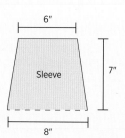

Clarke Sweater and Hat

Designed by Brenda Patipa, Brenda Patipa Knits

A six-button cardigan is knit with an eyelet check pattern in the body and a wide striped rib in the sleeves. The coordinated but varied buttons make the sweater unique, and it's topped off with a simple cap.

SIZE AND FINISHED MEASUREMENTS
To fit 0–3 months: 18"/45.5 cm chest circumference; 14"/35.5 cm hat circumference

YARN
Lisa Souza Knitwear and Dyeworks Hardtwist Petite, 100% superwash merino wool, 500 yds (457 m)/3.5 oz (100 g), Fresh Avocado (1)

NEEDLES
US 2 (2.75 mm) circular needle 20"/50 cm long and set of five US 2 (2.75 mm) double-point needles *or size needed to obtain correct gauge*

GAUGE
28 stitches and 40 rows = 4"/10 cm in Eyelet Check pattern

OTHER SUPPLIES
Stitch holders or scrap yarn, six ½"/13 mm buttons, sewing needle and coordinating thread, yarn needle

Pattern Essentials

EYELET CHECK
(back and forth; multiple of 8 stitches)

Row 1: *K5, p3; repeat from * to end of row.

Row 2: *K3, p5; repeat from * to end of row.

Row 3: *K5, p1, yo, p2tog; repeat from * to end of row.

Row 4: *Repeat Row 2.

Row 5: Repeat Row 1.

Row 6: Purl.

Row 7: *K1, p3, k4; repeat from * to end of row.

Row 8: *P4, k3, p1; repeat from * to end of row.

Row 9: *K1, p1, yo, p2tog, k4; repeat from * to end of row.

Row 10: Repeat Row 8.

Row 11: Repeat Row 7.

Row 12: Purl.

Work Rows 1–12 for pattern.

EYELET CHECK
(in the round; multiple of 8 stitches)

Rounds 1 and 2: *K5, p3; repeat from * to end of round.

Round 3: *K5, p1, yo, p2tog; repeat from * to end of round.

Rounds 4 and 5: Repeat Round 1.

Round 6: Knit.

Rounds 7 and 8: *K1, p3, k4; repeat from * to end of round.

Round 9: *K1, p1, yo, p2tog, k4; repeat from * to end of round.

Rounds 10 and 11: Repeat Round 7.

Round 12: Knit.

Work Rounds 1–12 for pattern.

BORDER
(back and forth; multiple of 4 stitches)

Rows 1–3: Knit.

Row 4: Purl.

Row 5: K1, p3; repeat from * to end of row.

Row 6: K3, p1; repeat from * to end of row.

Row 7: K1, p1, yo, p2tog; repeat from * to end of row.

Row 8: K3, p1; repeat from * to end of row.

Row 9: K1, p3; repeat from * to end of row.

Row 10: Purl.

Rows 11–14: Knit.

Work Rows 1–14 for pattern.

BORDER
(in the round; multiple of 4 stitches)

Rounds 1, 3, and 4: Knit.

Round 2: Purl.

Rounds 5 and 6: *K1, p3; repeat from * to end of round.

Round 7: *K1, p1, yo, p2tog; repeat from * to end of round.

Rounds 8 and 9: Repeat Rounds 5 and 6.

Rounds 10, 11 and 13: Knit.

Rounds 12 and 14: Purl.

Work Rounds 1–14 for pattern.

SLEEVE
(back and forth; multiple of 4 + 2 stitches)

Row 1 (RS): P1, *p2, k1, p1; repeat from * to last stitch, p1.

Row 2: K1, *k1, p1, k2; repeat from * to last stitch, k1.

Work Rows 1–12 for pattern.

KNITTING THE SWEATER

Note: Sweater is knit back and forth on circular needle to accommodate the number of stitches.

- With circular needle, cast on 120 stitches. Following chart or line-by-line instructions, work Rows 1 through 14 of Border stitch, then work Rows 1 through 12 of Eyelet Check pattern 4 times.

Dividing for Front and Back

- Continuing in Eyelet Check pattern as established, work 24 right front stitches and place on hold; bind off 8; work 56 back stitches and place on hold; bind off 8; work in pattern to end of row. *You now have* 24 stitches for the left front.

The Left Front

- Work even in pattern as established until armhole measures 2½"/6.5 cm, ending with a WS row. At the beginning of the next 4 WS rows, bind off for neck shaping as follows: 3 stitches once, 2 stitches once, then 1 stitch two times. *You now have* 17 shoulder stitches. Work even until armhole measures 3½"/9 cm. Bind off.

The Right Front

- Place 24 held right front stitches on needle. With WS facing, join yarn and work in pattern as established until armhole measures 2½"/6.5 cm, ending with a RS row. At the beginning of the next 4 RS rows, bind off for neck shaping as follows: 3 stitches once, 2 stitches once, then 1 stitch two times. *You now have* 17 shoulder stitches. Work even until armhole measures 3½"/9 cm. Bind off.

The Back

- Place 56 held back stitches on needle. With WS facing, join yarn and work in pattern as established until armhole measures 3"/7.5 cm, ending with a WS row.
- **Next Row (RS):** Work 21 stitches in pattern and place on hold for right neck and shoulder; bind off 14; work in pattern to end of row. *You now have* 21 stitches for left back. Work 1 WS row. At the beginning of the next 2

RS rows, bind off for neck shaping as follows: 3 stitches, then 1 stitch. *You now have* 17 left shoulder stitches. Work in pattern until armhole measures 3½"/9 cm, ending on a RS row. Bind off.

- Place 21 held right neck and shoulder stitches on needle. With WS facing, join yarn and bind off for neck shaping at the beginning of the next 2 WS rows as follows: 3 stitches, then 1 stitch. *You now have* 17 right shoulder stitches. Work in pattern until armhole measures 3½"/9 cm, ending on a RS row. Bind off.

The Sleeves (make 2)

- Cast on 42 stitches. Work Rows 1 through 12 of Border stitch. Beginning with a RS row, work in Sleeve pattern for 2 rows.
- **Next Row (RS):** K1, M1, continue in pattern as established to last stitch, M1, K1. *You now have* 44 stitches.

- Continue in this manner, increasing 1 stitch at the beginning and end of every 8 rows 5 more times, incorporating new stitches into pattern. *You now have 54 stitches.*
- Work even in pattern until sleeve measures 6¾"/17 cm. Bind off.

Finishing

- Block pieces to size. Sew shoulder and sleeve seams. Sew in sleeves.

Knitting the Left Front Band

- With RS facing and beginning at neck edge, pick up and knit (see page 281) 64 stitches to bottom edge.
- Rows 1–3: Knit.
- Row 4 (RS): K1, *k1, p3; repeat from * to last 3 stitches, k3.
- Row 5: P3, *k3, p1; repeat from * to last stitch, p1.
- Rows 6 and 7: Repeat Rows 4 and 5.
- Rows 8–11: Knit.
- Bind off.

The Right Front Band

- With RS facing and beginning at bottom edge, pick up and knit 64 stitches to neck edge.
- Rows 1–3: Knit.
- Row 4 (RS): K2, *k1, p3; repeat from * to last 2 stitches, k2.
- Row 5: P2, *K3, p1; repeat from * to last 2 stitches, p2.
- Row 6 (Buttonhole Row): K2, *k1, p1, yo, p2tog, (k1, p3) twice; repeat from * to last 2 stitches, k2.
- Row 7: Repeat Row 5.
- Row 8: Repeat Row 4.
- Rows 9–11: Purl.
- Bind off.

The Neck

- With RS facing, pick up and knit 79 stitches around neckline.
- Row 1 (WS): Knit.
- Row 2: K2, p1, yo, p2tog, knit to end of row.
- Rows 3 and 5: Knit to last 7 stitches, p2, k3, p2.
- Row 4: K2, p3, knit to end of row.
- Rows 6 and 7: Knit.
- Bind off.
- Sew buttons to left front opposite buttonholes. Weave in ends. Block.

KNITTING THE HAT

- With double-point needles, cast on 96 stitches. Divide stitches evenly onto 4 needles. Place marker and join into a round, being careful not to twist the stitches.
- Work Rounds 1 through 14 of Border pattern.
- Work Rounds 1 through 12 of Eyelet Check pattern twice, then work Rounds 1 through 6 once.

Decreasing for the Crown

- Slip marker, k1, pm to move beginning of round one stitch to the left.
- Round 1: *P3, k3, k2tog; repeat from * to end of round. *You now have 84 stitches.*
- Round 2: *P3, k4; repeat from * to end of round.
- Round 3: *P1, yo, p2tog, k2, k2tog; repeat from * to end of round. *You now have 72 stitches.*

- **Round 4:** *P3, k3; repeat from * to end of round.
- **Round 5:** *P3, k1, k2tog; repeat from * to end of round. *You now have* 60 *stitches.*
- **Round 6:** Knit.
- **Round 7:** *P3, k2tog; repeat from * to end of round. *You now have* 48 *stitches.*
- **Round 8:** *P3, k1; repeat from * to end of round.
- **Round 9:** *P2, k2tog; repeat from * to end of round. *You now have* 36 *stitches.*
- **Round 10:** *P2, k1; repeat from * to end of round.
- **Round 11:** *P1, k2tog; repeat from * to end of round. *You now have* 24 *stitches.*
- **Round 12:** *P1, k1; repeat from * to end of round.

- **Round 13:** *K2tog; repeat from * to end of round. *You now have* 12 *stitches.*
- **Round 14:** Knit.
- **Round 15:** *K2tog; repeat from * to end of round. *You now have* 6 *stitches.*

Finishing

- Cut yarn leaving a 6"/15 cm tail. Thread tail onto yarn needle and draw through remaining stitches. Pull up snug and fasten off. Weave in ends.

EYELET CHECK

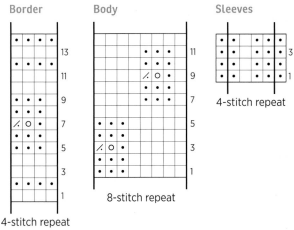

knit on RS, purl on WS

purl on RS, knit on WS

yo

p2tog on RS

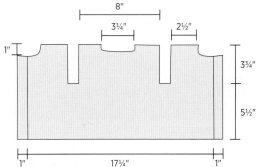

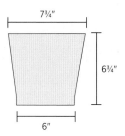

Birthday Baby

Designed by Melissa Morgan-Oakes

Melissa created this while waiting for her newest grandbaby to arrive. May you knit into your version all the joyous thoughts that babies bring. The best days are days when babies come!

SIZE AND FINISHED MEASUREMENTS

To fit newborn: 14"/35.5 cm chest circumference; 14"/35.5 cm hat circumference

YARN

Kangaroo Dyer Franklin, 75% wool/25% nylon, 450 yds (411 m)/4oz (113 g), Flower Garden ❶

NEEDLES

US 3 (3.25 mm) circular needle 24"/60 cm long and set of five US 3 (3.25 mm) double-point needles *or size needed to obtain correct gauge*

GAUGE

28 stitches and 40 rows = 4"/10 cm in stockinette stitch
31 stitches and 36 rows/rounds = 4"/10 cm in pattern stitch

OTHER SUPPLIES

Stitch markers, stitch holders or scrap yarn, four ½"/13mm buttons, 14"/35.5 cm of ⅜"/10 mm ribbon, sewing needle and coordinating thread, yarn needle

Note: The photographed sample used more ribbon for longer ties. However, we recommend keeping ties on items for young children to 6"/15 cm or less.

Pattern Essentials

PATTERN STITCH

(back and forth; multiple of 4 stitches)

Row 1 (RS): *P1, k1, p2; repeat from * to end of row.

Row 2: *K2, p1, k1; repeat from * to end of row.

Row 3: *P1, k1, p1 k1; repeat from * to end of row.

Row 4: *P1, k1, p1, k1; repeat from * to end of row.

Row 5: *P3, k1; repeat from * to end of row.

Row 6: *P1, k3; repeat from * to end of row.

Row 7: *P1, k1, p1, k1; repeat from * to end of row.

Row 8: *P1, k1, p1, k1; repeat from * to end of row.

Repeat Rows 1–8 for pattern.

PATTERN STITCH

(in the round; multiple of 4 stitches)

Rounds 1 and 2: *P1, k1, p2; repeat from * to end of row.

Rounds 3 and 4: *P1, k1; repeat from * to end of row.

Rounds 5 and 6: *P3, k1; repeat from * to end of row.

Rounds 7 and 8: *P1, k1; repeat from * to end of row.

Repeat Rounds 1–8 for pattern.

KNITTING THE SWEATER

- The sweater is knit from the top down, beginning with the yoke. A circular needle is used to accommodate the large number of stitches for the body.

- **Row 1 (RS):** K5, purl to last 5 stitches, slipping markers as you come to them, k5.
- **Row 2:** Knit to 1 stitch before marker, *yo, k1, sm, k1, yo, knit to 1 stitch before marker; repeat from * to 1 stitch before last marker, yo, k1, sm, k1, yo, knit to end of row.
- Repeat rows 1 and 2 sixteen more times, then work Row 1 once more. *You now have* 194 stitches.
- Knit 3 rows.

The Body

- Divide sleeve stitches and set aside to work body in one piece to hem as follows, knitting the stitch pattern by following chart or line-by-line instructions.
- **Dividing Row (RS):** K5, work 24 stitches in pattern Row 1, place 40 left sleeve stitches on a holder, work 56 center back stitches in pattern Row 1, place 40 right sleeve stitches on a holder, work 24 stitches in pattern Row 1, k5. *You now have* 114 stitches.
- **Next row:** Knit 5, work 104 stitches in pattern Row 2, knit 5.
- Continue in this manner, knitting the first and last 5 stitches of every row and working in pattern as established on center 104 stitches, until piece measures 8"/20.5 cm from cast-on edge.
- Knit 5 rows. Bind off.

The Sleeves (make 2)

- Place 40 held stitches onto 4 double-point needles with 8 stitches on three needles and 16 stitches on one needle.

The Yoke

- With circular needles, cast on 58 stitches.
- **Rows 1 and 2:** Knit.
- **Row 3 (RS):** (Buttonhole row) K2, yo, k2tog, k1, knit to end of row.
- **Rows 4 and 5:** Knit.

Note: Work a buttonhole as for the first 5 stitches of Row 3 every 20th row three more times.

- **Next row (WS):** K12, pm, k6, pm, k22, pm, k6, pm, k12.
- Begin shaping yoke as follows.

Sewing Buttons

We highly recommend sewing buttons onto baby clothes with a sewing needle and thread. Repeat the thread path many times to be sure the button will not come off, even if baby uses it for teething. If your buttons have large holes, you can sew first with thread, then cover the thread with yarn.

Note: If following the chart, work all chart rows from right to left.

- Work pattern stitch in the round over 40 stitches until sleeve measures 4½"/11.5 cm.

The Cuff

- **Round 1:** Purl.
- **Round 2:** *K2, k2tog; repeat from * to end of round. *You now have* 30 stitches.
- **Round 3:** Purl.
- **Round 4:** Knit.
- **Round 5:** Purl.
- Bind off.

Finishing

- Weave in ends, gently wash and block sweater. Sew buttons opposite buttonholes.

KNITTING THE HAT

- With circular needle, cast on 72 stitches. Work back and forth in pattern stitch until piece measures 4½"/11.5 cm from cast-on edge, ending on a WS row.
- **Next Row:** With RS facing, bind off 24; work center 24 stitches in pattern as established; bind off remaining 24 sts. Cut yarn. With WS facing, rejoin yarn and work in pattern as established on 24 center stitches until this new section (top of hat) measures 4"/10 cm. Bind off.
- Fold bound-off edges (arms of the T) to sides of center section and seam.

- With RS facing and beginning at lower right corner of hat, pick up and knit (see page 281) 24 stitches along right side, 18 stitches across top, and 24 stitches along left side.
- **Next Row:** *K1, p1; repeat from * to end of row.
- Repeat this row 7 more times. Bind off loosely in pattern.
- With RS facing, pick up and knit 64 stitches along bottom edge of hat. Knit 6 rows. Bind off.

Finishing

- Weave in ends, then wash and gently block hat. Attach ribbon at sides.

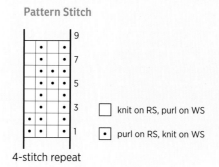

Pattern Stitch

☐ knit on RS, purl on WS

▣ purl on RS, knit on WS

4-stitch repeat

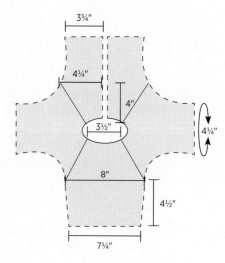

Little

TOPS

Sleeveless Baby Tees

Designed by Gail Gelin, Cottontail Creations

A simple waffle stitch is used to create these his and her baby tees. His armholes are finished with a simple knitted edging, while hers have a crocheted picot finish.

SIZE AND FINISHED MEASUREMENTS

To fit 0–3 months: 16"/40.5 cm chest circumference

YARN

Hers: Knit Picks Stroll, 75% superwash merino wool/25% nylon, 231 yds (211 m)/1.75 oz (50 g), Rouge

His: Knit Picks Essential Solid, 75% superwash wool, 25% nylon, 231 yds (211 m)/1.75 oz (50 g), Forest Heather

NEEDLES

Size US 3 (3.25 mm) straight needles for body, set of two US 3 (3.25 mm) double-point needles for His finishing, US D-3 (3.25 mm) crochet hook for Hers finishing *or size needed to obtain correct gauge*

GAUGE

24 stitches and 32 rows = 4"/10 cm in pattern, washed and blocked

OTHER SUPPLIES

Stitch holders, yarn needle, rosebud decoration (optional for Hers)

Pattern Essentials

WAFFLE STITCH

(multiple of 3 + 1 stitches)

Row 1 (RS): Knit.

Row 2 (WS): Purl.

Row 3: K1, *p2, k1; repeat from * to end of row.

Row 4: Purl.

ATTACHED I-CORD EDGING

Cast on desired number of I-cord stitches onto a double-point needle. *Slide the stitches to the other end and use a second needle to knit to the last stitch. Slip the last stitch knitwise onto the right needle. Pick up and knit one stitch from the garment edge. Pass the slipped stitch over this stitch. Repeat from * to the end of the edge you're covering. Bind off. If edging a circular piece, sew bind off to cast on.

KNITTING THE BACK

- Cast on 49 stitches using the long-tail cast on method (see page 279). Work Rows 2 through 4 of Waffle Stitch, then work Rows 1 through 4 of pattern 20 times.

Shaping the Back Neck

- **Row 1 (RS):** Work Row 1 of pattern over 18 stitches and place them on a holder for the right shoulder; bind off 13 stitches; work Row 1 of pattern over remaining stitches. *You now have* 18 stitches for the left shoulder.

- **Rows 2–4:** Keeping 3 stitches at neck edge in stockinette stitch throughout remainder of shoulder, work in pattern as established.

- **Rows 5 and 7:** K1, ssk, work in pattern as established to end of row.

- **Rows 6 and 8:** Work even in pattern. *You have* 16 stitches at the end of Row 8.

- **Rows 9–12:** Work even in pattern.

- Place stitches on holder and cut yarn leaving a 10"/25.5 cm tail.

- Place held right shoulder stitches on a needle and join yarn.

- With WS facing, work Rows 2–4 of pattern.

- **Decrease Row (RS):** Work in pattern to last 3 stitches, k2tog, k1.

- **Next Row:** Keeping 3 stitches at neck edge in stockinette stitch throughout remainder of shoulder, work even in pattern.

- Repeat last two rows once more. *You now have* 16 stitches.

- Work 4 rows even in pattern as established.

- Place stitches on holder and cut yarn leaving a 10"/25.5 cm tail.

KNITTING THE FRONT

- Cast on 49 stitches using the long-tail method. Work Rows 2 through 4 of Waffle Stitch, then work Rows 1 through 4 of pattern 18 times.

Shaping the Front Neck

- **Row 1 (RS):** Work Row 1 of pattern over 18 stitches and place them on a holder for the left shoulder; bind off 13 stitches; work Row 1 of pattern over remaining stitches. *You now have* 18 stitches for the right shoulder.

- **Rows 2–4:** Keeping 3 stitches at neck edge in stockinette stitch throughout remainder of shoulder, work in pattern as established.

- **Rows 5 and 7:** K1, ssk, work in pattern as established to end of row.

- **Rows 6 and 8:** Work even in pattern. *You have* 16 stitches at the end of Row 8.

- **Rows 9–20:** Work even in pattern.

- Place stitches on holder and cut yarn leaving a 10"/25.5 cm tail.

- Place held left shoulder stitches on a needle and join yarn.

- With WS facing, work Rows 2–4 of pattern, keeping 3 stitches at neck edge in stockinette stitch throughout remainder of shoulder.

- **Decrease Row (RS):** Work in pattern to last 3 stitches, k2tog, k1.

- **Next Row:** Work even in pattern.

- Repeat last two rows. *You now have* 16 stitches.

- Work 12 rows even in pattern as established.

- Place stitches on holder and cut yarn leaving a 10"/25.5 cm tail.

BLOCKING THE PIECES

- Block the front and back pieces to match the schematic.

JOINING THE FRONT AND BACK

- Join front and back shoulders with three-needle bind off (see page 282). Sew side seams 6½"/16.5 cm up from lower edge, leaving the remaining 5½"/14 cm open for the armholes.

FINISHING

- Beginning at underarms and back neck respectively, work edgings along armholes and neck opening as follows.

- *His:* Work a 3-stitch attached I-cord edging (see page 50).

- *Hers:* Join yarn with RS facing. With crochet hook, *chain 5, skip 1, single crochet in next stitch; repeat from * around. Sew rosebud to center front neck edge (optional).

Waffle Stitch

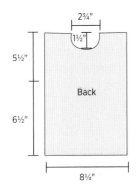

3-stitch repeat

□ k on RS, p on WS

• p on RS, k on WS

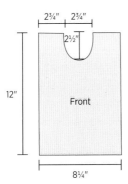

Back

5½"

6½"

2¾"

1½"

8¼"

Front

12"

2¾" 2¾"

2½"

8¼"

Baby Crown Tee

Designed by Jenise Reid

Baby Crown Tee is a delicate little top with a pretty lace yoke. If you do not like the nupps in the lace, you can simply leave them out or replace them with beads. Baby Crown Tee is knit from the bottom up, in the round, and there's a little bit of grafting at the underarm.

....
SIZES AND FINISHED MEASUREMENTS
To fit 12 (24) months: 20 (22)"/51 (56) cm chest circumference
....
YARN
The Uncommon Thread Merino Fingering, 100% superwash merino wool, 437 yds (400 m)/3.5 oz (100 g), Confetti ①

....
NEEDLES
US 5 (3.75 mm) circular needle 16"/40 cm long and set of four or five US 5 (3.75 mm) double-point needles *or size needed to obtain correct gauge*

....
GAUGE
24 stitches and 36 rows = 4"/10 cm in stockinette stitch, blocked

....
OTHER SUPPLIES
Stitch marker, scrap yarn for holders, yarn needle, three ½"/ 13 mm buttons

KNITTING THE SLEEVES (make 2)

- With double-point needles, cast on 35 (43) stitches and join into a round, being careful not to twist the stitches.

- **Rows 1–9:** *K2, p1; repeat from * to last 2 (1) stitches, k2 (1).

- Cut yarn leaving about a 1 yd/1 m tail. Place stitches on holder and set aside.

KNITTING THE BODY

- With circular needles, cast on 120 (132) stitches. Place marker and join into a round, being careful not to twist the stitches.

- **Rows 1–18:** *K2, p1; repeat from * to end of round.

- Work in stockinette stitch until piece measures 6 (7)"/15 (18) cm from beginning. If you want to change the length of the sweater, do it here. Adding a couple inches will allow the child to wear the sweater for an extra year or two, and one skein is more than enough yarn for either size.

Pattern Essentials

Nupp-7 [(Knit 1, yo) 3 times, k1] all into the same stitch, making 7 stitches from 1 stitch. On the next row, knit the 7 stitches together as 1.

KNITTING THE YOKE

- Using a tail from one sleeve, graft the next 9 stitches from one sleeve to the first 9 body stitches with Kitchener stitch (see page 278); using the body yarn, knit the remaining sleeve stitches onto the circular needle (*you now have 26 (34) additional sleeve stitches on the body needle*); k51 (57) body stitches; using the tail from the remaining sleeve, graft next 9 stitches from the second sleeve to the next 9 body stitches; using the body yarn, knit the remaining sleeve stitches onto the circular needle; k51 (57) body stitches. *You now have* 154 (182) stitches.

- *Size 12 months only:* Remove marker, k3, pm to move the beginning of the round.

Begin Lace Pattern

Note: At the ends of Rounds 6, 8, 10, 12, and 14, remove marker, slip 1st stitch of next round to right needle, and replace marker, moving start of round one stitch forward.

- **Rounds 1–2:** Knit.

- **Round 3:** *K6, yo, ssk, k6; repeat from * to end of round.

- **Rounds 4, 6, 8, 10, 12, and 14:** Knit.

- **Round 5:** *K4, k2tog, yo, k1, yo, ssk, k5; repeat from * to end of round.

- **Round 7:** *Yo, k2, k2tog, yo, k3, yo, ssk, k2, yo, s2kp; repeat from * to end of round.

- **Round 9:** *Yo, k1, k2tog, yo, k1, yo, s2kp, yo, k1, yo, ssk, k1, yo, s2kp; repeat from * to end of round.

- **Round 11:** *Yo, k2tog, yo, k2, yo, s2kp, yo, k2, yo, ssk, yo, s2kp; repeat from * to end of round.

- **Round 13:** *Yo, k2, nupp-7, k1, yo, s2kp, yo, k1, nupp-7, k2, yo, s2kp; repeat from * to end of round.

- **Round 15:** *Yo, k1, nupp-7, k2, yo, s2kp, yo, k2, nupp-7, k1, yo, s2kp; repeat from * to end of round.

- Knit 4 of the next round, cast on 6 stitches. *You now have* 160 (188) stitches. Turn and begin knitting back and forth.

- **Row 16:** Purl.

- **Row 17:** Slip 1, *k7, yo, s2kp, yo, k4; repeat from * to last 5 stitches, p1, k4.

- **Row 18:** Slip 1 wyif, p2, k1, purl to end of row.

- **Row 19:** Slip 1, k5, k2tog, yo, *k3, yo, ssk, k2, yo, s2kp, yo, k2, k2tog, yo; repeat from * to last 12 stitches, k3, yo, ssk, [k1, p1, k1] twice, k1.

- **Row 20:** Slip 1 wyif, (k1, p2) twice, purl to end of row.

- **Row 21:** Slip 1, k4, k2tog, yo, k2, *(k3, yo, s2kp, yo) twice, k2; repeat from * to last 11 stitches, k3, yo, ssk, k2, p1, k3.

- **Row 22:** Slip 1 wyif, (p1, k1, p1) twice, purl to end of row.

- **Row 23:** Slip 1, k1, ssk, yo, k1, yo, ssk, k2tog, k1, ssk, *(k2tog, yo, k1) twice, k1, yo, ssk, k2tog, k1, ssk; repeat from * to last 8 stitches, k2tog, yo, (k1, p1, k1) twice. *You now have* 138 (162) stitches.

- **Row 24:** Slip 1 wyif, p2, k1, purl to end of row.

- **Row 25:** S1, k2, *k3, yo, ssk, k1, k2tog, yo, k2, ssk, yo; repeat from * to last 15 stitches, k3, yo, ssk, k1, k2tog, yo, (k1, p1, k1) twice, k1.

- **Row 26:** Slip 1 wyif, (k1, p2) twice, purl to end of row.

- **Row 27:** Slip 1, k2, *k4, yo, s2kp, yo, k3, ssk, yo; repeat from * to last 15 stitches, k4, yo, s2kp, yo, k4, p1, k3.

- **Row 28:** Slip 1 wyif, (p1, k1, p1) twice, purl to end of row.

- **Row 29:** Slip 1, k1, *k5, yo, s2kp, yo, k2, k2tog, yo; repeat from * to last 16 stitches, k5, yo, s2kp, yo, k2, (k1, p1, k1) twice.

- **Row 30:** Slip 1 wyif, p2, k1, purl to end of row.

- **Row 31:** S1, k1, ssk, yo, k3, yo, s2kp, yo, *k5, yo, ssk, k2, yo, s2kp, yo; repeat from * to last 8 stitches, (k2, p1) twice, k2.

- **Row 32:** Slip 1 wyif, (k1, p2) twice, purl to end of row.

- **Row 33:** Slip 1, k1, *k3, ssk, yo, s2kp, yo, k2tog twice, yo; repeat from * to last 16 stitches, k3, ssk, yo, s2kp, yo, k2tog, k2, p1, k3. *You now have* 116 (136) stitches.

- **Row 34:** Slip 1 wyif, (p1, k1, p1) twice, purl to end of row.

- **Row 35:** Slip 1, *k5, yo, s2kp, yo, k2; repeat from * to last 5 stitches, p1, k2, p1, k1.

- **Row 36:** Slip 1 wyif, p2, k1, purl to end of row.

- **Row 37:** Slip 1, *k3, ssk, yo, s2kp, yo, k2tog; repeat from * to last 5

stitches, k2, p1, k2. *You now have 94 (110) stitches.*

- **Row 38:** Slip 1 wyif, (k1, p2) twice, purl to end of row.

- **Row 39:** Slip 1, k1, ssk, yo, k2, ssk, *k1, k2tog, k1, ssk, k2; repeat from * to last 6 stitches, k2, p1, k3. *You now have 73 (85) stitches.*

- **Row 40:** Slip 1 wyif, p1, k1, purl to end of row.

- **Row 41:** Slip 1, k66 (78), (k1, p1, k1) twice.

- **Row 42:** Slip 1 wyif, p2, k1, purl to end of row.

- **Row 43:** Slip 1, k69 (81), p1, k2.

- **Row 44 (turning ridge):** Bind off 5 stitches, knit.

- **Row 45:** Knit.

- **Row 46:** Purl.

FINISHING

- Fold the neck edge to the inside at the turning ridge. Sew each live stitch loosely to the back of the purl bumps to allow the neckline to stretch. Weave in ends.

- Sew three buttons to the button band opposite buttonholes.

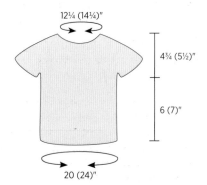

Warm Heart Baby Vest

Designed by Ellen Harvey

A simple surplice-wrap vest is designed to keep a baby warm without having to fuss with sleeves. Knit in washable wool in seed stitch and seed stitch variation, this is an easy-to-knit but handsome garment.

Pattern Essentials

SEED STITCH

(odd number of stitches)

Row 1: *K1, p1; repeat from * to last stitch, k1.

Repeat Row 1 for pattern.

DOT STITCH

(multiple of 4 + 3 stitches)

Row 1 (RS): K1, *p1, k3; repeat from * to last 2 stitches, p1, k1.

Row 2: Purl.

Row 3: *K3, p1; repeat from * to last 3 stitches, k3.

Row 4: Repeat Row 2.

Repeat Rows 1–4 for pattern.

SIZE AND FINISHED MEASUREMENTS

To fit 6–12 months: 20"/51 cm chest circumference

YARN

Carodan Farms Yarns Chincoteague Colors, 100% superwash merino wool, 250 yds (229 m)/4 oz (118 g), Chincoteague Waters (3)

NEEDLES

US 6 (4 mm) straight needles *or size needed to obtain correct gauge*

GAUGE

20 stitches and 32 rows = 4"/10 cm in Dot Stitch pattern, blocked

OTHER SUPPLIES

Stitch holders or scrap yarn, yarn needle, two ⁷⁄₁₆"/11 mm buttons, sewing needle and coordinating thread

KNITTING THE BACK

- Cast on 51 stitches. Work in Seed Stitch for 1"/2.5 cm, ending with a WS row. Work in Dot Stitch until piece measures 7"/18 cm from cast-on edge.

Shaping the Armholes and Back Neck

- Continuing in Dot Stitch as established and maintaining 1 stockinette stitch at each edge, decrease 1 stitch at the beginning and end of every RS row 4 times, working k1, ssk at the beginning and k2tog, k1 at the end of the decrease rows. *You now have* 43 stitches.

- Continue in Dot Stitch until armholes measure 3¾"/9.5 cm.

- **Next Row:** Work 13 stitches in pattern as established and place them on hold; bind off 17 stitches; work to end of row and place remaining 13 stitches on hold.

KNITTING THE RIGHT FRONT

- Cast on 47 stitches. Work in Seed Stitch for 1"/2.5 cm, ending with a WS row.

- **Buttonhole Row (RS):** K2, yo, k2tog, work Row 1 of Dot Stitch to last 4 stitches, k2tog, yo, k2.

- **Next row (WS):** Work in established Dot Stitch.

- **Next row (decrease row):** K1, k2tog, work in pattern to end of row. *You now have* 46 stitches.

- Maintaining pattern, continue to decrease 1 st at beginning of each RS row until piece measures 7"/18 cm from cast-on edge, ending with a WS row.

Shaping the Armhole

- **Row 1 (RS):** K1, k2tog, work in pattern to last 3 stitches, k2tog, k1.

- **Row 2:** P2, work in pattern to end.

- **Rows 3–8:** Repeat Rows 1 and 2 three more times.

- Continue in Dot Stitch as established, decreasing at the beginning of every RS row, until 13 stitches remain. Work even in pattern until armhole measures 3¾"/9.5 cm. Place stitches on hold.

KNITTING THE LEFT FRONT

- Cast on 47 stitches. Work in Seed Stitch for 1"/2.5 cm, ending with a WS row.
- **Row 1 (RS, decrease row):** Work Row 1 of Dot Stitch to last 3 stitches, ssk, k1. *You now have 46 stitches.*
- **Row 2:** Work in established pattern.
- Maintaining pattern, continue to decrease 1 stitch at end of each right side row until piece measures 7"/18 cm from cast-on edge, ending with a wrong side row.

Shaping the Armhole

- **Row 1 (RS):** K1, ssk, work in pattern to last 3 stitches, ssk, k1.
- **Row 2:** Work in pattern to last 2 stitches, p2.
- **Rows 3–8:** Repeat Rows 1 and 2 three more times.
- Continue in Dot stitch as established, decreasing at the end of every right side row, until 13 stitches remain. Work even in pattern until armhole measures 3¾"/9.5 cm. Place stitches on hold.

FINISHING

- Join fronts to back at shoulder with three-needle bind off (see page 282).
- With RS facing and beginning at underarm, pick up and knit (see page 281) 3 of every 4 stitches around armhole, ending with an odd number of stitches. Work seed stitch for 6 rows. Bind off in pattern. Repeat for second armhole.
- With RS facing and beginning at lower right front edge, pick up and knit 3 of every 4 stitches up to shoulder, pick up and knit 17 back neck stitches, pick up and knit 3 of every 4 stitches along left front to same number picked up for right front, ending with an odd number of stitches. Work Seed Stitch for 6 rows. Bind off in pattern.
- Sew side seams. Sew buttons to lower left-front edge to align with buttonholes on lower right-front edge. Weave in ends. Block.

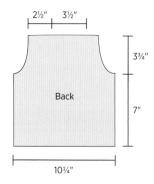

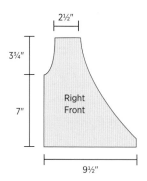

Diamond Vest

Designed by Jenny Snedeker, Cutie Pie Fashions

This easy-to-knit vest is worked in pieces and seamed and features a unique button closure. The self-striping yarn makes it fun to knit, and no two will be exactly alike.

SIZES AND FINISHED MEASUREMENTS

To fit 6 (12) months: 18 (20)"/45.5 (51) cm chest circumference. Sample shown is 12 months.

YARN

Knit One Crochet Too Ty-Dy Sandbox, 70% acrylic/30% wool, 251 yds (230 m)/3.5 oz (100 g), Color 5875 Olive Taupe (4)

NEEDLES

US 8 (5 mm) straight needles *or size needed to obtain correct gauge*

GAUGE

16 stitches and 24 rows = 4"/10 cm in stockinette stitch

OTHER SUPPLIES

Two locking stitch markers, stitch holders or scrap yarn, spare needle for bind off, yarn needle, three ¾"/19 mm buttons

KNITTING THE BACK

- Cast on 36 (40) stitches. Knit 7 rows, increasing 4 stitches evenly spaced on last row. *You now have* 40 (44) stitches.

- Work in stockinette stitch until piece measures 5½ (6¼)"/14 (16) cm from cast-on edge, ending with a wrong side row.

Shaping the Armholes

- Bind off 4 stitches at the beginning of the next 2 rows. *You now have* 32 (36) stitches.
- **Decrease Row (RS):** K2, ssk, knit to last 4 stitches, k2tog, k2. *You now have* 30 (34) stitches.
- **Next Row:** Purl.
- Repeat these two rows once more. *You now have* 28 (32) stitches.
- Work even in stockinette stitch until piece measures 10 (11)"/25.5 (28) cm from cast-on edge. Place stitches on hold.

KNITTING THE LEFT FRONT

- Cast on 14 (16) stitches. Knit 7 rows, increasing 4 stitches evenly spaced on last row. *You now have* 18 (20) stitches.
- Work in stockinette stitch until piece measures 5½ (6¼)"/14 (16) cm from cast-on edge, ending with a wrong side row.

Shaping the Armhole and Neck

- Bind off 4 stitches at the beginning of the next RS row, knit to last 3 stitches, k2tog, k1. Place a locking stitch marker at the end of this row.
- **Next Row (WS):** Purl.
- **Decrease Row:** K2, k2tog, knit to last 3 stitches, k2tog, k1.
- Repeat armhole decrease at the beginning of every RS row 0 (1) more time and *at the same time* work neck decreases every 6th row once then every 4th row 3 times. *You now have* 7 (8) stitches.
- Work even until left front measures 10 (11)"/25.5 (28) cm from cast-on edge. Place stitches on hold.

KNITTING THE RIGHT FRONT

- Work as for left front until piece measures 5½ (6¼)"/14 (16) cm from cast-on edge, ending with a WS row.

Shaping the Armhole and Neck

- **Next Row (RS):** K1, ssk, knit to end of row. Place a locking stitch marker at the beginning of this row.
- **Next Row (WS):** Bind off 4 stitches, purl to end of row.
- **Decrease row (RS):** K1, ssk, knit to last 4 stitches, k2tog, k2.
- Purl 1 row.
- Repeat armhole decrease at the end of every RS row 0 (1) more time and *at the same time* work neck decreases every 6th row once then every 4th row 3 times. *You now have* 7 (8) stitches.
- Work even until right front measures same as left front.

JOINING THE SHOULDERS

- Place 7 (8) back right shoulder stitches on needle. Using three-needle bind off (see page 282), join right front and back shoulders. Leaving next 14 (16) back neck stitches on hold, place last 7 (8) back left shoulder stitches on needle; place front left shoulder stitches on second needle. Using three-needle bind off, join left front and back shoulders.

KNITTING THE BANDS

The Armbands

- With right side facing and beginning at underarm, pick up and knit (see page 281) 3 stitches out of every 4 rows around armhole. Knit 2 rows, bind off knitwise on a wrong side row. Repeat for other armhole.

The Neck Band

- With right side facing and beginning at right front neck decrease marker, pick up and knit 3 stitches out of every 4 rows to shoulder seam, knit 14 (16) back neck stitches from holder, pick up and knit 3 stitches out of every 4 rows to left front neck decrease marker. Knit 2 rows, bind off knitwise on a wrong side row.

The Buttonhole Bands

Note: Consider working buttonholes on both sides for easily converting for a boy or girl.

- With right side facing and beginning at lower edge of right front, pick up and knit 24 (30) stitches along center front, ending with 2 stitches in end of neck band.

- Working 8 (10) stitches at a time, continue as follows.

- **Row 1:** Slip 1 wyif, k7 (9), turn, leaving remaining stitches unworked.

- **Row 2:** Slip 1 wyif, k3 (4), kfb, k3 (4). *You now have* 9 (11) stitches.

- **Row 3:** Slip 1 wyif, ssk, k3 (5), k2tog, k1. *You now have* 7 (9) stitches.

- *Larger size only:*

- **Row 4:** Slip 1 wyif, knit to end of row.

- **Row 5:** Slip 1 wyif, ssk, k3, k2tog, k1. *You now have* 7 stitches.

- **Row 6:** Repeat Row 4.

- *Both Sizes:*

- **Row 7:** Slip 1 wyif, ssk, yo, k2tog twice (buttonhole made). *You now have* 5 stitches.

- **Row 8:** Slip 1 wyif, knit to end of row.

- **Row 9:** Slip 1 wyif, ssk, k2tog. *You now have* 3 stitches.

- **Row 10:** Repeat Row 8.

- **Row 11:** Slip 1 wyif, k2tog, psso. Cut yarn and fasten off.

- With right side facing, rejoin yarn at front edge and repeat Rows 1–11 for remaining 2 groups of stitches.

- Repeat buttonhole band sequence for left front.

FINISHING

- Sew buttons opposite buttonholes, on right front for boys and on left front for girls. Sew underarm seams. Weave in ends. Block to measurements.

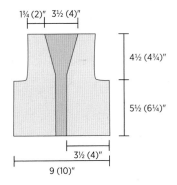

Lacy Baby Top

Designed by Carol J. Sorsdahl

This lovely lacy baby top is knit from the top down with an increasing rib worked back and forth for the yoke and a lace pattern worked circularly for the body. The subtle hand-dyed yarn adds highlights.

KNITTING THE NECKBAND

- With circular needle, cast on 64 stitches using the cable cast on method (see page 276). Do not join; the yoke is worked back and forth in rows.

- **Row 1 (RS):** Knit.

- **Row 2:** Knit.

- **Rows 3 and 4:** Repeat Rows 1 and 2.

KNITTING THE YOKE

- **Row 1 (RS, increase row):** K4, (M1, k1) 7 times, (M1, k2) 21 times, (M1, k1) 7 times, k2tog, yo, k2 (buttonhole made). *You now have* 99 stitches.

- **Row 2 (WS):** K4, *k1, p1; repeat from * to last 5 stitches, k5.

- **Row 3:** K4, p1, *k1, p1; repeat from * to last 4 stitches, k4.

- **Rows 4–9:** Repeat Rows 2 and 3 three times.

- **Row 10:** Repeat Row 2.

- **Row 11 (increase row):** K4, *p1, M1, k1; repeat from * to last 5 stitches, p1, k2tog, yo, k2 (buttonhole made). *You now have* 144 stitches.

- **Row 12:** K5, *p2, k1; repeat from * to last 4 stitches, k4.

- **Row 13:** K4, *p1, k2; repeat from * to last 5 stitches, p1, k4.

- **Rows 14–19:** Repeat Rows 12 and 13 three times.

- **Row 20:** Repeat Row 12.

- **Row 21 (increase row):** K4, p1, *k1, kfb, p1; repeat from * to last 7 stitches, k2, p1, k2tog, yo, k2 (buttonhole made). *You now have* 188 stitches.

SIZE AND FINISHED MEASUREMENTS
To fit 6–24 months: 19"/48 cm chest circumference

YARN
Wonderland Yarns Hand-dyed "Cheshire Cat" sock/fingering, 100% superwash merino wool, 512 yds (468 m)/4 oz (113 g), Cherry Tarts, [1]

NEEDLES
US 3 (3.25 mm) circular needle 24"/60 cm long and set of four US 3 (3.25 mm) double-point needles *or size needed to obtain correct gauge*

GAUGE
28 stitches and 36 rows = 4"/10 cm in 2x2 rib
27 stitches and 36 rows = 4"/10 cm in lace pattern

OTHER SUPPLIES
Four locking stitch markers, 20 regular stitch markers (one in a unique color for marking beginning of round), scrap yarn for holders, yarn needle, three ⅜"/10 mm buttons, sewing needle and coordinating thread

Pattern Essentials

LACE
(multiple of 10 stitches)

Round 1: Knit.

Round 2: *Yo, k3, sk2p, k3, yo, k1; repeat from * to end of round.

Round 3: Knit.

Round 4: *K1, yo, k2, sk2p, k2, yo, k2; repeat from * to end of round.

Round 5: Knit.

Round 6: *K2, yo, k1, sk2p, k1, yo, k3; repeat from * to end of round.

Round 7: Knit.

Round 8: *K3, yo, sk2p, yo, k4; repeat from * to end of round.

Repeat Rounds 1 through 8 for pattern.

- **Row 22:** K5, p2, *k2, p2; repeat from * to last 5 stitches, k5.
- **Row 23:** K4, *p1, k2, p1; repeat from * to last 4 stitches, k4.
- **Rows 24–25:** Repeat Rows 22 and 23.
- **Row 26:** Repeat Row 22.
- **Round 27 (joining round):** K4, *p1, k2, p1; repeat from * to last 4 stitches; place last 4 stitches onto a double-point needle and hold needles so that the first 4 stitches of the round are behind the last 4 stitches; knit these last 4 stitches together with first 4 stitches (buttonhole band now overlaps button band). Place marker to indicate beginning of round. *You now have 184 stitches.*
- **Round 28:** *P1, k2, p1; repeat from * to last 4 stitches, p4.
- **Round 29:** *P1, k2, p7; repeat from * to last 4 stitches, k4.
- **Round 30:** Purl.
- **Round 31:** Knit.
- **Round 32:** Purl.

DIVIDING THE SLEEVES FROM THE BODY

- Work Round 1 (increase round) as follows.
- **Right Front:** K1, (M1L, k2) fourteen times, M1L, k1; place next 32 stitches on scrap yarn for sleeve; cast on 10 underarm stitches using backward loop cast on (see page 276).
- **Back:** K1, (M1L, k2) 29 times, M1L, k1; place next 32 stitches on scrap yarn for sleeve; cast on 10 underarm stitches using backward loop cast on.
- **Left Front:** K1, (M1L, k2) 14 times, M1L, k1. *You now have 200 stitches.*

KNITTING THE BODY

Note: You will now begin the Lace pattern; pm after each 10-stitch repeat.

- Work the 8-round lace pattern 6 times, 48 rounds total.
- **Round 49:** Knit, removing all but beginning marker.

- **Round 50:** Purl.
- **Round 51:** Knit.
- Bind off purlwise.

KNITTING THE SLEEVE BANDS (make 2)

- With double-point needles and beginning at center of underarm, pick up and knit (see page 281) 6 underarm stitches, knit the 32 held sleeve stitches, then pick up and knit 6 underarm stitches. *You now have 44 stitches.*
- Bind off purlwise.

FINISHING

- Weave in ends. Sew buttons to the button band, opposite the button-holes. Wet block and lay flat to dry, shaping as necessary.

Lace Pattern

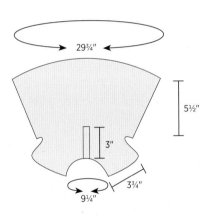

10-stitch repeat

☐ k on RS, p on WS

⅄ sk2p

○ yo

Entrechat Shrug

Designed by Lisa Chemery, Frogginette Knitting Patterns

Both the heartwarming style and the textured stitch are evocative of the "entrechat," a ballet jump where the legs cross each other mid-air in a flutter. The shrug is knit seamlessly from the top down to the underarms. The raglan cap sleeves are then bound off and the back is worked together with stitches picked up along the front sleeve edges to form the body in one piece.

29¾"

5½"

3"

3¾"

9¼"

SIZES AND FINISHED MEASUREMENTS

To fit 3 (6, 12, 18) months: 16 (17, 18, 19)"/40.5 (43, 45.5, 48.5) cm chest circumference; 9 (9¾, 10¾, 11½)"/23 (25, 27.5, 29) cm cross-back measurement

YARN

Malabrigo Merino Worsted, 100% merino wool, 210 yds (192 m)/3.5 oz (100 g), Color 17 Pink Frost 4

NEEDLES

US 8 (5 mm) cm circular needle 24"/60 long *or size needed to obtain correct gauge*

GAUGE

18 stitches and 28 rows = 4"/10 cm in stockinette stitch

OTHER SUPPLIES

2 stitch markers, yarn needle, one ⅝"/15 mm button

SPECIAL ABBREVIATIONS

inc-1
   Increase 1 by placing a backwards loop onto the right needle (see page 276).

KNITTING THE YOKE AND THE SLEEVES

- Cast on 22 (24, 26, 34) stitches.
- **Set-Up Row 1 (RS):** K4 (4, 4, 6), pm, k14 (16, 18, 22), pm, k4 (4, 4, 6).
- **Set-Up Row 2:** Knit.

Working the Raglan Increases

- **Row 1 (Increase Row):** K2, M1R, *knit to 1 stitch before marker, M1L, k1, sm, k1, M1R; repeat from * once more, knit to last 2 stitches, M1L, k2. *You now have* 28 (30, 32, 40) stitches.
- **Row 2:** Knit.
- **Rows 3–6:** Repeat Rows 1 and 2 two more times. *You now have* 40 (42, 44, 52) stitches.
- **Row 7:** Repeat Row 1. *You now have* 46 (48, 50, 58) stitches.
- **Row 8:** Purl.
- Repeat Rows 7 and 8 seven (eight, nine, nine) more times, then work Row 7 once more. *You now have* 38 (42, 46, 50) back stitches and 28 (30, 32, 34) stitches for each sleeve.

- **Next Row (WS):** K28 (30, 32, 34), sm, p38 (42, 46, 50), sm, k28 (30, 32, 34).
- **Increase Row (RS):** Repeat Row 1. *You now have* 40 (44, 48, 52) back stitches and 30 (32, 34, 36) stitches for each sleeve, 100 (108, 116, 124) stitches total.
- **Next Row:** Bind off 30 (32, 34, 36) sleeve stitches knitwise, p40 (44, 48, 52) back stitches, bind off 30 (32, 34, 36) sleeve stitches. *You now have* 40 (44, 48, 52) stitches. Cut yarn, leaving a 6"/15 cm tail. Leave stitches on needle.

PICKING UP FRONT SLEEVE STITCHES

- With right side facing and beginning at left neck edge, join yarn and pick up and knit 15 (16, 17, 17) stitches for the left front by picking up 1 stitch for every garter ridge and 1 stitch for every 2 stockinette rows along front sleeve, then 1 stitch for every garter ridge at the bound-off sleeve edge.
- Fold left sleeve in half with wrong sides together and k40 (44, 48, 52) back stitches from left underarm to right underarm. **Note:** Be sure and work the first back stitch snugly to prevent any gap from forming at the transition.
- Fold right sleeve in half with wrong sides together and, with same working yarn, pick up and knit 15 (16, 17, 17) stitches for the right front, beginning at the underarm and working up to the neck edge. *You now have* 70 (76, 82, 86) stitches.

KNITTING THE BODY

- **Row 1 (WS):** Knit to last stitch, slip 1 purlwise wyif.

- **Rows 2–4:** Repeat Row 1.

- **Row 5:** K4, purl to last 4 stitches, k3, slip 1 purlwise wyif.

Begin Textured Pattern

- **Row 1 (RS):** K4, *yo, k2, pass yo over the k2; repeat from * to last 4 stitches, k3, slip 1 purlwise wyif.

- **Row 2:** K4, purl to last 4 stitches, k3, slip 1 purlwise wyif.

- **Row 3:** K5, *yo, k2, pass yo over the k2; repeat from * to last 5 stitches, k4, slip 1 purlwise wyif.

- **Row 4:** Repeat Row 2.

- **Rows 5 and 6:** Repeat Rows 1 and 2.

- *For largest size only,* repeat Rows 3 and 4.

- **Next 3 Rows:** Knit to last stitch, slip 1 purlwise wyif

- **Next Row (WS):** K15 (16, 17, 17), pm, k40 (44, 48, 52) back stitches, pm, k14 (15, 16, 16), slip 1 purlwise wyif.

Increasing for the Back Ruffle

- **Increase Row (RS):** Knit to marker, sm, (inc-1, k2) 3 times, (inc-1, k1) to 6 stitches before marker, (inc-1, k2) 3 times, m1, sm, knit to last stitch, slip 1 purlwise wyif. *You now have 105 (115, 125, 133) stitches.*

- **Next Row (WS):** Removing markers, k4, purl to last 4 stitches, k3, slip 1 purlwise wyif.

- **Next Row (RS):** Knit to last stitch, slip 1 purlwise wyif.

- Repeat these 2 rows until piece measures 1 (1, 1½, 1½)"/2.5 (2.5, 4, 4) cm from increase row, ending with a RS row.

The Garter Edge

- **Rows 1–3:** Knit to last stitch, slip 1 purlwise wyif.

- **Row 4 (RS):** Knit to last 4 stitches, k2tog, yo, k1, slip 1 purlwise wyif (buttonhole made).

- **Rows 5 and 6:** Knit to last stitch, slip 1 purlwise wyif.

- Bind off knitwise on wrong side.

FINISHING

- Weave in ends. Firmly sew button on left neck edge opposite buttonhole. Wet block.

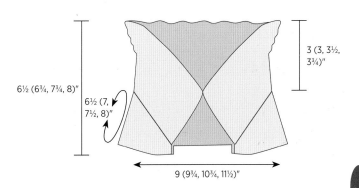

6½ (6¾, 7¾, 8)"

6½ (7, 7½, 8)"

3 (3, 3½, 3¾)"

9 (9¾, 10¾, 11½)"

Saint Catherine's Cache-Coeur

Designed by Ranée Mueller

A lovely little shrug knit in one piece with a crossover front will hold baby's heart and keep it warm. The back features a lace heart motif.

SIZES AND FINISHED MEASUREMENTS
To fit 0–6 (6–12) months: 16 (18)"/40.5 (45.5) cm chest circumference. Sample shown in larger size.

YARN
Madelinetosh Tosh Vintage, 100% superwash merino wool, 200 yds (183 m)/3.5 oz (100 g), Dr. Zhivago's Sky (4)

NEEDLES
US 6 (4 mm) straight needles *or size needed to obtain correct gauge*

GAUGE
21 stitches and 32 rows = 4"/10 cm in stockinette stitch

OTHER SUPPLIES
Stitch markers, two ¾"/19 mm buttons

SPECIAL ABBREVIATIONS
Dec 4 (decrease 4)

    Slip three stitches purlwise from left needle to right needle. Pass second stitch on right needle over the last stitch and off the needle. Slip the last stitch to the left needle and pass the next stitch over it and off the needle. Slip the stitch back to the right needle and pass the first slipped stitch over it and off the needle. Slip the stitch back to the left needle and pass the following stitch over it and off the needle. Knit the stitch.

W3 (wrap 3)

    With yarn in back, slip next 3 stitches purlwise from left needle to right needle. Bring yarn to front and slip the stitches back to the left needle. Bring yarn to back and knit the 3 stitches.

KNITTING THE CACHE-COEUR

- Cast on 45 (51) stitches.

- **Rows 1–4:** Knit.

- **Row 5:** K3, M1R, knit to last 3 stitches, M1L, k3. *You now have 47 (53) stitches.*

- **Row 6:** K3, purl to last 3 stitches, k3.

- Repeat Rows 5 and 6 one (two) more times. *You now have 49 (57) stitches.*

- **Next Row:** K3, M1R, k9 (13), pm, work Row 1 of Lace Heart chart (see page 70) over next 25 stitches, pm, k9 (13), M1L, k3. *You now have 51 (59) stitches.*

- Continuing to increase at each edge of RS rows as established and working stockinette stitch at the beginning and end of all rows and working Lace Heart chart over center 25 stitches, work through Row 34 of chart. Remove markers.

- Continuing to increase at each edge of RS rows as established, work in stockinette stitch until you have 89 (97) stitches, ending on a RS row.

Shaping the Neck

- **Row 1 (WS):** K3, p34 (35), pm, k15 (21), pm, p34 (35), k3.

- **Row 2:** Knit.

- **Row 3:** K3, p34 (35), k15 (21), p34 (35), k3.

- Repeat Rows 2 and 3 one more time.

- **Next Row (RS):** K40 (41), bind off 9 (15), knit to end of row.

Working the Fronts

Note: The fronts are worked one side at a time; place unworked stitches on holder if necessary.

Left Front

- Maintaining 3 garter edge stitches, work even in stockinette stitch for 3 more rows. Begin decrease rows as follows.

- **Row 1 (RS):** K3, k2tog, knit to end of row. *You now have 39 (40) sts.*

- **Row 2:** K3, purl to last 3 stitches, k3.

- Repeat Rows 1 and 2 until you have 30 (31) stitches, ending on Row 2.

- **Next Row (RS):** K3, M1R, ssk, knit to last 5 stitches, k2tog, k3. *You now have 29 (30) stitches.*

- **Next Row (WS):** K3, purl to last 3 stitches, k3.

- Repeat these last 2 rows until 17 stitches remain, ending with a WS row.

- Now work double decreases at the neck edge and single decreases at the arm edge as follows.

- **Row 1 (RS):** K3, sk2p, knit to last 5 stitches, k2tog, k3. *You now have* 14 stitches.

- **Row 2:** K3, purl to last 3 stitches, k3.

- **Row 3:** Knit.

- **Row 4:** Repeat Row 2.

- Repeat Rows 1–4 until 8 stitches remain, ending with Row 4.

- **Next Row (RS):** K1, sk2p, k2tog, k2. *You now have* 5 stitches.

- Knit 5 rows.

- **Buttonhole Row:** K2, yo, k2tog, k1.

- Knit 4 rows. Bind off.

Right Front

- With WS facing, join yarn at neck edge and work 3 rows even as established. Then begin decrease rows as follows.

- **Row 1:** K3, knit to last 5 stitches, ssk, k3.

- **Row 2:** K3, purl to last 3 stitches, k3.

- Repeat Rows 1 and 2 until you have 30 (31) stitches, ending on Row 2.
- **Next Row (RS):** K3, ssk, knit to last 5 stitches, k2tog, M1L, k3.
- **Next Row (WS):** K3, purl to last 3 stitches, K3.
- Repeat these last 2 rows until 17 stitches remain, ending with a WS row.
- Now work double decreases at the neck edge and single decreases at the arm edge as follows.
- **Row 1 (RS):** K3, ssk, knit to last 6 stitches, sk2p, k3.

- **Row 2:** K3, purl to last 3 stitches, k3.
- **Row 3:** Knit.
- **Row 4:** Repeat Row 2.
- Repeat Rows 1–4 until 8 stitches remain, ending with Row 4.
- **Next Row (RS):** K2, ssk, sk2p, k1.
- Knit 5 rows.
- **Buttonhole Row:** K2, yo, k2tog, k1.
- Knit 4 rows. Bind off.

FINISHING

- Weave in all ends. Block lightly. Sew buttons to back bottom corners opposite buttonholes.

Lace Heart

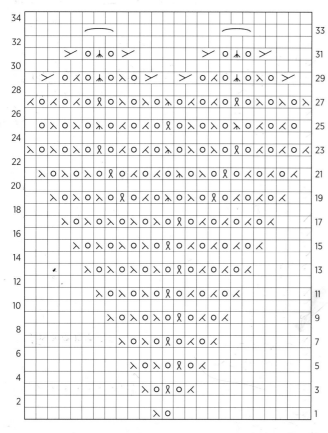

25-stitch panel

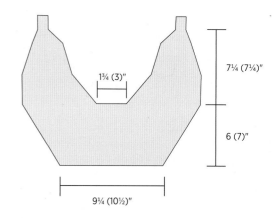

1¾ (3)"

7¼ (7¼)"

6 (7)"

9¼ (10½)"

	k on RS, p on WS		ktbl		wrap 3
o	yo		sk2p		
	ssk		kfb		
	k2tog		decrease 4		

Sail Away with Me

Designed by Janice Bye

Reverse stockinette stitch creates a sailboat motif on the front of this sweater and the sleeve ridges are suggestive of waves. The sweater features a button-up shoulder for easy access.

SIZE AND FINISHED MEASUREMENTS

To fit 3–6 months: 19"/48.5 cm chest circumference

YARN

Zwerger Garn Opal 4 Ply, 75% wool/25% nylon, 465 yds (425 m)/3.5 oz (100 g), Color 1290 Petticoat ②

NEEDLES

US 2½ (3 mm) straight needles *or size needed to obtain correct gauge*

GAUGE

28 stitches and 36 rows = 4"/10 cm in stockinette stitch
28 stitches and 46 rows = 4"/10 cm in Wave Pattern

OTHER SUPPLIES

Stitch markers, stitch holders or scrap yarn, extra needle for three-needle bind off, yarn needle, three ⅜"/10 mm buttons, ⅜"/10 mm snap, sewing needle and coordinating thread

Pattern Essentials

WAVE PATTERN

Row 1 (RS): Knit.

Row 2 (WS): Purl.

Rows 3 and 4: Knit.

Repeat Rows 1 through 4 for pattern.

KNITTING THE BACK

- Cast on 72 stitches.
- **Row 1 (WS):** P2, *k2, p2, k1, p2; repeat from * to end of row.
- **Row 2:** K2, *p1, k2, p2, k2; repeat from * to end of row.
- Repeat Rows 1 and 2 three more times.
- **Next Row:** Purl.
- Work Rows 1 through 4 of Wave pattern 11 times, then work Rows 1 and 2 once more.
- **Next 2 Rows:** Bind off 8, knit to end of row. *You now have* 56 stitches.
- Work even in Wave pattern until armhole measures 4"/10 cm.
- **Next Row (RS):** K15 and place on holder for right shoulder, bind off 26, knit to end of row.
- Knit 5 rows on remaining stitches for button band. Bind off.

KNITTING THE FRONT

- Cast on 72 stitches.
- **Row 1 (WS):** P2, *k2, p2, k1, p2; repeat from * to end of row.
- **Row 2:** K2, *p1, k2, p2, k2; repeat from * to end of row.
- Repeat Rows 1 and 2 three more times.
- **Next Row:** Purl.
- Work Rows 1 through 4 of Wave pattern 3 times.
- **Next Row (RS):** K15, pm, work Row 1 of Sail Away Pattern chart (see page 74) across next 42 stitches, pm, k15.

- Keeping the first and last 15 stitches in stockinette stitch, work Rows 2 through 34 of chart between markers.
- Continuing in chart pattern, bind off 8 stitches at the beginning of the next 2 rows. *You now have* 56 stitches.
- Work even through Row 54 of chart.
- Work 4 rows in stockinette stitch.
- **Next Row:** K21 and place on a holder for left shoulder, bind off 14, knit to end of row.

Working the Right Shoulder

- **Row 1 (WS):** Purl.
- **Row 2:** K1, ssk, knit to end of row. *You now have* 20 stitches.
- **Row 3:** Purl.
- Repeat Rows 2 and 3 five more times. *You now have* 15 stitches.
- Work even in stockinette stitch until armhole measures 4"/10 cm, ending with a WS row.
- Join right front and back shoulder stitches together with three-needle bind off (see page 282).

Working the Left Shoulder

- Place held stitches on needle and join yarn with WS facing.
- **Row 1 (WS):** Purl.
- **Row 2:** Knit to last 3 stitches, k2tog, k1. *You now have* 20 stitches.
- **Row 3:** Purl.
- Repeat Rows 2 and 3 five more times. *You now have* 15 stitches.
- Work even in stockinette stitch until armhole measures 4"/10 cm, ending with a WS row.
- Knit 4 rows for buttonhole band.
- **Next Row:** K3, (yo, k2tog, k2) three times for buttonholes.
- Knit 3 rows. Bind off.

KNITTING THE SLEEVES (make 2)

- Cast on 44 stitches.
- **Row 1 (WS):** P2, *k2, p2, k1, p2; repeat from * to end of row.
- **Row 2:** K2, *p1, k2, p2, k2; repeat from * to end of row.
- Repeat Rows 1 and 2 three more times.
- **Next Row:** Purl.
- Work Rows 1 through 4 of Wave pattern once, then work Rows 1 and 2 once more.
- **Next Row:** (Row 3 of Wave pattern) K1, kfb, knit to last 2 stitches, kfb, k1.
- **Next Row:** Work Row 4 of Wave pattern.
- Continue in this manner, increasing on Row 3 of every other Wave pattern repeat 3 more times, then on Row 3 of every Wave pattern repeat 4 times. *You now have 60 stitches.*
- Continue even in pattern as established until sleeve measures 6"/15 cm. Bind off.

KNITTING THE NECK

- With RS facing and beginning at front buttonhole band, pick up and knit 80 stitches evenly spaced through back button band.
- **Row 1 (WS):** Purl.
- **Row 2:** *K2, kfb, k2; repeat from * to end of row. *You now have* 96 stitches.
- **Row 3:** Purl.
- **Row 4:** Knit.
- **Row 5:** Purl.
- Repeat Rows 4 and 5 five more times. Bind off.

FINISHING

- Sew side seams. Sew top of right sleeve into armhole. Overlap button and buttonhole flaps, pin in place, and sew top of left sleeve into armhole, making sure that the flaps are smoothly and firmly attached to center of sleeve. Sew underarms to tops of side seams and sew arm seams down to the cuffs. Sew buttons to button flap opposite buttonholes. Roll the ends of the neck edge and tack each end of the roll in place with needle and thread; sew one half of the snap to each end.
- Weave in all ends. Wash and block.

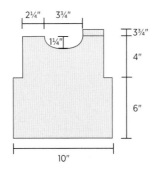

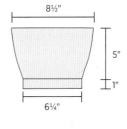

Sail Away Pattern

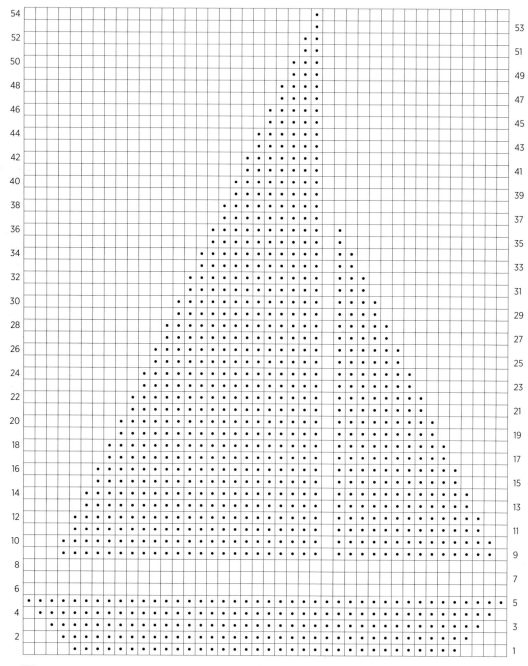

☐ k on RS, p on WS

• p on RS, k on WS

Playtime Sweater

Designed by René E. Wells, Granny an' Me Designs

This handsome pullover is knit with a combination of stockinette stitch and simple knit-purl textured patterns. Perfect for your active toddler.

SIZE AND FINISHED MEASUREMENTS
To fit a 2-year-old: 23"/58.5 cm chest circumference

YARN
Plymouth Yarn Select Worsted Merino Superwash Kettle Dyed, 100% super-wash fine merino wool, 436 yds (399 m)/7 oz (200 g), Kettle Cream (4)

NEEDLES
US 5 (3.75 mm) circular needle 20–24"/50–60 cm long and set of four US 5 (3.75 mm) double-point needles; US 7 (4.5 mm) circular needle 20–24"/50–60 cm long and set of four US 7 (4.5 mm) double-point needles *or size needed to obtain correct gauge*

GAUGE
22 stitches and 28 rows = 4"/10 cm in stockinette stitch on larger needles

OTHER SUPPLIES
Stitch markers, scrap yarn for holders, yarn needle

KNITTING THE SWEATER BODY

- With smaller circular needle, cast on 112 stitches. Place marker and join into a round, being careful not to twist the stitches.

- **Rounds 1–11:** To work rib, *k1, p1; repeat from * to end of round.

- **Round 12:** Rib 4, (M1, rib 8) thirteen times, M1, rib 4. *You now have* 126 stitches.

- Change to larger needle. K63, pm for side, knit to end of round. Work in stockinette stitch until piece measures 4½"/11.5 cm from cast-on edge.

- Work Round 1 of Playtime Pattern chart to marker, sm, work in stitch pattern to end of round. Continue working stitch pattern chart until piece measures 7"/18 cm from cast-on edge.

Dividing for Front and Back

- Bind off 2 stitches, work in pattern as established to next marker, place remaining 63 stitches on holder. Turn, bind off 2 stitches, work in pattern to end of row. *You now have* 59 stitches for the back. Work even in pattern until piece measures 11"/28 cm.

- **Next Row:** Work 18 stitches in pattern and place on hold for shoulder; work 23 stitches and place on hold for back neck; work 18 stitches and place on hold for shoulder.

- Place held front stitches on larger needle. With RS facing, attach yarn and work as for back until piece measures 8½"/21.5 cm.

- Work 23 stitches in pattern, place center 13 stitches on hold for front neck, attach new yarn and work 23 stitches in pattern. Working both sides with separate yarn, keep 1 stitch in stockinette at each neck edge and decrease 1 stitch at each neck edge on RS rows 5 times. *You now have* 18 stitches for each shoulder. Work even in pattern until front length matches back.

- Join front and back at shoulders using three-needle bind off (see page 282).

KNITTING THE SLEEVES (make 2)

- With larger double-point needles, right side facing, and beginning at the underarm, pick up and knit (see page 281) 52 stitches evenly spaced around to underarm. Place marker and join. Knit 1 round.

- **Decrease Round:** K1, k2tog, knit to last 2 stitches, ssk.

- Repeat decrease round every other round once more, then every 4th round 8 times. *You now have* 32 stitches.

- Continue even in stockinette stitch until sleeve measures 6½"/16.5 cm.

- Change to smaller double-point needles.

- **Next Round:** K5, k2tog, k4, (k2tog, k5) three times. *You now have* 28 stitches.

- **Next Round:** *K1, p1; repeat from * to end of round.

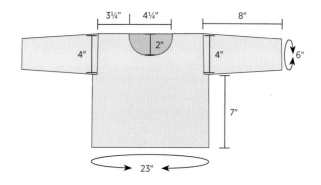

• Repeat this last round 10 more times. Bind off loosely using Jeny's Surprisingly Stretchy Bind Off (see page 277).

FINISHING

• With smaller needles, RS facing, and beginning at right shoulder, pick up and knit 23 stitches for back neck, 16 stitches for left front neck, knit 13 held front stitches, pick up and knit 16 stitches for right front neck. *You now have* 68 stitches. Place marker, join, and work k1, p1 rib for 1"/2.5 cm. Bind off loosely using Jeny's Surprisingly Stretchy Bind Off.

Playtime Pattern

Repeat Rounds 7-14 for pattern

Work Rows 1-6 once

63-stitch repeat

Column numbers: 13, 11, 9, 7, 5, 3, 1 (top); 12, 10, 8, 6, 4, 2 (bottom)

Legend:
☐ k on RS, p on WS
• p on RS, k on WS

Sunday Sweater

Designed by René E. Wells, Granny an' Me Designs

Perfect for showing off at family gatherings, Sunday Sweater combines seed stitch with cables in a slightly flared shape with a cable detail on the back. It is knit from the top down with raglan sleeves.

SIZE AND FINISHED MEASUREMENTS

To fit 0–3 months: 16"/40.5 cm chest circumference

YARN

OnLine Supersocke 100 Emotion II-Color, 50% superwash merino wool/25% bamboo/25% nylon, 240 yds (219 m)/3.5 oz (100 g), Color 1218 **1**

NEEDLES

US 3 (3.25 mm) straight needles, US 2 (2.75 mm) straight needles, set of four US 3 (3.25 mm) double-point needles, and set of four US 2 (2.75 mm) double-point needles *or size needed to obtain correct gauge*

GAUGE

30 stitches and 42 rows = 4"/10 cm in stockinette stitch on larger needles

34 stitches and 39 rows = 4"/10 cm in lower body cable pattern

OTHER SUPPLIES

Stitch markers, stitch holders or scrap yarn, two ½"/13 mm buttons, sewing needle and coordinating thread, yarn needle, US size C-2 (2.75 mm) crochet hook

SPECIAL ABBREVIATIONS

1/2 LC
 Slip 1 stitch to cable needle and hold in front, k2 from left needle, k1 from cable needle

1/2 RC
 Slip 2 stitches to cable needle and hold in back, k1 from left needle, k2 from cable needle

p-yo-pb
 (Purl 1, yarn over, purl 1 through back loop) all in the next stitch (2 stitches increased)

k-b-k
 (Knit 1, knit 1 through the back loop, knit 1) into the p-yo-p of previous row

Pattern Essentials

SEED STITCH
(odd number of stitches)

Row 1: *K1, p1; repeat from * to last stitch, k1.

Repeat Row 1 for pattern.

YOKE CABLE PANEL
(worked over 11 stitches)

Row 1 (RS): P2, k3, p1, k3, p2.

Row 2: K2, p3, k1, p3, k2.

Row 3: P2, 1/2 RC, p1, 1/2 LC, p2.

Row 4: Repeat Row 2.

Repeat Rows 1–4 for pattern.

LOWER BODY CABLE
(multiple of 10 stitches + 11)

Row 1 (RS): P2, k3, p1, k3, *p3, k3, p1, k3; repeat from * to last 2 stitches, p2.

Row 2: K2, p3, k1, p3, *k3, p3, k1, p3; repeat from * to last 2 stitches, k2.

Row 3: P2, 1/2 RC, p1, 1/2 LC, *p3, 1/2 RC, p1, 1/2 LC; repeat from * to last 2 stitches, p2.

Row 4: Repeat Row 2.

Repeat Rows 1–4 for pattern.

- **Row 2:** Seed stitch 5 as established, work Row 2 of Yoke Cable Panel, p4, sm, purl to next marker, sm, p6, work Row 2 of Yoke Cable Panel, purl to marker, sm, purl to next marker, sm, p4, work Row 2 of Yoke Cable Panel, seed stitch 5 as established.

- Maintaining seed stitch borders, stockinette stitch, and cable patterns as established, work raglan increases as follows.

- **Row 3:** (Work to 1 stitch before marker, kfb, sm, kfb) four times, work to end of row.

- **Row 4:** Work even in patterns as established.

- Repeat Rows 3 and 4 fifteen more times. *You now have* 213 stitches — 55 back stitches, 36 stitches each front, 43 stitches each sleeve.

Dividing for Sleeves and Body

- **Row 1 (RS):** Seed stitch 5, work established pattern over next 11 stitches, working pfb into last stitch, (k2, kfb, k3, p-yo-pb) twice, k2, kfb, k3; place 43 sleeve stitches on hold; p1, pfb, (k2, kfb, k3, p-yo-pb) twice, k2, kfb, k3, work established pattern over next 11 stitches working pfb into first and last stitches, (k2, kfb, k3, p-yo-pb) twice, k2, kfb, k3, pfb, p1; place 43 sleeve stitches on hold; (k2, kfb, k3, p-yo-pb) twice, k2, kfb, k3, work established pattern over next 11 stitches working pfb into first stitch, seed 5. *You now have* 161 stitches.

KNITTING THE YOKE

- With smaller straight needles, cast on 77 stitches.

- Work 4 rows of Seed Stitch.

- Change to larger needle.

- **Row 1 (RS):** Seed stitch 5 as established, work Row 1 of Yoke Cable Panel, k2, kfb, pm, kfb, k7, kfb, pm, kfb, k4, work Row 1 of Yoke Cable Panel, k4, kfb, pm, kfb, k7, kfb, pm, kfb, k2, work Row 1 of Yoke Cable Panel, work seed stitch as established on last 5 stitches. *You now have* 85 stitches.

- **Row 2:** Seed stitch 5, knit the knits and purl the purls to last 5 stitches, working k-b-k into the p-yo-pb from the previous row, seed stitch 5.

KNITTING THE LOWER BODY

- **Next Row (RS):** Seed stitch 5, work Row 1 of Lower Body Cable Pattern to last 5 stitches, seed stitch 5.

- Work in established patterns until Rows 1-4 of Lower Body Cable Pattern have been worked 14 times, then work Rows 1 and 2 once more.

- Change to smaller needle and work 7 rows of seed stitch. Bind off in pattern.

KNITTING THE SLEEVES

- With larger double-point needles, RS facing, and beginning at underarm, pick up and knit 1 stitch, knit 43 held stitches, pick up and knit 1 stitch. *You now have 45 stitches.*

- Arrange stitches evenly onto 3 double-point needles, pm, and join into a round, being careful not to twist the stitches.

- **Rows 1–9:** Knit.

- **Row 10:** K1, k2tog, knit to last 3 stitches, ssk, k1. *You now have 43 stitches.*

- Repeat Rows 1 through 10 three more times. *You now have 37 stitches.*

- Continue even in stockinette stitch until sleeve measures 5½"/14 cm from underarm. Change to smaller double-point needles and work 7 rows of seed stitch. Bind off in pattern.

FINISHING

- Sew buttons to left front yoke. Make crochet chain (see page 276) loops on right front yoke opposite buttons, anchoring the loops in the 3rd stitch of the 5-stitch seed border.

- Weave in ends. Block.

Lower Body Cable

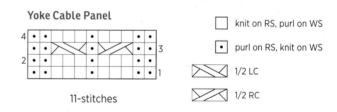

10-stitch repeat

Yoke Cable Panel

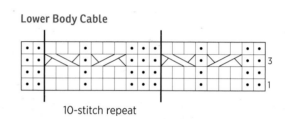

11-stitches

- ☐ knit on RS, purl on WS
- ▣ purl on RS, knit on WS
- ⬚ 1/2 LC
- ⬚ 1/2 RC

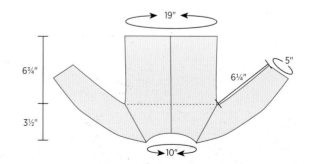

Vertical Lace Baby Cardigan

Designed by Vicki K. Byram

Further proof that sock yarn is not just for socks, here it is knitted up into this side-to-side cardigan worked from the left front to the right front. And with all the colorways available, you can knit a unique garment for every baby you know.

SIZE AND FINISHED MEASUREMENTS

To fit 0-6 months: 16"/40.5 cm chest circumference, buttoned

YARN

Ellen's 1/2 Pint Farm Merino, Tencel & Nylon Sock, 75% merino wool/10% tencel/15% nylon, 465 yds (425 m)/4 oz (113 g), Mexican Siesta ⬛❶

NEEDLES

US 4 (3.5 mm) and US 5 (3.75 mm) straight needles *or size needed to obtain correct gauge*

GAUGE

26 stitches and 52 rows = 4"/10 cm in garter stitch on larger needle
24 stitches and 42 rows = 4"/10 cm in pattern on larger needle

OTHER SUPPLIES

Stitch holders or scrap yarn, three ½"/13 mm buttons, yarn needle

KNITTING THE LEFT FRONT

- Using the cable cast on method (see page 276) and smaller needle, cast on 60 stitches. Knit 7 rows and change to larger needles. See page 282 for explanation of WT, wrap and turn.

- Rows 1 and 2: Knit.
- Row 3 (RS): K54, WT, leaving remaining neck stitches unworked.
- Row 4: K54.
- Row 5: K44, WT.
- Row 6: K44.
- Row 7: (K2tog, yo) 16 times, k1, WT.
- Row 8: K33.
- Row 9: Knit.
- Row 10: Knit.
- Rows 11–42: Work Rows 3–10 four more times.
- Row 43: K33, place remaining 27 stitches on hold. Continue on underarm stitches as follows.
- Rows 44–46: K33.
- Row 47: (K2tog, yo) 16 times, k1.
- Rows 48–51: K33. Cut yarn and place 33 left underarm stitches just worked on hold.

KNITTING THE LEFT SLEEVE

- Using the cable cast on method (see page 276) and larger needle, cast on 38 stitches.
- Rows 1–4: Knit.
- Row 5 (RS): K38; place 27 held yoke stitches on left needle, k21 yoke stitches, WT, leaving 6 remaining stitches unworked for neck. *You now have* 65 stitches.
- Row 6: K54, WT, leaving 5 stitches unworked for cuff.
- Row 7: K44, WT.
- Row 8: Knit.
- Row 9: K5, (k2tog, yo) 16 times, k1, WT.
- Row 10: K33, WT.
- Row 11: Knit.
- Row 12: Knit.
- Rows 13–68: Repeat Rows 5–12 seven more times, working Row 5 as K59, WT.
- Row 69: K38, turn.

- Rows 70–72: K38.
- Bind off these 38 stitches, cut yarn, and sew underarm of sleeve.

KNITTING THE BACK

- Slip 27 held yoke stitches onto needle and join yarn with right side facing.
- Row 1 (RS): K21, WT.
- Row 2: K21 yoke stitches, k33 body stitches from holder.
- Row 3: K44, WT.
- Row 4: Knit.
- Row 5: (K2tog, yo) 16 times, k1, WT.
- Row 6: Knit.
- Row 7: Knit.
- Row 8: Knit.
- Row 9: K54, WT.
- Row 10: Knit.
- Rows 11–16: Repeat Rows 3–8.
- Rows 17–88: Work Rows 9–16 nine more times.

- **Row 89:** K33, place next 27 yoke stitches on hold, turn.
- **Rows 90–92:** K33.
- **Row 93:** (K2tog, yo) 16 times, k1.
- **Rows 94–97:** K33. Cut yarn and place 33 stitches on hold.

KNITTING THE RIGHT SLEEVE

- Work as for left sleeve.

KNITTING THE RIGHT FRONT

- Slip 27 held yoke stitches onto needle and join yarn with right side facing as for back.
- Work Rows 1–48 as for Back (5 pattern repeats complete)
- Knit 2 rows.
- Change to smaller needles for front band.
- **Rows 1–4:** Knit.
- **Row 5 (buttonhole row):** K31, (yo, k2tog, k10) twice, yo, k2tog, k3.
- **Rows 6–7:** Knit.
- Bind off.

FINISHING

- Weave in ends. Sew buttons to left front band opposite buttonholes. Block.

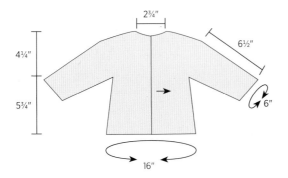

2¾"

4¼"

5¾"

6½"

6"

16"

Baby in Red

Designed by Liz Nields

A ruffled and lacy sweater makes a bold statement in red. This one is knitted side to side, beginning at the sleeve edges, and the ruffles are formed onto picked-up stitches once the garment pieces are completed.

SIZE AND FINISHED MEASUREMENTS
To fit 12 months: 20"/51 cm chest circumference, buttoned

YARN
Zwerger Garn Opal 4 Ply, 75% superwash wool/25% nylon, 465 yds (425 m)/3.5 oz (100 g), Color 5180 Red (1)

NEEDLES
US 1 (2.25 mm) straight needles *or size needed to obtain correct gauge*

GAUGE
30 stitches and 52 rows = 4"/10 cm in lace pattern, lightly blocked

OTHER SUPPLIES
Stitch holders or scrap yarn, four ⅜"/10 mm buttons, sewing needle and coordinating thread

Pattern Essentials

LACE
(multiple of 8 stitches)

Row 1 (RS): *Yo, ssk, k3, k2tog, yo, k1; repeat from * to end of row.

Row 2: Purl.

Row 3: *K1, yo, ssk, k1, k2tog, yo, k2; repeat from * to end of row.

Row 4: Purl.

Row 5: *K2, yo, s2kp, yo, k3; repeat from * to end of row.

Rows 6–8: Purl.

Repeat Rows 1–8 for pattern.

KNITTING THE RIGHT SLEEVE

- Cast on 53 stitches. Knit 9 rows. Knit 1 row, increasing 6 stitches evenly spaced. *You now have* 59 stitches. Purl 1 row.

- Work Lace pattern from chart on page 87 or line-by-line instructions as follows.

- **RS Rows:** K2, work in Lace pattern to last stitch, k1.

- **WS Rows:** P1, work in Lace pattern to last 2 stitches, p2.

- Continuing with edge stitches and lace pattern as established, work rows 1–8 twice, then work rows 1–6 once more.

- **Next Row (Pattern Row 7):** K1, M1, k1 work in pattern to last stitch, M1, k1. *You now have* 61 stitches.

- **Next Row:** Work pattern Row 8.

- Work Rows 1–8 of pattern as established 3 more times, increasing in Row 7 of each repeat and working new stitches in stockinette stitch. *You now have* 67 stitches.

- Work Rows 1–5 of Lace pattern once more.

KNITTING THE RIGHT FRONT AND BACK

- **Next Row:** With wrong side facing and using the purlwise cable cast on method (see page 276), cast on 20 stitches to beginning of row; work pattern Row 6 as established; turn and using the knitwise cable cast on method (see page 276), cast on 20 stitches to the end of the row. *You now have* 107 stitches.

- Work pattern Rows 7 and 8 across all stitches.

- Work Rows 1–8 of Lace pattern 5 more times as follows.

- **RS Rows:** K2, work Row 7 of Lace pattern to last stitch, k1.

- **WS Rows:** P1, work Row 8 of Lace pattern to last 2 stitches, p2.

Divide for Front and Back

- Work edge stitches and pattern Row 1 on 54 stitches and place these stitches on hold for the front. *You now have* 53 stitches for right back.

The Right Back

- Maintain established stockinette edge stitches throughout.

- **Row 1:** Bind off 2, work in Lace pattern Row 1 as established to end of row. *You now have* 51 stitches.

- **Row 2:** Work Lace pattern Row 2 as established.

- **Row 3:** Bind off 1, work in pattern to end of row. *You now have* 50 stitches.

- Continuing with patterns and maintaining established stockinette edge stitches, work Rows 4–8 of Lace pattern, then work Rows 1–8 of Lace pattern 2 more times.

- Place stitches on hold.

The Right Front

- Place 54 held right front stitches onto needle. With WS facing, join yarn and bind off 10 stitches, work pattern Row 2 and edge stitches as established to end of row. *You now have* 44 stitches.

- Continuing with pattern and edge stitches, decrease for the neck as follows.

- **RS Rows:** Work in pattern to last 3 stitches, k2tog, k1.

- **WS Rows:** Work even in pattern as established.

- Continue in this manner, decreasing on RS rows, until you have 36 stitches. Work even until Row 5 of the 8th repeat for the front is complete. Place remaining 36 stitches on hold.

KNITTING THE LEFT SLEEVE

- Work as for right sleeve.

KNITTING THE LEFT FRONT AND BACK

- Work as for right front and back.

Dividing for Front and Back

- Work edge stitches and pattern Row 1 across 54 stitches, place remaining 53 stitches onto holder for front. *You now have* 54 stitches for left back.

The Left Back

- Maintain established stockinette edge stitches throughout.

- With WS facing, bind off 2, work pattern Row 2 to end of row.

- Continue in pattern with edge stitches as established as follows.

- **Next Row:** Work even pattern Row 3.

- **Next Row:** Bind off 1, work pattern Row 4 to end of row. *You now have* 51 stitches.

- Continuing with patterns and maintaining 1 edge stitch at neck in stockinette and 2 at lower edge in stockinette as established, work Rows 5–8 of pattern, then work Rows 1–8 of pattern 2 more times.

- Place stitches on hold.

The Left Front

- Place 53 held left front stitches onto needle. With RS facing, bind off 10 stitches, work pattern Row 1 and edge stitches as established to end of row. *You now have* 43 stitches.

- Continuing with pattern and edge stitches, decrease for the neck as follows.

- **WS Rows:** Work even in pattern as established.

- **RS Rows:** K1, ssk, work in pattern to end of row.

- Continue in this manner, decreasing on RS rows, until you have 36 stitches. Work even until Row 5 of the 8th pattern repeat is complete. Place remaining 36 stitches on hold.

KNITTING THE SLEEVE RUFFLES

- With RS facing, pick up and knit 53 stitches from cast-on edge.

- **Row 1 (WS):** *K2, kfb; repeat from * to last 2 stitches, k2. *You now have* 70 stitches.

- **Row 2:** Knit.

- **Row 3:** Purl.

- **Row 4:** K3, *yo, k1; repeat from * to last 2 stitches, k2. *You now have* 135 stitches.

- Bind off knitwise on WS.

- Repeat on other sleeve.

Babies and Lace

In general, when knitting lace for babywear or blankets, choose patterns that have holes on the small side. Tiny fingers and toes can easily get tangled in fabric with a large openwork pattern.

FINISHING

- Join right and left sections down the center back with Kitchener stitch (see page 278). Sew sleeve and side seams. Weave ends.

The Bottom Border

- With RS facing and beginning at bottom left edge, pick up and knit (see page 281) 136 stitches. Work garter stitch for 4 rows. Bind off knitwise on WS.

The Neck Border

- With RS facing and beginning at right front neck edge, pick up and knit 76 stitches around neck. Knit 4 rows. Bind off knitwise on WS.

The Button Band

- With RS facing and beginning at left neck edge, pick up and knit 3 stitches from neck band edge, knit held left front stitches, pick up and knit 3 stitches from bottom border. *You now have* 42 stitches. Work garter stitch for 4 rows. Bind off knitwise on WS.

Buttonhole Band

- With RS facing and beginning at lower right edge, pick up and knit 3 stitches from bottom border, knit held right front stitches, pick up 3 stitches from front neck border. *You now have* 42 stitches.

- **Next Row (WS):** Knit.

- **Next Row (buttonhole row):** K2, yo, ssk, k10, yo, ssk, k10, yo, ssk, k10, yo, ssk, k2.

Lace Pattern

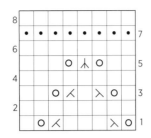

	k on RS, p on WS
o	yo
╱	k2tog
╲	ssk
⋏	s2kp

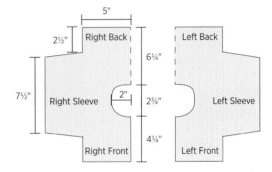

- Knit 2 rows.
- Bind off knitwise on WS.

The Neck Ruffle

- With RS facing and beginning at right front neck, pick up and knit 76 stitches from neck border by knitting through the purl bumps of first border row.

- **Row 1 (WS):** *K3, kfb; repeat from * to last 4 stitches, k4. *You now have* 94 stitches.

- **Row 2:** Knit.

- **Row 3:** Purl.

- **Row 4:** K3, *yo, k1; repeat from * to last 3 stitches, k3. *You now have* 182 stitches.

- Bind off knitwise on WS.

Babe in Bloom Cardigan

Designed by Caroline Perisho

Adding knitted flower petals and a flouncy fabric ruffle to this sweet cardigan takes a little extra time, but it's time well spent. This one puts the "A" in adorable.

SIZES AND FINISHED MEASUREMENTS

To fit 18 (24) months: 20 (22)"/51 (56) cm chest circumference

YARN

Swans Island Natural Colors, 100% organic merino wool, 525 yds (480 m)/3.5 oz (100 g), Color 129

NEEDLES

US 4 (3.5 mm) straight needles and US 2 (2.75 mm) straight needles for flowers *or size needed to obtain correct gauge*

GAUGE

28 stitches and 40 rows = 4"/10 cm in stockinette stitch

OTHER SUPPLIES

25 (28)"/63.5 (71) cm of 2½"/6.5 cm (or wider) trim, four ½"/13 mm buttons, 1 small snap (optional), sewing needle and coordinating thread, yarn needle

KNITTING THE BACK

Note: Before starting, wind off a ball of approximately 30 yds/27 m and set aside.

- Cast on 70 (78) stitches. Work in stockinette stitch for 3 (3½)"/7.5 (9) cm.

- Work in Seed Stitch until piece measures 7½ (8)"/19 (20.5) cm, ending with a WS row.

- Continuing in Seed Stitch, work 23 (25) stitches, bind off 24 (28) stitches in pattern, work to end of row.

- Using extra ball of yarn to work each shoulder separately, work 3 more rows of seed stitch. Bind off on RS.

KNITTING THE LEFT FRONT

- Cast on 47 (53) stitches. Work in stockinette stitch for 3 (3½)"/7.5 (9) cm.

- Work in Seed Stitch until piece measures 7 (7½)"/18 (19) cm, ending with a WS row.

- Continuing in Seed Stitch, work 31 (37) stitches, join extra ball of yarn and bind off 8 (4) stitches in pattern, work to end of row.

- Working both sides at once with separate balls of yarn, bind off 4 stitches at each neck edge 2 (3) times. Bind off remaining 23 (25) shoulder stitches.

KNITTING THE RIGHT FRONT

- Work as for left front until piece measures 4"/10 cm from cast-on edge, ending with a WS row.

Pattern Essentials

SEED STITCH
(even number of stitches)

Row 1: *K1, p1; repeat from * to end of row.

Row 2: *P1, k1; repeat from * to end of row.

Repeat Rows 1 and 2 for pattern.

SEED STITCH
(odd number of stitches)

Row 1: *K1, p1; repeat from * to last stitch, k1.

Repeat Row 1 for pattern.

- **Buttonhole Row (RS):** K4 (5), work a 3-stitch one-row buttonhole (see page 281), k17 (20), make buttonhole, work to end of row.

- Continue in Seed Stitch until piece measures 6 (6¼)"15 (16) cm.

- Repeat Buttonhole Row.

- Continue in Seed Stitch until piece measures 7 (7½)"/18 (19) cm, ending with a WS row.

- Continuing in Seed Stitch, work 8 (12) stitches, join a second piece of yarn and bind off 8 (4) stitches in pattern, work to end of row.

- Working both sides at once with separate balls of yarn, bind off 4 stitches at each neck edge 2 (3) times. Bind off remaining 23 (25) shoulder stitches.

KNITTING THE SLEEVES (make 2)

- Cast on 35 stitches.

- **Row 1:** *K1, p1; repeat from * to last stitch, k1.

- **Row 2:** *P1, k1; repeat from * to last stitch, p1.

- Repeat Rows 1 and 2 two times.

- Work in Seed Stitch and *at the same time* increase 1 stitch at the beginning and end of every 5th row 10 (14) times. *You now have* 55 (63) stitches. Continue even in Seed Stitch until piece measures 7½ (7¾)"/19 (19.5) cm. Work in stockinette stitch until piece measures 8¼ (8¾)"/21 (22) cm. Bind off.

ASSEMBLING THE GARMENT

- Seam the fronts and back together at shoulders. Place each sleeve with center at shoulder seam and ends 3½ (4½)"/9 (11.5) cm from front and back lower edges and sew in place. Sew underarm and side seams.

KNITTING THE COLLAR

- With RS facing and beginning at right front neck edge, pick up and knit 3 of every 4 stitches along front and back decrease edges and pick up all stitches from bound off center neck edges. Work Seed Stitch for 7 rows, increasing 1 stitch at the beginning and end of rows 2 and 3 and decreasing 1 stitch at the beginning and end of row 6. Bind off.

KNITTING THE BUTTONHOLE FLOWER PETALS (make 20)

- With smaller needle, cast on 2 stitches.
- **Row 1 (RS):** Knit.
- **Row 2 and all WS rows:** Purl.
- **Row 3:** K1, M1, K1. *You now have* 3 stitches.
- **Row 5:** K1, (M1, k1) twice. *You now have* 5 stitches.
- **Rows 7 and 9:** Knit.
- **Row 10:** Purl.
- Bind off leaving a tail long enough to sew petal to garment. Weave in cast-on tail. Use bind-off tails to sew the bases of 5 petals around each buttonhole, overlapping if necessary, then tacking down other areas of petals as desired.

KNITTING THE CUFF FLOWER PETALS (make 20)

- Work as for Buttonhole petals through Row 7. Bind off.
- Sew 10 petals to each sleeve, positioning them just above the ribbing.

FINISHING

- Sew on buttons, sew snap in top front corner (optional). Sew trim to cast-on edge.

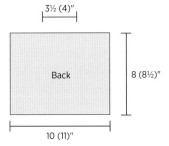

3½ (4)"

Back

8 (8½)"

10 (11)"

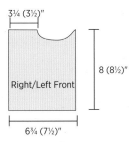

3¼ (3½)"

Right/Left Front

8 (8½)"

6¾ (7½)"

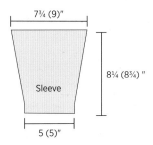

7¾ (9)"

Sleeve

8¼ (8¾) "

5 (5)"

Elizabeth, a Springtime Cardigan

Designed by Sarah Grieve

This side-to-side sweater starts at the cuffs and is worked to the center back. Plenty of knitting interest awaits you here — underarm gussets, short row shaping, and Kitchener stitch to name a few!

SIZES AND FINISHED MEASUREMENTS

To fit newborn (6 mos, 12 mos): 18 (19, 20)"/45.5 (48.5, 51) cm chest circumference, buttoned

YARN

Manos Del Uruguay Alegria, 75% superwash wool/25% nylon, 445 yds (407 m)/3.5 oz (100 g), Color A-401 (2)

NEEDLES

US 3 (3.25 mm) circular needle 40"/100 cm long and set of four or five US 3 (3.25 mm) double-point needles (optional) *or size needed to obtain correct gauge*

GAUGE

28 stitches and 40 rows = 4"/10 cm in stockinette stitch

OTHER SUPPLIES

Stitch markers, yarn needle, five ½"/13 mm buttons, sewing needle and coordinating thread

Pattern Essentials

TRAVELING LACE

(multiple of 2 stitches)

Row 1 (RS): *K2tog, yo; repeat from * to end of row.

Row 2 (WS): Purl.

Row 3: *Yo, ssk; repeat from * to end of row.

Row 4: Purl.

Repeat Rows 1–4 for pattern.

KNITTING THE RIGHT TOP

Note: Sleeves are knitted in the round on double-point needles or with the Magic Loop method (see page 280).

- Cast on 36 (36, 40) stitches. Place marker and join into a round, being careful not to twist stitches.

- **Rounds 1–9:** *K1, p1; repeat from * to end of round.

- **Rounds 10–16:** Knit.

- **Round 17:** K1, M1L, knit to last stitch, M1R, k1. *You now have* 38 (38, 42) stitches.

- Repeat Rounds 10–17, four more times. *You now have* 46 (46, 50) stitches.

- Knit 7 more rounds.

The Armhole Gusset

- **Round 1:** K1, M1L, knit to last stitch, M1R, k1. *You now have* 48 (48, 52) stitches.

- **Round 2:** K3, M1L, knit to last 3 stitches, M1R, k3. *You now have* 50 (50, 54) stitches.

Begin Short Rows

Note: The short rows will be worked over stitches from both sides of the marker. Begin working back and forth, changing to circular needle if necessary. See page 282 for explanation of WT.

- **Short Row 1:** K4, WT.

- **Short Row 2:** P8, WT.

- **Short Row 3:** K6, WT.

- **Short Row 4:** K4, WT.

- **Short Row 5:** K2.

The Top Body

- With right side facing, use the cable cast on method (see page 276) to cast on 6 stitches at beginning of the next row. *You now have* 56 (56, 60) stitches.

- **Next Row:** Knit, working the wraps together with the stitches when they appear.

- Turn work and cable cast on 6 stitches. *You now have* 62 (62, 66 stitches).

The Back and Front

- Begin working back and front in stockinette stitch starting with a purl row.**

- Work 2¾ (3, 3¼)"/7 (7.5, 8.5) cm in stockinette stitch, ending with a wrong side row.

Shape Front Neck

- **Short Rows 1 and 2:** K4, WT; purl to end of row.

- **Short Rows 3 and 4:** K9, knitting the wrap together with its stitch, WT; purl to end of row.

- **Short Rows 5 and 6:** K14, knitting the wrap together with its stitch, WT; purl to end of row.

- **Short Rows 7 and 8:** K19, knitting the wrap together with its stitch, WT; purl to end of row.

- **Short Rows 9 and 10:** K24, knitting the wrap together with its stitch, WT; purl to end of row.

- **Short Rows 11 and 12:** K29, knitting the wrap together with its stitch, WT; purl to end of row.

- **Short Rows 13 and 14:** K31 (31, 33), knitting the wrap together with its stitch, WT; purl to end of row. Slip these last 31 (31, 33) stitches onto a stitch holder. Knit remaining 31 (31, 33) stitches of row.

The Back

- Continue working in stockinette stitch over 31 (31, 33) stitches, beginning with a purl row, until work measures 4½ (4¾, 5)"/11.5 (12, 12.5) cm from underarm cast on stitches.

- Place stitches on a holder.

KNITTING THE LEFT TOP

- Work as for Right Top to **.

- Work 2¾ (3, 3¼)"/7 (7.5, 8.5) cm in stockinette stitch, ending with a right side row.

Shape Front Neck

- **Short Rows 1 and 2:** P4, WT; knit to end of row.

- **Short Rows 3 and 4:** P9, purling the wrap together with its stitch, WT; knit to end of row.

- **Short Rows 5 and 6:** P14, purling the wrap together with its stitch, WT; knit to end of row.

- **Short Rows 7 and 8:** P19, purling the wrap together with its stitch, WT; knit to end of row.

- **Short Row 9 and 10:** P24, purling the wrap together with its stitch, WT; knit to end of row.

- **Short Row 11 and 12:** P29, purling the wrap together with its stitch, WT; knit to end of row.

- **Short Row 13:** P31 (31, 33). Slip these last 31 (31, 33) stitches onto a stitch holder. Purl remaining 31 (31, 33) stitches of row.

The Back

- Continue working in stockinette stitch, beginning with a knit row, until work measures 4½ (4¾, 5)"/11.5 (12, 12.5) cm from underarm cast on stitches.

JOINING RIGHT AND LEFT TOPS

- Use Kitchener stitch (see page 278) to graft the two pieces together at the center back and to graft the underarm seams together.

KNITTING THE LOWER BODY

- Using the circular needle with RS facing, pick up and knit (see page 281) 125 (133, 141) stitches along lower edge of sweater top.

- **Row 1:** *K2, k2tog; repeat from * to last stitch, k1. *You now have* 94 (100, 106) stitches.

- **Rows 2 and 3:** Knit.

The Lace Pattern

- Maintaining 2 stockinette stitches at the beginning and end of every row, work Rows 1 through 4 of Traveling Lace pattern until piece measures 3½ (4, 4½)"/9 (10, 11.5) cm from pick up, ending with Row 3 of pattern.

- Knit 5 rows. Bind off.

KNITTING THE BUTTON BAND

- With RS facing and beginning at lower edge of right side, pick up and knit 181 (187, 193) stitches to lower left edge.

- **Row 1:** P1, *k1, p1; repeat from * to end of row.

- **Rows 2–3:** Work in rib as established.

- **Row 4:** Rib 3 stitches, *yo, k2tog (buttonhole made), rib 8 (8, 10); repeat from * 4 more times, rib to end of row.

- Work 3 more rows in k1, p1 ribbing as established. Bind off in pattern.

FINISHING

- Using a yarn needle, weave in ends. Sew buttons opposite buttonholes. Wash and block to measurements.

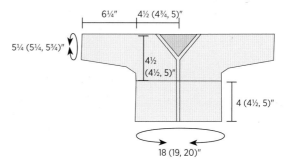

Baby Gansey Crossover Coat

Designed by Deborah Hess

The body of this unique coat is knitted in one piece from the bottom up for the back, over the shoulder, and then from the top down for the front. Sleeve stitches are picked up at the shoulder and knit down to the wrist.

SIZE AND FINISHED MEASUREMENTS
To fit 6–9 months: 20"/51 cm chest circumference

YARN
Imperial Yarn Tracie Too, 100% wool, 395 yds (361 m)/4 oz (113 g), Color 127 Marionberry Pie (2)

NEEDLES
US 5 (3.75 mm) straight needles *or size needed to obtain correct gauge*

GAUGE
23 stitches and 32 rows = 4"/10 cm in pattern

OTHER SUPPLIES
Stitch holders or scrap yarn, stitch markers, two ½"/13 mm buttons, yarn needle

KNITTING THE BACK

- Before beginning, wind off about 2 yds (2 m) of yarn and set aside.

- Cast on 57 stitches. Knit 8 rows. Note: If you cast on with the long-tail method, knit only 7 rows.

- Work Rows 1 through 8 of Diamond pattern (see page 98) 3 times, then work Row 1 once more.

- Knit 3 rows (this forms a definition ridge), increasing 1 stitch in 3rd row. *You now have* 58 stitches.

- Work Rows 1 through 4 of Box Stitch pattern (see page 98) 7 times.

- Knit 4 rows (definition ridge), increasing 1 stitch on 4th row. *You now have* 59 stitches.
- Work Rows 1 through 8 of Zigzag pattern (see page 98) 3 times.
- Work Rows 1 through 4 of Shoulder Ridge pattern (see page 98) twice.
- Piece should now measure about 9½"/24 cm.

Shaping Back Neck and Shoulders

- **Row 1 (RS):** P22, k15, p22.
- **Rows 2 and 3:** Knit.
- **Row 4:** P21, k17, p21.
- **Row 5:** P20, k19, p20.
- **Rows 6 and 7:** Knit.
- **Row 8:** P19, k21, p19.
- **Row 9:** P19, k4, place these stitches on a holder for right shoulder; bind off 13, k the next 3 stitches (*you now have* 4 stitches on needle), p19.

KNITTING THE LEFT FRONT

- Continue on 23 stitches over the shoulder and down the front as follows.

Left Shoulder

- Working with 23 left shoulder stitches, proceed as follows.
- **Row 1 (WS):** Knit.
- **Row 2:** Slip 1, k2, ssk, knit to end of row. *You now have* 22 stitches.
- **Row 3:** Purl to last 4 stitches, k4.
- **Row 4:** Slip 1, k2, ssk, purl to end of row. *You now have* 21 stitches.
- **Rows 5–8:** Repeat Rows 1–4. *You now have* 19 stitches.

Left Front Neck

- **Row 1 (WS):** Knit to last 4 stitches, pm, k4.
- **Row 2:** Slip 1, k3, sm, M1L, knit to end of row. *You now have* 20 stitches.

- **Row 3:** Purl to last 4 stitches, k4.
- **Row 4:** Slip 1, k3, M1LP, purl to end of row. *You now have* 21 stitches.
- **Rows 5–7:** Repeat Rows 1–3. *You now have* 22 stitches.
- **Next Row:** Slip 1, k3, sm, M1L; beginning with stitch #2, work Row 1 of Zigzag pattern to end of row. *You now have* 23 stitches.
- Maintaining 4 neck edge stitches in garter stitch, slipping the 1st stitch and increasing on RS rows, work Rows 2–8 of Zigzag once, then Rows 1–8 two more times, incorporating new stitches into pattern. *You now have* 34 stitches. Maintaining slip stitch and increases on RS rows, knit 4 rows (definition ridge). *You now have* 36 stitches.

The Left Box Section with Tab and Slot

- Using the cable cast on method (see page 276), cast on 9 stitches at beginning of row. *You now have* 45 stitches.
- **Row 1 (RS):** K13, sm, work Row 1 of Box Stitch over 10 stitches, k1, turn. Place remaining 21 stitches on hold. *You now have* 24 stitches on needle.
- **Row 2:** K1, Box Stitch 10, sm, k12, kfb. *You now have* 25 stitches on needle.
- **Row 3:** Kfb, k13, sm, Box Stitch 10, k1. *You now have* 26 stitches.
- **Row 4:** K1, Box Stitch 10, sm, k11, yo, k2tog (buttonhole made), k2.
- **Row 5:** K15, sm, Box Stitch 10, k1.

- **Row 6:** K1, Box Stitch 10, sm, k13, k2tog. *You now have 25 stitches.*

- **Row 7:** Ssk, k12, sm, Box Stitch 10, k1. *You now have 24 stitches.*

- **Row 8:** K1, Box Stitch 10, sm, knit to end of row. Place 24 stitches on hold. Do not cut yarn.

- Return 21 held stitches to needle. With RS facing, attach the small ball of yarn.

- **Row 1 (RS):** K1, work Row 1 of Box Stitch to end of row.

- **Row 2:** Box Stitch to last stitch, k1.

- Maintaining garter edge stitch as established, work 6 more rows of Box Stitch.

- Return 24 held stitches to needle. *You now have 45 stitches.* Continue with main yarn.

- **Next Row (RS):** Bind off 9, knit to marker, sm, work in Box Stitch as established to end of row. *You now have 36 stitches.*

- Continue in patterns as established with 4 garter stitches at front edge until 7 repeats of Box Stitch have been completed in this section, 28 rows total.

- Knit 4 rows (definition ridge), increasing 1 st in center of last row. *You now have 37 stitches.*

- Maintaining 4 garter stitches as front edge, work Rows 1 through 8 of Diamond pattern 3 times, then work Row 1 once more.

- Knit 7 rows. Bind off on RS.

KNITTING THE RIGHT FRONT

- Place 23 held stitches on needle. With WS facing, join yarn.

Right Shoulder

- **Row 1 (WS):** Slip 1, knit to end of row.

- **Row 2:** Knit to last 5 stitches, k2tog, k3. *You now have 22 stitches.*

- **Row 3:** Slip 1, k3, purl to end of row.

- **Row 4:** Purl to last 5 stitches, k2tog, k3. *You now have 21 stitches.*

- **Rows 5–8:** Repeat Rows 1–4. *You now have 19 stitches.*

- **Row 9:** Slip 1, k3, pm, knit to end of row.

Right Front Neck

- **Row 1 (RS):** Knit to marker, M1R, sm, k4. *You now have 20 stitches.*

- **Row 2:** Slip 1, k3, sm, purl to end of row.

- **Row 3:** Purl to marker, M1R, sm, k4. *You now have 21 stitches.*

- **Row 4:** Slip 1, k3, sm, knit to end of row.

- **Rows 5 and 6:** Repeat Rows 1 and 2. *You now have 22 stitches.*

- Maintaining 4 neck edge stitches in garter stitch, slipping the 1st stitch on WS rows and increasing on RS rows, work Rows 1–8 of Zigzag pattern three times, incorporating new stitches into pattern. *You now have 34 stitches.* Maintaining slip stitch and increases as established, knit 4 rows (definition ridge). *You now have 36 stitches.*

The Right Box Section with Tab

- **Row 1 (RS):** Work Row 1 of Box Stitch to marker, sm, k4; turn and cast on 9 stitches using the purlwise cable cast on method (see page 276). *You now have 45 stitches.*

- **Row 2:** Kfb, k12, work Box Stitch to end of row. *You now have 46 stitches.*

- **Row 3:** Box Stitch to marker, sm, knit to last stitch, kfb. *You now have 47 stitches.*

- **Row 4:** K2, k2tog, yo (buttonhole made), knit to marker, sm, Box Stitch to end of row.

front edge until 7 repeats of Box Stitch have been completed in this section, 28 rows total.

- Knit 4 rows (definition ridge), increasing 1 st in center of last row. *You now have* 37 stitches.

- Maintaining 4 garter stitches as front edge, work Rows 1 through 8 of Diamond pattern 3 times, then work Row 1 once more.

- Knit 7 rows. Bind off on RS.

KNITTING THE SLEEVES (make 2)

- With RS facing, pick up and knit 51 stitches between bottoms of Zigzag patterns on front and back (approximately 4"/10 cm down from shoulder on each side).

- **Rows 1–5:** Work Rows 2 through 4 of Shoulder Ridge pattern, then work rows 1 and 2 once more.

- **Row 6 (RS):** P1, ssp, purl to last 3 stitches, p2tog, p1. *You now have* 49 stitches.

- **Rows 7, 9 and 11:** Purl.

- **Rows 8 and 10:** Knit.

- **Row 12:** K1, ssk, knit to last 3 stitches, k2tog, k1. *You now have* 47 stitches.

- **Row 13 and 15:** Purl.

- **Row 14:** Knit.

- Beginning with a RS row, work 14 rows of Sleeve Chart (see next page). *You now have* 41 stitches.

- Continuing in stockinette stitch, work 2 rows even. Decrease 1 st each side on next row and then every 4th row 2 more times. *You now have* 35 stitches.

- Continue even in stockinette stitch until sleeve measures 5¼"/13.5 cm from shoulder. Knit 7 rows. Bind off.

FINISHING

- Sew sleeves and side seams. Sew buttons on fronts to correspond with buttonholes. Wash and block.

(Continued on next page)

- **Row 5:** Box Stitch to marker, sm, knit to end of row.

- **Row 6:** Ssk, knit to marker, sm, Box Stitch to end of row. *You now have* 46 stitches.

- **Row 7:** Box Stitch to marker, sm, k12, k2tog. *You now have* 45 stitches.

- **Row 8:** K13, sm, Box Stitch to end of row.

- **Row 9:** Box Stitch to marker, sm, k13.

- **Row 10:** Bind off 9, knit to marker, sm, Box Stitch to end of row.

- Continue in patterns as established with 4 garter stitches at

Diamond Pattern

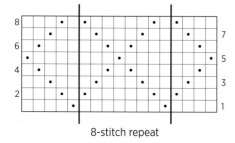

8-stitch repeat

Zigzag Pattern

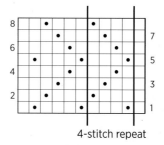

4-stitch repeat

Sleeve Chart

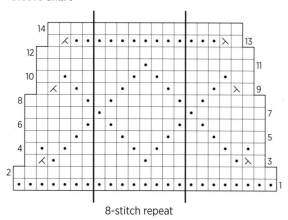

8-stitch repeat

Shoulder Ridge

Box Stitch

4-stitch repeat

☐ k on RS, p on WS

• p on RS, k on WS

╱ k2tog

╲ ssk

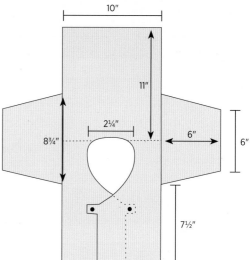

No-Sew Taiyo Baby Jacket

Designed by Brigitte Lang

Complete with button bands and a collar, this little jacket is surprisingly easy to knit. Worked on a chunky yarn and large needles, it knits up quickly, too.

SIZE AND FINISHED MEASUREMENTS

To fit 0–6 months: 18"/45.5 cm chest circumference, 10"/25.5 cm long

YARN

Noro Taiyo, 40% cotton/30% silk/15% wool/15% nylon, 220 yds (200 m)/3.5 oz (100 g), Color 66 (4)

NEEDLES

US 9 (5.5 mm) circular needle 24"/60 cm long and set of four US 9 (5.5 mm) double-point needles *or size needed to obtain correct gauge*

GAUGE

16 stitches and 24 rows = 4"/10 cm in stockinette stitch

OTHER SUPPLIES

Scrap yarn or stitch holders, stitch markers, five ⅝"/16 mm buttons, yarn needle

KNITTING THE FRONTS AND BACK

- With circular needle, cast on 76 stitches. Work back and forth in Seed Stitch (see Pattern Essentials on next page) for 1"/2.5 cm.

- Continue in stockinette stitch until piece measures 6¼"/16 cm, ending with a WS row.

Divide for Armholes

- **Next Row (RS):** K16, k2tog, k1; place 18 stitches just worked on holder for right front; k1, ssk, k32, k2tog, k1; place remaining 19 stitches on holder for left front. *You now have* 36 stitches for the back.

- Continue in stockinette stitch on these 36 stitches for 3¾"/9.5 cm, ending with a WS row. Cut yarn and place stitches on holder.

The Right Front

- Place 18 right front stitches on needle. With WS facing, attach yarn at armhole edge and continue in stockinette stitch for 2"/5 cm, ending with a WS row.

- **Next Row (RS):** Bind off 5 stitches, knit to end of row. *You now have* 13 stitches.

- **Next Row:** Purl.

Pattern Essentials

SEED STITCH
(even number of stitches)

Row 1: *K1, p1; repeat from * to end of row.

Row 2: *P1, k1; repeat from * to end of row.

Repeat Rows 1 and 2 for pattern.

....

SEED STITCH
(odd number of stitches)

Row 1: K1, *p1, k1; repeat from * to end of row.

Repeat Row 1 for pattern.

....

SEED STITCH
(in the round; odd number of stitches)

Round 1: K1, *p1, k1; repeat from * to end of round.

Round 2: P1, *k1, p1; repeat from * to end of round.

Repeat Rounds 1 and 2 for pattern.

- **Next Row:** K1, ssk, knit to end of row. *You now have 12 stitches.*
- **Next Row:** Purl.
- Repeat the last 2 rows 2 more times. *You now have 10 stitches.*
- Continue even until piece measures same as back. Place stitches on holder.

The Left Front

- Place 19 left front stitches on needle. With RS facing, attach yarn at armhole edge. K1, ssk, k16. *You now have 18 stitches.*
- Continue in stockinette stitch for 2"/5 cm, ending with a RS row.
- **Next Row (WS):** Bind off 5 purlwise, purl to end of row. *You now have 13 stitches.*
- **Next Row (RS):** Knit to last 3 stitches, k2tog, k1. *You now have 12 stitches.*
- **Next Row:** Purl.
- Repeat the last 2 rows 2 more times. *You now have 10 stitches.*

- Continue even until piece measures same as back. Leave stitches on needle

JOINING THE SHOULDERS

- Join 10 front and back shoulder stitches on each side using three-needle bind off (see page 282), leaving remaining 16 back stitches on hold for collar pick up.

KNITTING THE BUTTON BANDS

Note: Work 5 buttonholes into 3rd row of Seed Stitch (right front for girls, left front for boys) as follows: K1, yo, k2tog, *seed 6, yo, k2tog; repeat from * 3 more times, k1.

- With RS facing and beginning at lower right front edge, pick up and knit (see page 281) 36 stitches to neck. Work Seed Stitch for 5 rows, placing buttonholes appropriately. Bind off on RS.
- With RS facing and beginning at the upper left front edge, pick up and knit 36 stitches to lower edge. Work Seed Stitch for 5 rows, placing buttonholes appropriately. Bind off on RS.

KNITTING THE SLEEVES (make 2)

- With double-point needles and RS facing, beginning at underarm, pick up and knit 32 stitches around armhole. Place marker and join into a round. Work in stockinette stitch and decrease 1 stitch at underarm every 5 rows five times. *You now have 27 stitches.*

Work even until sleeve measures 5"/12.5 cm. Work 6 rounds of Seed Stitch. Bind off in pattern.

KNITTING THE COLLAR

- With RS facing and beginning at right front neck, pick up and knit 14 stitches from right front neck, knit 16 held stitches, pick up and knit 14 stitches from left front neckline. *You now have* 44 stitches. Work in Seed Stitch until collar measures 2½"/6.5 cm, ending on a WS row. Bind off in pattern.

FINISHING

- Weave in ends. Sew buttons opposite buttonholes.

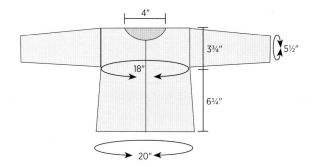

Boon Island Hoodie

Designed by Susan Boye

An adorable basket weave jacket that's appropriate for both girls and boys, this hoodie is knit seamlessly from the bottom up. Using simple knit and purl stitches, even a novice can succeed.

SIZE AND FINISHED MEASUREMENTS
To fit 2–4 years: 24"/61 cm chest circumference

YARN
Bernat Big Ball Handicrafter Cotton, 100% cotton, 710 yds (650 m)/14 oz (397 g), Color 27224 Grass (4)

NEEDLES
US 7 (4.5 mm) circular needle 24"/60 cm long, set of four US 7 (4.5 mm) double-point needles, and US 7 (4.5 mm) straight needles (for grafting, optional) *or size needed to obtain correct gauge*

GAUGE
18 stitches and 24 rows = 4"/10 cm in Basket Weave pattern

OTHER SUPPLIES
Stitch holders or scrap yarn, clasp fastener, yarn needle, stitch markers

KNITTING THE SLEEVES (make 2)

- With double-point needles, cast on 36 stitches. Place 12 stitches on each of 3 needles and join into a round, being careful not to twist the stitches.
- **Rounds 1–7:** Work Basket Weave pattern in the round.
- **Round 8 (Increase Round):** K1, M1, work in established pattern around, M1. *You now have* 38 stitches.
- Bringing new stitches into pattern, continue to increase 1 st at beginning and end of round every 8 rounds two more times. *You now have* 48 stitches.
- Work Rounds 1–7 once more.
- **Next Round:** K3, place last 6 stitches on hold. Cut yarn leaving a 16"/40.5 cm tail.

KNITTING THE BODY

- With circular needle, cast on 108 stitches.

Pattern Essentials

BASKET WEAVE
(back and forth; multiple of 12 stitches)

Rows 1–6: *K6, p6; repeat from * to end of row.

Row 7: Knit.

Rows 8: Purl.

Rows 9–14: *P6, k6; repeat from * to end of row.

Row 15: Knit.

Row 16: Purl.

Repeat Rows 1–16 for pattern.

··

BASKET WEAVE
(in the round; multiple of 12 stitches)

Rounds 1–6: *K6, p6; repeat from * to end of round.

Round 7 and 8: Knit.

Rounds 9–14: *P6, k6; repeat from * to end of round.

Rounds 15 and 16: Knit.

Repeat Rounds 1–16 for pattern.

- Work Rows 1–16 of Basket Weave pattern back and forth 3 times, then work Rows 1–6 once more (54 rows total).
- **Next Row (RS):** K30, place last 6 stitches on holder, k54, place last 6 stitches on holder, knit to end of row.

JOINING SLEEVES TO BODY

- With wrong side facing, purl 24 body stitches, pm, purl 42 sleeve stitches, pm, purl 48 back stitches, pm, purl 42 sleeve stitches, pm, purl 24 body stitches. *You now have* 180 stitches.
- Work 2 rows in pattern as established.

KNITTING THE YOKE

- Continuing in Basket Weave pattern as established, work decreases as follows.
- **Row 1 (RS):** *Work to 4 stitches before marker, k2tog, k2, sm, k2, ssk; repeat from * 3 more times, work in pattern to end of row. *You now have* 172 stitches.

- **Row 2 (WS):** Work even in pattern as established.
- Repeat Rows 1 and 2 twelve more times. *You now have 76 stitches.*
- **Next Row (RS):** *Work to 4 stitches before marker, k2tog, k2, sm, knit to marker, sm, k2, ssk; rep from * once more, work in pattern to end of row. *You now have 72 stitches.*
- Work 3 rows of established Basket Weave pattern.

KNITTING THE HOOD

- Work even in pattern as established until hood measures approximately 9"/23 cm, ending with Row 7 or 15 of Basket Weave pattern.
- **Next Row:** Place 36 stitches each onto two straight needles. Graft top of hood stitches together with Kitchener stitch (see page 278).

FINISHING

- Graft underarm stitches together with Kitchener stitch. Attach fastener to front of coat, just below the hood. Weave in all ends.

Basket Weave

☐ k on RS, p on WS

⊡ p on RS, k on WS

12-stitch repeat

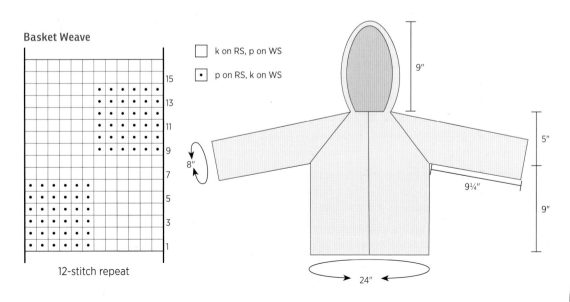

Into the Woods Baby Poncho

Designed by Ellen Harvey

Simple top-down raglan shaping is featured in this easy-to-wear poncho. Stitches for the hood are picked up along the neck and worked up from there, finishing with a Kitchener stitch join. No seams to wrangle with here!

SIZE AND FINISHED MEASUREMENTS
To fit 6–12 months: 9½"/24 cm length

YARN
Blue Moon Fiber Arts Socks that Rock Heavyweight, 100% superwash merino wool, 350 yds (320 m)/7 oz (198 g), Brick

NEEDLES
US 6 (4 mm) circular needles 24"/60 cm and 29"/74 cm long *or size needed to obtain correct gauge*

GAUGE
20 stitches and 30 rows = 4"/10 cm in stockinette stitch

OTHER SUPPLIES
Stitch markers, yarn needle

KNITTING THE YOKE

- With shorter needle, cast on 40 stitches. Do not join.
- **Set-Up Row:** P2, pm, p10, pm, p16, pm, p10, pm, p2.
- **Row 1 (RS):** Knit to 1 st before marker, kfb, sm, kfb; repeat from * three more times, knit to end. *You now have* 48 stitches.
- **Row 2:** Purl.
- Repeat Rows 1 and 2 four more times. *You now have* 80 stitches.
- Using the backward loop method (see page 276), cast on 4 stitches at the beginning of the next two rows for front bands. *You now have* 88 stitches.
- Keeping the first and last 4 stitches of each row in garter stitch, continue with Rows 1 and 2 as established eight more times. *You now have* 152 stitches.

JOINING THE FRONT PLACKET AND KNITTING THE BODY

- **Next Row (RS):** Work as established to last 4 stitches; place last 4 stitches on a separate needle and hold in front of first 4 stitches of row; knit the first and last 4 stitches together. *You now have* 148 stitches. Place marker and begin working in the round.

- Continue body increases as follows.

- **Round 1:** Knit.

- **Round 2:** Knit to 1 st before marker, kfb, sm, kfb; repeat from * three more times, knit to end of round. *You now have* 156 stitches.

- Repeat Rows 1 and 2 two more times, changing to longer needle when necessary. *You now have* 172 stitches.

- Continue body increases as follows.

- **Round 1:** Knit.

- **Round 2 (Increase Round):** *Knit to 1 stitch before next marker, kfb, sm, work to next marker, sm, kfb; repeat from * once, knit to end of round. *You now have* 176 stitches.

- Repeat Rounds 1 and 2 three more times. *You now have* 188 stitches. Work the increase round every 4th round twice, then every 6th round twice. *You now have* 204 stitches.

- Work 5 rounds garter stitch (knit 1 round, purl 1 round).

- Bind off loosely knitwise.

KNITTING THE HOOD

- With shorter needle, RS facing, and beginning at right front neck edge, pick up and knit 64 stitches evenly spaced to left front neck edge. Work back and forth in rows as follows.

- **Row 1 (WS):** K4, purl to last 4 stitches, k4.

- **Row 2:** Knit.

- Repeat Rows 1 and 2 until piece measures 3"/7.5 cm from picked up stitches.

- **Next Row (WS):** K4, p28, pm, p28, k4.

- **Next Row (Increase Row, RS):** Knit to 1 st before marker, kfb, sm, kfb, knit to end. *You now have* 66 stitches.

- **Next Row (WS):** K4, purl to last 4 stitches, k4.

- Repeat these two rows two more times. *You now have* 70 stitches.

- Work even until hood measures 6½"/16.5 cm.

- Arrange stitches evenly on two ends of one needle. Holding stitches parallel, graft the two halves together with Kitchener stitch (see page 278).

FINISHING

- Weave in ends. Block.

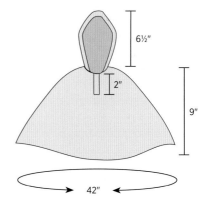

Little

BOTTOMS

Ruffle Bumpkin

Designed by Lindsay Lewchuk, Knit Eco Chic

Precious ruffles adorn the booty of your cute little bumpkin in this organic cotton design. Completely seamless and super comfy, Ruffle Bumpkin finishes your little one's outfit in style.

SIZES AND FINISHED MEASUREMENTS
To fit preemie (newborn): 10 (12½)"/ 25.5 (31.5) cm waist

YARN
Classic Elite Yarns Seedling, 100% organic cotton, 110 yds (101 m)/1.75 oz (50 g), Color 4561 Zephyr (4)

NEEDLES
Set of five US 6 (4 mm) double-point needles, set of five US 7 (4.5 mm) double-point needles, and US G-6 (4 mm) crochet hook *or size needed to obtain correct gauge*

GAUGE
18 stitches and 28 rounds = 4"/10 cm in stockinette stitch

OTHER SUPPLIES
2 stitch markers in different colors, 20"/51 cm of ⅜"/10 mm ribbon (optional), F-5 (3.75 mm) crochet hook, yarn needle

Pattern Essentials

pfbf (purl front, back, front) Purl in the (front, back, front) of one stitch, then drop stitch from needle

KNITTING THE WAISTBAND

Note: Before beginning, wind off approximately 10 yards/10 meters of yarn into a separate ball for use when knitting the crotch.

- With smaller needle, cast on 48 (56) stitches. Divide evenly onto double-point needles, pm to indicate beginning of round and center back. Join into a round, being careful not to twist the stitches.

- Round 1: (K2, p2) 6 (7) times, pm for center front, (k2, p2) 6 (7) times.

- Rounds 2–5: *K2, p2; repeat from * to end of round.

- Round 6 (folding round): Purl.

- Rounds 7 and 8: *K2, p2; repeat from * to end of round.

- Round 9 (eyelet round): Work rib as established to 4 stitches before center front marker, k2tog, yo, work 4 stitches in rib as established, removing marker, yo, p2tog, work rib as established to end of round.

- **Rounds 10 and 11:** Work in rib as established.
- Cut a ribbon 20 (22½)"/51 (57) cm long.
- Thread ribbon through the front eyelets and tie into a circle. Fold the ribbed band in half to the inside at the folding round (Round 6).
- **Next Round:** Knit the next stitch together with the corresponding stitch from the cast-on edge; repeat from * to end of round, seaming the waistband to the inside of the pants.

KNITTING THE BODY

- Change to larger needles.
- **Set-Up Round:** Knit, increasing 6 stitches evenly spaced. *You now have* 54 (62) stitches. Remove end of round marker, k14 (15), replace marker to indicate new beginning of round.
- **Rounds 1–3:** Knit.
- **Round 4:** K27 (31), purl to end of round.
- **Round 5–7:** Knit.
- Repeat Rounds 1–7 once more, then work Rounds 1–4 once. Work even in stockinette stitch until piece measures 4 (4¼)"/10 (11) cm or desired length, ending last round 4 (7) stitches before end of round.

KNITTING THE CROTCH

- **Next Round:** Bind off 8 (14) right leg stitches, k19 (17), join new yarn and bind off 8 (14) left leg stitches, knit to end. *You now have* two sections of 19 (17) stitches each.
- Work the front and back sections at the same time with separate balls of yarn back and forth in rows as follows.
- **Row 1 and all WS rows:** Purl.
- **Row 2 (RS):** On front stitches, k1, ssk, knit to last 3 stitches, k2tog, k1; on back stitches, k1, ssk, knit to last 3 stitches, k2tog, k1. *You now have* two sections of 17 (15) stitches each.
- **Rows 3–10:** Repeat Rows 1 and 2 four more times. *You now have* two sections of 9 (7) stitches each.

- Work even in stockinette stitch until piece measures 6"/15 cm or desired length.
- Graft front and back sections together with Kitchener stitch (see page 278).

RUFFLING THE BOOTY

- With smaller needle and RS facing, pick up and knit the purl bumps, along one of the purl ridges at the back.
- **Row 1 (WS):** *Pfbf; repeat from * to end of round. *You now have* 81 (93) stitches.
- **Row 2:** Knit.
- Bind off all stitches purlwise.
- Repeat for two more ruffles.

FINISHING

- With right side facing, work single crochet around leg openings.
- Weave in ends.

Baby Atelier Pants

Designed by Izumi Ouchi

The pants begin at the bottom, are worked back and forth, and then joined at the hip and worked in the round. There's ribbing around waist and legs, and a crocheted drawstring in the waistband makes them adjustable.

SIZE AND FINISHED MEASUREMENTS

To fit 6–12 months: 18¾"/47.5 cm hip circumference

YARN

Zitron Opus 1, 100% merino wool, 208 yds (190 m)/3.5 oz (100 g), Color 200 Harvest (4)

NEEDLES

US 7 (4.5 mm) circular needle 16"/40 cm long and set of four US 7 (4.5 mm) double-point needles *or size needed to obtain correct gauge*

GAUGE

18½ stitches and 27 rows/rounds = 4"/10 cm in stockinette stitch

OTHER SUPPLIES

US G-6 (4 mm) crochet hook, scrap yarn, yarn needle

Pattern Essentials

TUBULAR BIND OFF

This method is used to bind off K1, P1 ribbing. Working a comfortable number of stitches at a time, separate the knits onto one needle and hold in front and the purls onto a separate needle and hold in back. Graft stitches together using Kitchener stitch (see page 278).

KNITTING THE PANTS

- Using the crochet hook and scrap yarn, cast on 40 stitches using the crochet chain provisional cast on method (see page 281). Do not join. Purl 1 row.
- **Row 1 (RS):** K1, ssk, knit to last 3 stitches, k2tog, k1. *You now have* 38 stitches.
- **Row 2 (WS):** Purl.
- Repeat Rows 1 and 2 six more times. *You now have* 26 stitches.
- Work even in stockinette stitch until piece measures 7½"/19 cm, ending with WS row.
- **Next Row (RS):** K1, M1, knit to last stitch, M1, k1. *You now have* 28 stitches.
- **Row 2 (WS):** Purl.
- Repeat these 2 rows 6 more times. You now have 40 stitches.
- **Joining Round:** With RS facing, cast on 2 stitches, place 40 live stitches from provisional cast on onto needle, cast on 2 stitches. *You now have* 84 stitches.
- Working in round, continue in stockinette stitch until piece measures 4"/10 from the join.

- **Next Round:** *K1, p1; repeat from * to end of round.
- Repeat this round until ribbing measures 1¼"/3 cm.
- **Next Round:** Work ribbing over 10 stitches, p2tog, yo; repeat from * to end of round.
- Work even in ribbing as established until ribbing measures 2¼"/5.5 cm or desired length. With yarn needle, bind off using the tubular bind off method (see opposite page).

FINISHING

- With double-point needles and RS facing, pick up and knit 60 stitches around leg opening and join into a round. Work (k1, p1) ribbing for 6 rows. Bind off using the tubular bind off method. Repeat for second leg opening.
- Using a crochet hook, chain 180 stitches or desired length for drawstring. Weave in ends and block. Thread drawstring through eyelets in ribbing.

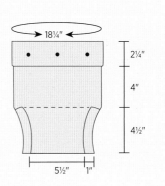

Old-School Baby Soaker

Designed by Diana Foster

This soaker, made of 100% pure wool, will keep baby warm even when wet. If using a greasy wool, the lanolin will neutralize baby's urine, keeping the soaker fresh between washings.

SIZE AND FINISHED MEASUREMENTS
To fit 0–6 months: 19"/48.5 cm hip circumference

YARN
Kerry Woollen Mills Aran Wool, 100% wool, 365 yds (334 m)/7 oz (200 g), White (4)

NEEDLES
US 5 (3.75 mm) circular needle 16"/40 cm long *or size needed to obtain correct gauge*

GAUGE
20 stitches and 40 rounds = 4"/10 cm in garter stitch

OTHER SUPPLIES
Stitch marker, stitch holder or scrap yarn, yarn needle

Pattern Essentials

TWISTED CORD

Twisted cord can be made with one or more lengths of yarn, depending on desired thickness. Cut a piece (or pieces) of yarn approximately four times longer than desired cord length. Fold the length in half and loop the center over a hook, doorknob or other stationary holder. Hold the ends together and begin to twist in the same direction. When yarn is very twisted, remove the end from the hook and, continuing to hold the other ends, allow the cord to fold back on itself. Tie the end to secure.

KNITTING THE SOAKER

- Cast on 96 stitches. Place a marker and join into a round, being careful not to twist the stitches.

- **Rounds 1–4:** *K2, p2; repeat from * to end of round.

- **Round 5:** *K2, yo, p2tog; repeat from * to end of round.

- **Rounds 6–9:** Repeat Rounds 1–4.

- **Round 10:** Knit.

- **Round 11:** Purl.

- Repeat Rounds 10 and 11 until piece measures 7"/18 cm from cast-on edge.

The Bottom Ribbing

- From here you'll work back and forth in rows.

- **Row 1:** *K2, p2; repeat from * 11 more times, turn. Place remaining 48 stitches on hold.

- Repeat Row 1 until piece measures 6"/15 cm from beginning of bottom ribbing.

- Join stitches to held stitches. To graft with Kitchener stitch (see page 278) hold the work with the ribbed stitches in front and the garter stitches in back;

work as instructed for the knit stitches on front needle; make first pass through purl stitches on front needle as if to knit and leave them on needle, then pass through them as if to purl and remove them from the needle; work all stitches on back needle as instructed.

FINISHING

• Weave in ends. Cut four 1½ yd/1.5 m lengths of yarn and make a twisted cord (see opposite page), tying knots at the ends. Thread drawstring cord through eyelets.

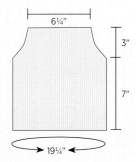

Perfect Baby Soakers

Soakers are made to be used over cloth diapers. When knitted with pure wool, preferably in worsted weight, they will absorb much of the moisture from a wet diaper. And since wool retains approximately 80% of its insulating value when wet, baby will stay warm. Washing them in a lanolin solution occasionally will keep them performing at their best.

Ruffles and Beads

Designed by Judith Durant

A little girl will feel like a princess with all the shiny beads on this three-tiered skirt. A headband with a large beaded flower tops off the outfit.

SIZE AND FINISHED MEASUREMENTS

To fit 12–24 months: 20"/51 cm waist, 9"/23 cm skirt length; 14"/35.5 cm headband circumference (will stretch to 18"/45.5 cm), 1¼"/3 cm headband width

YARN

Cascade Yarns Heritage 150 Sock Yarn, 75% superwash wool/25% nylon, 492 yds (450 m)/5.25 oz (150 g), Color 5605 Plum (1)

NEEDLES

Two US 3 (3.25 mm) circular needles 16"/40 cm long *or size needed to obtain correct gauge*

GAUGE

24 stitches and 38 rounds = 4"/10 cm in stockinette stitch

OTHER SUPPLIES

353 size 4 x 7 mm magatama beads (approximately 50 g), big eye beading needle, 21"/53.5 cm length of ⅝"/16 mm elastic, yarn needle, sewing needle and thread

Pattern Essentials

SEED STITCH

(in the round; even number of stitches)

Round 1: *K1, p1; repeat from * to end of round.

Round 2: *P1, k1; repeat from * to end of round.

Repeat Rounds 1 and 2 for pattern.

SEED STITCH

(back and forth; odd number of stitches)

Row 1: *K1, p1; repeat from * to last stitch, k1.

Repeat Row 1 for pattern.

KNITTING THE SKIRT

Stringing the Beads and Casting On

- Thread yarn onto big eye beading needle and string 99 beads, pushing the beads down toward the yarn ball as necessary. Using the long-tail cast on method (see page

279) cast on 1 stitch, slide bead up to needle, *making sure this and remaining beads stay to the back as you cast on the next stitches, cast on 2 stitches, slide bead up to needle; repeat from * 97 more times, cast on 1 stitch. *You now have 198 stitches*

- Turn and knit 1 row.

The First Ruffle

- Place marker, join into a round, and work 3 rounds of Seed Stitch.

- Work in stockinette stitch (knit every round) until piece measures 3½"/9 cm.

- **Decrease Round:** *K1, k2tog; repeat from * to end of round. *You now have 132 stitches.*

- Work even in stockinette stitch for 3"/7.5 cm. Leave stitches on needle and set aside.

The Second Ruffle

- With second needle, cast on and work as for first ruffle through the Decrease Round.

- Hold the two ruffles together with the second ruffle in front of the first ruffle and knit 1 stitch from second ruffle together with 1 stitch of first ruffle until all stitches are joined. Work even in stockinette stitch for 1¼"/3 cm.

- Leave the stitches on one needle and set aside.

The Third Ruffle

- With second needle, cast on and work as for first ruffle until piece measures 2½"/6.5 cm. Work the Decrease Round, then place the third ruffle in front of the ruffles on the other needle and join as for Second Ruffle.

The Waistband

- Work stockinette stitch for ¾"/2 cm.

- Purl 1 round.

- Work stockinette stitch for ¾"/2 cm, binding off the last 5 stitches of the last round. Bind off 5 more stitches and pull yarn through the last stitch.

- Cut yarn, leaving a long tail. Thread tail onto yarn needle and join live stitches to the beginning round of the waistband on the inside, leaving the 10 bound-off stitches free for inserting elastic.

Finishing

- Cut elastic to 21"/53.5 cm. Thread elastic through waistband. Overlap ½"/13 mm ends of elastic and stitch them together with needle and thread. Use yarn tail to sew the 10 bound-off stitches to beginning round of waistband.

- Weave in ends, steam block.

KNITTING THE HEADBAND

- Cast on 9 stitches. Work in Seed Stitch until band measures 14"/35.5 cm. Bind off and cut yarn, leaving a tail for sewing. Thread tail onto yarn needle and join bind off edge to cast-on edge.

The Flower

- String 56 beads onto yarn. Using the long-tail method, *cast on 3 stitches, slide bead up to needle; repeat from * 55 more times, cast on 3 stitches. *You now have 171 stitches.*

- Turn and bind off all stitches.

- Fold the beaded cord into 8 loops, each with 7 beads, and stitch them together to form a flower.

- Stitch flower to headband, covering the seam. Weave in ends.

Wee Britches

Designed by Melissa Morgan-Oakes

If you're saying this out loud, be sure to apply a bit of a brogue, as in "wee breetches." These are practical and deliciously warm. The pattern is written for Magic Loop knitting and the pants are worked from the waist to the ankles.

SIZE AND FINISHED MEASUREMENTS
To fit 3-6 months: 20"/51 cm hip circumference, 15½"/39.5 cm length

YARN
Valley Yarns/Kangaroo Dyer Franklin, 75% wool/25% nylon, 450 yds (411 m)/4 oz (113 g), Twilight 🔲1

NEEDLES
US 2 (2.75 mm) circular needle 40"/100 cm long *or size needed to obtain correct gauge*

GAUGE
28 stitches and 36 rounds = 4"/10 cm in stockinette stitch

OTHER SUPPLIES
Removable stitch marker, 32"/81.5 cm of ⅜"/10 mm ribbon, yarn needle

KNITTING THE BRITCHES

- Cast on 152 stitches. Divide and join for working in the round Magic Loop style (see page 280). Place marker in first stitch to note beginning of round and move it up every few inches.

- **Rounds 1–6:** *K1, p1; repeat from * to end of round.

- **Row 4:** P54, WT.
- **Row 5:** K45, WT.
- **Row 6:** P36, WT.
- **Row 7:** K27, WT.
- **Row 8:** P18, WT.
- Return to working in the round, picking up wraps and knitting them together with their respective stitches as you come to them. Continue working in stockinette stitch until work measures 6½"/16.5 cm from cast-on edge when measured at center front.

Dividing for the Legs

- From marker, knit 38 and drop yarn. Attach new yarn from opposite end of ball and knit 38. Turn and reorient your work to continue Magic Loop style; knit 38 more stitches with the same yarn (these 76 stitches are leg 1). Drop this yarn, pick up previously dropped yarn, and knit remaining 38 stitches to complete leg 2.
- **Next round:** Knit 38 stitches of leg 2, drop yarn; pick up next yarn and knit 38 stitches of leg 1; knit 38 stitches of leg 1, drop yarn; pick up previously dropped yarn and knit remaining 38 stitches of leg 2.

Note: Some of you may know that you're now working 2-at-a-time-sock style. For those of you who didn't know it, congratulations; now you know how it works! *You now have* 2 legs, divided on your long circular needle. Work even on both legs for ½"/13 mm.

Shaping the Legs

- Leg decreases are worked at the inside of the leg as follows.
- **Decrease Round:** Knit to 3 stitches before crotch of garment (center of needle), k2tog, k1; move to next leg and k1, ssk, knit to end of needle; turn and reorient, knit to 3 stitches before crotch, k2tog, k1; move next leg and k1, ssk, knit to end of needle. *You now have* 74 stitches on each leg.
- Knit 2 rounds even.
- Continue in this manner, decreasing every 3rd round 16 more times. *You now have* 42 stitches on each leg.

- **Round 7:** (eyelet round) *K1, p1, yo, k2tog; repeat from * to end of round.
- **Rounds 8–16:** *K1, p1; repeat from * to end of round.
- Work in stockinette stitch (knit every round) for ½"/13 mm.
- Use short rows on the back of the pants to create extra space for baby's bottom as follows. (See explanation of WT on page 282.)
- **Row 1:** K74, WT.
- **Row 2:** P71, WT.
- **Row 3:** K63, WT.

- Work even in stockinette stitch for 1"/2.5 cm.

The Ankle Cuffs

- **Round 1:** *K1, p1; repeat from * to end of round.
- Repeat Round 1 for 2"/10 cm. Bind off.

FINISHING

- Thread ribbon through the eyelets in the waistband.
- Weave in ends. Block.

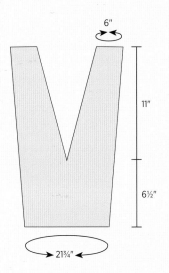

Baby Green Jeans

Designed by Judith Durant

Captain Kangaroo was a favorite TV show for many baby-boomer babies, and at least one of them wished she could have overalls like Mr. Green Jeans. The legs are knit circularly from the bottom and then joined together above the crotch for circular knitting from the hips to the waist.

SIZE AND FINISHED MEASUREMENTS
To fit 3–6 months: 19"/48.5 cm waist, 13"/33 cm from waist to ankle

YARN
Imperial Yarn Tracie Too, 100% wool, 395 yds (361 m)/4 oz (113 g), Color 331 Honeydew (2)

NEEDLES
Set of five US 3 (3.25 mm) double-point needles and one US 3 (3.25 mm) circular needle 16"/40 cm long *or size needed to obtain correct gauge*

GAUGE
24 stitches and 37 rounds = 4"/10 cm in stockinette stitch

OTHER SUPPLIES
Stitch marker, scrap yarn for stitch holder, two ½"/13 mm buttons, sewing needle and coordinating thread, 20"/51 cm of ¾"/19 mm elastic, yarn needle

KNITTING THE LEGS

- With double-point needles, cast on 60 stitches. Join into a round, being careful not to twist the stitches. Work 12 rounds of Moss Stitch (see opposite page).
- **Next Round:** Knit 30, pm, knit to last 2 stitches, kfb, k1. *You now have* 61 stitches and the round begins at the inside leg.

Pattern Essentials

MOSS STITCH
(in the round; multiple of 4 stitches)

Rounds 1 and 2: *K2, p2; repeat from * to end of round.

Rounds 3 and 4: *P2, k2; repeat from * to end of round.

Repeat Rounds 1 through 4 for pattern.

....

MOSS STITCH
(back and forth; multiple of 4 + 2 stitches)

Row 1 (WS): *K2, p2; repeat from * to last 2 stitches, k2.

Rows 2 and 3: *P2, k2; repeat from * to last 2 stitches, p2.

Row 4: Repeat Row 1.

Repeat Rows 1 through 4 for pattern.

- **Round 1:** K1, M1L, knit to marker, sm, slip 1, knit to last stitch, M1R, k1. *You now have* 63 stitches.

- **Round 2:** Knit.

- Continue in stockinette stitch, slipping the marked stitch on every other round and *at the same time* increasing at the beginning and end of every 4th round 5 more times, then at the beginning and end of every 6th round 2 times. *You now have* 77 stitches. Work even until piece measures 7½"/19 cm.

SHAPING THE CROTCH

- Work 2 rounds as established, continuing the slip stitches on every other round at the outer leg "seam," and ending last round 4 stitches before end of round. Bind

off next 8 stitches. *You now have* 69 stitches. Work back and forth as follows.

- **Row 1 (RS):** K1, ssk, knit to last 3 stitches, k2tog, k1. *You now have* 67 stitches.

- **Row 2:** Purl.

- **Rows 3–8:** Repeat Rows 1 and 2 three times. *You now have* 61 stitches. Cut yarn leaving a tail long enough to sew the crotch seam and place stitches on hold. Knit a second leg to this point but do not cut yarn.

JOINING THE LEGS

- Place stitches of both legs side-by-side onto a circular needle. With attached yarn and RS facing, continue as established to last stitch of first leg, pm for center front, knit the last stitch together with the first stitch of second leg; work to last stitch of second leg, pm for center back, knit last stitch of second leg together with first stitch of first leg. *You now have* 120 stitches.

KNITTING THE HIPS

- Work in rounds of stockinette stitch for 1"/2.5 cm, continuing to slip stitches at the outside legs *and also* at the center back and center front of every other round. Piece should measure approximately 9¾"/25 cm.

- **Increase Round:** (K6, M1R) 4 times, work in established pattern to last 24 stitches, (M1L, k6) 4 times. *You now have* 128 stitches.

- Work even in pattern as established until piece measures 13"/33 cm.

KNITTING THE WAISTBAND

- Discontinue slip stitches; purl 1 round for turning ridge.

- Work even in stockinette stitch for 1"/2.5 cm, ending last round 4 stitches before end of round. Bind off next 8 stitches. Cut the yarn, leaving a 30"/76 cm tail, and pull the tail through the last bound-off stitch.

- Fold waistband to wrong side at turning ridge. Thread tail onto yarn needle and sew live stitches to the inside, making sure you join to the same round throughout, and join one live stitch to each stitch in the round. You now have a casing with an opening to insert elastic. Do not weave in end; leave the remainder of tail for finishing.

KNITTING THE BIB

- With circular needle, RS facing and beginning in the stitch after the left side "seam" stitch, pick up and knit 58 stitches to 1 stitch before right side "seam" stitch, skipping the center front stitch. Work back and forth as follows.

- **Row 1 (WS):** Work Moss Stitch over 6 stitches, p46, Moss Stitch over 6 stitches.

- **Row 2:** Moss Stitch 6, k46, Moss Stitch 6.

- **Row 3:** Moss Stitch 6, purl to last 6 stitches, Moss Stitch 6.

- **Row 4:** Moss Stitch 6, ssk, knit to last 8 stitches, k2tog, Moss Stitch 6.

- Repeat Rows 3 and 4 thirteen more times. *You now have* 30 stitches.

- Work in Moss Stitch for 10 rows. Bind off in pattern.

KNITTING THE STRAPS

- With circular or double-point needles and RS of center back facing, skip 13 stitches to left of right side "seam" stitch, then pick up and knit 10 stitches. Work in Moss Stitch for 5"/12.5 cm or to desired length. Place stitches on hold. Repeat for second strap, beginning in the 11th stitch to the left of the center back stitch.

Joining the Straps

- Place stitches for both straps side-by-side on a needle. Continue in Moss Stitch as established for 8 stitches; place next 2 stitches on a spare double-point needle

and hold in back of and parallel to the following 2 stitches; work the next 2 pairs of stitches together in pattern to join straps, work in Moss Stitch to end of row. *You now have* 18 stitches. Work even in Moss Stitch until piece measures approximately 1"/2.5 cm from the join.

Continuing the Straps

- **Next Row:** Moss Stitch 8; place these stitches on hold, bind off 2, Moss Stitch 8.

- Continue in pattern as established until strap measures 5"/12.5 cm from separation.

- **Next Row:** Pattern 3, yo, k2tog, pattern 3 (buttonhole made).

- Work in pattern as established for 4 more rows, decreasing 1 stitch at the beginning and end of every RS row. *You now have* 4 stitches. Bind off in pattern.

- Place held strap stitches back onto needle and repeat for second strap.

KNITTING THE POCKETS (make 2)

- Cast on 22 stitches, leaving a long tail for sewing. Work Moss Stitch for 8 rows.

- **Next Row (RS):** Moss Stitch 4, k14, Moss Stitch 4.

- **Next Row:** Moss Stitch 4, p14, Moss Stitch 4.

- Repeat these 2 rows two more times, then decrease as follows.

- **Row 1 (RS):** Moss Stitch 4, ssk, knit to last 6 stitches, k2tog, Moss Stitch 4.
- **Row 2:** Moss Stitch 4, purl to last 4 stitches, Moss Stitch 4.
- Repeat Rows 1 and 2 five more times. *You now have* 10 stitches.
- Work 4 rows in Moss Stitch. Bind off in pattern.

FINISHING

- Thread yarn tail from first leg onto yarn needle and sew the crotch seam together. Thread elastic through waistband, overlap the edges by ½"/13 mm, and stitch the ends together. Thread waistband yarn tail onto yarn needle and sew the bound-off stitches to the bottom of the waistband. Use yarn tails to sew pockets in place using the photograph as a guide. Use sewing needle and thread to sew buttons to top of bib. Weave in all ends. Block.

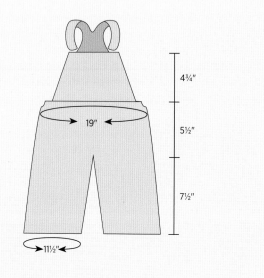

Confetti and Lace Baby Dress

Designed by Carol J. Sorsdahl

The body of this festive and lacy top is knit from the bottom up in two pieces and seamed together. The sleeves and collar are knit separately and attached. Perfect for baby's first birthday party.

SIZE AND FINISHED MEASUREMENTS
To fit 6–24 months: 21"/53.5 cm chest circumference and 12½"/31.5 cm long

YARN
Fancy Image Hand-dyed Yarn, 100% superwash merino wool, 420 yds (384 m)/4 oz (113 g), Confetti

NEEDLES
Two US 4 (3.5 mm) circular needles 16"/40 cm long; US 6 (4 mm) circular needle 16"/40 cm long *or size needed to obtain correct gauge*

GAUGE
25 stitches and 36 rows = 4"/10 cm in stockinette stitch with smaller needle
33 stitches and 30 rows = 4"/10 cm in Lace pattern with larger needles

OTHER SUPPLIES
Stitch holders, yarn needle, one ⅜"/10 mm button

Pattern Essentials

LACE
(multiple of 11 stitches)

Row 1 (RS): *K2tog twice, (yo, k1) three times, yo, ssk twice; repeat from * to end of row.

Row 2 (WS): Knit.

Repeat Rows 1 and 2 for pattern.

KNITTING THE BACK

- Before beginning, wind off approximately 25 yds/ 23 m of yarn into a second ball.
- With larger needle cast on 90 stitches using backward loop cast on method (see page 276).
- **Next Row (RS):** Knit.
- **Next Row (WS):** P1, knit to last stitch, p1.
- Maintaining 1 stockinette edge stitch at each end of row, work Rows 1 and 2 of Lace pattern over center 88 stitches until piece measures 7"/18 cm from cast-on edge, ending with RS Row 1.

The Back Bodice

- **Next Row (WS):** P1, k2, k2tog, k1, k2tog, (k2, k2tog) 18 times, k2, k2tog, k1, k2tog, k2, p1. *You now have* 68 stitches.
- Change to smaller needle and knit 4 rows, ending with a WS row.
- Work in stockinette stitch until piece measures 8"/20.5 cm from cast-on edge.

Shape Armhole

- Continuing in stockinette stitch, decrease 1 stitch at each end of row on the next 8 rows. *You now have* 52 stitches.
- Continue in stockinette stitch until piece measures 10"/25.5 cm from cast-on edge, ending with a WS row.

Button Band Placket

- **Row 1 (RS):** K24, p5 for button band, place remaining 23 stitches on holder. *You now have* 29 right back stitches on needle.
- **Row 2:** Purl.
- **Row 3:** K24, p5.
- **Rows 4–19:** Repeat Rows 2 and 3 eight more times, ending with a RS row.
- **Next Row (WS):** Bind off 16 stitches at neck edge knitwise, purl remaining 13 stitches and place them on holder for right shoulder. Cut yarn leaving a long tail for three-needle bind off shoulder join.

Buttonhole Band Placket

- Return 23 held left back stitches to smaller needle and rejoin yarn at armhole edge with WS facing.
- **Row 1 (WS):** P23, pick up and purl 5 stitches from purl bumps in first row of button band. *You now have* 28 stitches.
- **Row 2:** P5, k23.
- **Row 3:** Purl.
- **Rows 4–16:** Repeat Rows 2 and 3 six more times, then work Row 2 once more.
- **Row 17 (WS, buttonhole row):** Purl to last 5 stitches, p2, yo, p2tog, p1.
- **Rows 18 and 19:** Repeat Rows 2 and 3 once more.
- **Next Row (RS):** Bind off 16 stitches at neck edge purlwise, knit remaining 13 stitches and place them on a holder for left shoulder. Cut yarn leaving a long tail for three-needle bind off shoulder join.

KNITTING THE FRONT

- Work as for back until armhole shaping has been completed, ending with a WS row; piece measures about 10"/25.5 cm from cast-on edge. *You now have* 52 stitches.

Neck Shaping

- **Next Row (RS):** K20, attach second ball of yarn, bind off 12 center front stitches, k20. *You now have* 20 stitches on each side.
- **Next Row:** Using second ball of yarn to work each side separately, purl.

- Continuing to work each side separately in stockinette stitch, decrease 1 stitch at each neck edge every other row 7 times. *You now have* 13 stitches on each side.
- Work even in stockinette stitch until piece measures same length as back. Place stitches on separate holders.

KNITTING THE SLEEVES (make 2)

- With larger needle cast on 46 stitches using backward loop cast on method (see page 276).
- **Next Row (RS):** Knit.
- **Next Row (WS):** P1, knit to last stitch, p1.
- Maintaining stockinette edge stitches and working center 44 stitches in pattern, work Rows 1 and 2 of Lace pattern three times. Change to smaller needle and knit 2 rows.

Shape Armhole

- Continuing in stockinette stitch, decrease 1 stitch at each end of every row 8 times. *You now have* 30 stitches.

Cap Shaping

- Decrease 1 stitch each side every other row 5 times. *You now have* 20 stitches.
- Decrease 1 stitch each side every 3rd row 2 times. *You now have* 16 stitches.
- Bind off 2 stitches at the beginning of next 4 rows; bind off remaining 8 stitches.

KNITTING THE COLLAR

- Place held stitches of back and front right shoulder on needles and join shoulder stitches using three-needle bind off method (see page 282). Join left shoulder in the same manner.
- With larger needle cast on 90 stitches using backward loop method. Knit 2 rows, keeping 1 edge stitch at each end of row in stockinette. Maintaining stockinette edge stitches and working center 88 stitches in pattern, work Rows 1 and 2 of Lace pattern twice, then work Row 1 once more.
- **Next Row (WS):** P1, (k1, k2tog) twice, (k2, k2tog, k1, k2tog) 11 times, k1, (k2tog) twice, p1. *You now have* 64 stitches.
- Change to smaller needle and knit 2 rows. Do not cut yarn; set aside.

Picking Up Neck Edge Stitches

Note: Do not pick up any neck edge stitches across the top of the buttonhole or button bands.

- With second smaller needle and second ball of yarn and beginning to the left of buttonhole band on left back, pick up and knit 11 stitches across back neck, 15 stitches down right side of front neck, 12 stitches across center front, 15 stitches up left side of neck, and 11 stitches across right back neck ending where button band begins. *You now have* 64 stitches.

Joining Collar to Neck

- Hold collar needle and neck edge pick-up needle together with RS of both pieces facing you and collar in front of bodice. Using the other end of one of the smaller needles, *insert needle tip into the first stitch on both the collar and neck pick-up needles and knit 1 stitch from collar together with 1 stitch from neck edge as k2tog; repeat from * until all stitches from both needles have been knit together. *You now have* 64 joined stitches on one needle. Knit 1 WS row. Bind off loosely.

FINISHING

* Sew sleeves into armholes. Sew sleeve and side seams. Weave in ends. Sew button to button band, opposite buttonhole. Wet block and lay flat to dry, shaping as necessary.

Lace Pattern

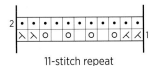

11-stitch repeat

☐	knit on RS, purl on WS
•	purl on RS, knit on WS
☐ o	yo
☐ ⋌	k2tog
☐ ⋋	ssk

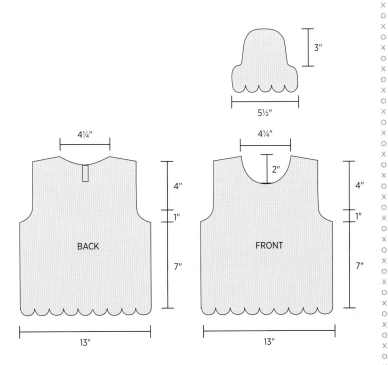

3"

5½"

4¼"

BACK

4"

1"

7"

13"

4¼"

2"

FRONT

4"

1"

7"

13"

Like Sleeves for Babies

Designed by Yumiko Sakurai, Harumidori Designs

A lovely tunic worked in the round from the bottom up, this is a fine example of how much you can do with simple knits and purls. Seed stitch weights the hem, the stockinette stitch body is decreased at the yoke, and garter stitch forms distinct sleeves.

SIZES AND FINISHED MEASUREMENTS
To fit 3–6 (6–12) months: 17 (18¼)"/43 (46.5) cm chest circumference

YARN
Madelintosh Tosh Merino Light, 100% superwash merino wool, 420 yds (384 m)/3.5 oz (100 g), Gilded **1**

NEEDLES
US 5 (3.75 mm) circular needle 16"/40 cm long or set of five US 5 (3.75 mm) double-point needles *or size needed to obtain correct gauge*

GAUGE
24 stitches and 36 rows = 4"/10 cm in stockinette stitch

OTHER SUPPLIES
Stitch markers, scrap yarn for holders, yarn needle

SPECIAL ABBREVIATIONS
sskp
  Slip 2 stitches knitwise one at a time, knit 1, pass the two slipped stitches over the knit stitch

KNITTING THE LOWER BODY

- Cast on 135 (143) stitches. Place marker and join into a round, being careful not to twist the stitches. Work in Seed Stitch (see Pattern Essentials) until piece measures 2 (2½)"/5 (6.5) cm.
- **Next Round:** K2tog, knit to end of round. *You now have 134 (142) stitches.* Continue in stockinette stitch until piece measures 7 (7¼)"/18 (18.5) cm from cast-on edge.
- **Decrease Round:** K4 (6), (s2kp, k5) seven times, s2kp, k4 (6), pm, k4 (6), (s2kp, k5) 7 times, s2kp, k4 (6). *You now have 51 (55) stitches between each pair of markers.*

KNITTING THE YOKE

- Knit to first marker, remove marker, turn. Work the back yoke back and forth as follows.
- **Row 1 (WS):** K3, purl to last 3 stitches, knit to marker, remove marker, turn. Place remaining 51 (55) front stitches on scrap yarn to hold.
- **Row 2 and all even-numbered (RS) rows:** Knit.
- **Row 3:** K5, purl to last 5 stitches, knit to end of row.
- **Row 5:** K7, purl to last 7 stitches, knit to end of row.
- **Row 7:** K9, purl to last 9 stitches, knit to end of row.
- **Row 9:** K10, purl to last 10 stitches, knit to end of row.
- **Row 11:** K11, purl to last 11 stitches, knit to end of row.
- **Row 13:** K12, purl to last 12 stitches, knit to end of row.
- **Row 15:** K13, purl to last 13 stitches, knit to end of row.
- **Row 17:** K13 (14), purl to last 13 (14) stitches, knit to end of row.
- Repeat Rows 16 and 17 until armhole (from first row of garter stitch) measures 2½ (3)"/6.5 (7.5) cm, ending with a WS row.

Shape Back Neck

- **Next Row (RS):** K18 (20), transfer the remaining stitches to scrap yarn to hold.
- Continue working in pattern as established for 1"/2.5 cm. Bind off, cut yarn.

SEED STITCH

Round 1: *K1, p1; repeat from * to last stitch, k1.

Round 2: *P1, k1; repeat from * to last stitch, p1.

Repeat Rounds 1 and 2 for pattern.

- Transfer 18 (20) stitches from the other shoulder onto the needle. With RS facing, attach new yarn, work 1"/2.5 cm in pattern as established.
- Bind off. Leave remaining 15 stitches on hold for the back neck.

The Front Yoke

- Place 51 (55) held stitches on needle for front yoke.
- With RS facing, attach new yarn and work as follows until armhole (from first row of garter stitch) measures 1½ (2)"/4 (5) cm, ending with a WS row. **Note:** Armhole patterning and neck shaping may take place at the same time; you may attain the measurement before you reach Row 22.
- **Row 1 and all following odd-numbered rows (RS):** Knit.
- **Row 2 (WS):** K4, purl to last 4 stitches, knit to end of row.
- **Row 4:** K5, purl to last 5 stitches, knit to end of row.
- **Row 6:** K6, purl to last 6 stitches, knit to end of row.
- **Row 8:** K7, purl to last 7 stitches, knit to end of row.
- **Row 10:** K8, purl to last 8 stitches, knit to end of row.

- **Row 12:** K9, purl to last 9 stitches, knit to end of row.
- **Row 14:** K10, purl to last 10 stitches, knit to end of row.
- **Row 16:** K11, purl to last 11 stitches, knit to end of row.
- **Row 18:** K12, purl to last 12 stitches, knit to end of row.
- **Row 20:** K13, purl to last 13 stitches, knit to end of row.

- **Row 22 (WS):** K13 (14), purl to last 13 (14) stitches, knit to end of row.

Shape Front Neck

- **Next Row (RS):** K21 (23), transfer the next 9 sts to scrap yarn to hold for neck and the remaining 21 (23) sts to another holder for right shoulder.
- Continue working remaining garter stitch rows if necessary to Row 22 and, *at the same time,* decrease at the neck edge by k2tog on every RS row 3 times. *You now have* 18 (20) sts.
- Work even in established pattern (Rows 21 and 22 of front yoke) until armhole measures 3½ (4)"/9 (10) cm. Bind off all stitches. Cut yarn.
- Transfer 21 (23) right shoulder stitches to needle.
- With RS facing, attach new yarn, continue working remaining front yoke rows for front until Row 22 if necessary and, *at the same time,* decrease at the neck edge by ssk on every RS rows 3 times. *You now have* 18 (20) sts.
- Work even in established pattern (Rows 21 and 22 of front yoke) until armhole measures 3½ (4)"/9 (10) cm.
- Bind off all stitches. Cut yarn.

FINISHING

- Sew front and back together at shoulders. With right side facing, knit 15 held stitches from for back neck, pick up and knit (see page 281) 8 stitches for left back neck edge, pick up and knit 19 stitches for left front neck edge, knit 9 held for front neck, then pick up and knit 19 stitches for right front neck, and pick up and knit 8 stitches for right back neck edge. *You now have* 78 stitches. Place marker and join into a round.
- **Round 1:** Purl.
- **Round 2:** Knit.
- **Round 3:** Purl.
- Bind off all stitches *loosely* knitwise, using a larger needle or Jeny's Surprisingly Stretchy Bind Off (see page 277). Weave in ends. Block.

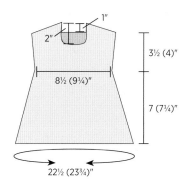

Lacy Silk Christening Gown

Designed by Judith Durant

Knit with luscious shiny silk, this christening gown can be worn by your baby today, then put away and worn again by your baby's baby years from now. The skirt is knitted with an open airy lace pattern and the bodice is a bit denser. A headband is included for a baby girl.

SIZE AND FINISHED MEASUREMENTS

To fit 0–3 months: 17"/43 cm chest circumference, 20"/51 cm length; 14"/35.5 cm head circumference

YARN

Habu Textiles NS-28, 21/132 Silk Tram degummed, 100% silk, 260 yds (232 m)/1 oz (28 g): one 3.6 oz (102 g) ball, White

NEEDLES

Two US 3 (3.25 mm) circular needles 16"/40 cm long, set of four US 3 (3.25 mm) double-point needles, and US 5 (3.75 mm) circular needle 16"/40 cm long *or size needed to obtain correct gauge*

GAUGE

24 stitches = 4"/10 cm in Little Petal Lace on smaller needles, blocked
22 stitches = 4"/10 cm in Bell Lace on larger needles, blocked

OTHER SUPPLIES

Stitch markers (one in a unique color), ⅜"/10 mm button, 1 yd of ½"/13 mm satin ribbon, ½ yd /0.5 m lining fabric, yarn needle, purchased rosette or other decoration for headband (optional), sewing needle and coordinating thread

Pattern Essentials

PICOT BIND OFF

Using the knitwise cable cast on method (see page 276), *cast on 2 stitches, bind off 4 stitches, transfer remaining stitch from right needle to left needle; repeat from * to end of round or row, cut yarn and pull through remaining stitch.

PURLWISE OPEN BAR INCREASE

Purl 1 into the strand between the stitch on the right needle and the stitch on the left needle.

KNITTING THE SKIRT

- With larger circular needles, cast on 126 stitches, placing a marker every 18 stitches with a unique color for end of round. Join into a round, being careful not to twist the stitches.

- Work Rounds 1–28 of the Bell Lace chart (see page 134) 4 times. On Rounds 13 and 21, remove end of round marker, slip 1 stitch to right needle, then replace marker. You will need to move markers and take one stitch from the following group to complete the sk2p for each repeat of the pattern.

- Change to smaller needles and knit 1 round, decreasing 22 stitches evenly spaced as follows: (K4, k2tog) 6 times, (k3, k2tog) 5 times, (k4, k2tog) 6 times, (k3, k2tog) 5 times, k4. *You now have* 104 stitches.

Working the Eyelet Border

- Round 1: Purl.
- Rounds 2 and 3: Knit.
- Round 4: K1, yo, k2tog, *k2, yo, k2tog; repeat from * to last stitch, k1.
- Round 5 and 6: Knit.
- Round 7: Purl.

KNITTING THE BODICE

Note: The bodice is worked back and forth on the smaller circular needle. Maintain 2 stockinette edge stitches at the beginning and end of every row.

- Row 1: K2, work Row 1 of Little Petals Lace (see page 134) to last 2 stitches, k2.
- Row 2: P2, work Little Petals Lace as established to last 2 stitches, p2.
- Row 3: K2, work Little Petals Lace as established to last 2 stitches, k2.
- Row 4: P2, work Little Petals Lace as established to last 2 stitches, p2.
- Continue in this manner, working 2 stockinette edge stitches at the beginning and end of every row and working lace pattern as established between them through Row 8 of pattern, then work Rows 1–4 of pattern once more.

Dividing for Backs and Front

- Work 23 stitches in pattern as established and place on hold for left back; bind off 6, work the next 46 stitches in pattern as established and place on hold for front, bind off 6, work remaining 23 stitches in pattern as established for right back.

The Right Back

- Continue in pattern as established, maintaining 2 edge stitches at back and 1 edge stitch at armhole edge, and *at the same time* decrease 1 stitch at the armhole edge every other RS row 3 times. *You now have* 20 stitches.
- Continue even in pattern until 4 complete repeats have been worked from Eyelet Border.
- Work Rows 1–4 of pattern one more time, binding off 5 stitches purlwise at the neck edge of (WS) rows 2 and 4. Work to end of row and place 10 stitches on hold for right shoulder.

The Left Back

- Place 23 held left back stitches on needle. With WS facing, attach yarn at armhole edge. Continue in pattern as established and *at the same time* decrease 1 stitch at the armhole edge every other RS row 3 times. *You now have* 20 stitches.

- Continue even in pattern until 4 complete repeats have been worked from Eyelet Border.

- Work Rows 1–4 of pattern one more time, binding off 5 stitches at the neck edge of (RS) Rows 1 and 3. Work Row 4 of pattern and place 10 stitches on hold for left shoulder.

The Front

- Place held 46 front stitches on needle. With WS facing, join yarn and work Row 2 of pattern. Maintaining 1 stockinette edge stitch at the beginning and end of every row, continue in pattern as established and *at the same time,* decrease 1 stitch at each side of every other RS row 2 times, ending with a WS row. *You now have* 42 stitches.

- **Next Row (RS):** K1 edge stitch, ssk, work 13 stitches in pattern as established and place these 15 stitches on hold for left front, bind off center 10 stitches, work 13 stitches in pattern as established, k2tog, k1 edge stitch.

The Right Front

- Maintaining edge stitches on armhole and neck edges and working in pattern as established, bind off 1 stitch at the beginning of every RS row 5 times. Work additional rows as necessary to match back.

The Left Front

- Place 15 held left front stitches on needles. Maintaining edge stitches on armhole and neck edges and working in pattern as established, bind off 1 st at the beginning of every WS row 5 times. Work additional rows as necessary to match back and right front.

Joining the Shoulders

- Join front and back at shoulders with the three-needle bind off method (see page 282).

KNITTING THE ARMHOLE TRIM

- With double-point needles, RS facing, and beginning at center of underarm bind off, use a pick-up rate of 2 of every 3 stitches to pick up and knit (see page 281) 40 stitches around armhole.
- Work Picot bind off on all stitches.
- Repeat for second armhole.

KNITTING THE NECK TRIM

- With double-point needles, RS facing, and beginning at right back neck edge, pick up and knit 22 stitches down center back edge, pick up 1 stitch in the gap between the edges, pick up and knit 22 stitches up other back edge. *You now have* 45 stitches.
- Knit 2 rows.

Picking Up the Neck Edge

Note: If the curve of the front neck is too sharp to pick up stitches onto a circular needle, pick up onto 2 or 3 double-point needles.

- With RS facing and using a new needle and the yarn attached to the left neck edge, pick up and knit 13 stitches to shoulder seam, 15 stitches to beginning of bound off stitches, 10 bound off stitches, 15 stitches to shoulder seam, and 13 stitches to right back neck edge. *You now have* 66 stitches. Do not turn.

- Next Row: Working along back opening, bind off 21 placket stitches, k3tog and pass stitch on right-hand needle over the resulting stitch to bind off 3 stitches together, bind off next 21 placket stitches to neck edge; continuing around neck edge, work a Picot bind off to the end of the stitches but do not cut the yarn and do not pull through the last stitch.

MAKING THE BUTTON LOOP

- Using the knitted on method (see page 279) and the live stitch from neck trim, cast on 10 stitches.
- Turn and bind off all stitches, pulling yarn through the last stitch.
- Cut yarn leaving an 8"/20.5 cm tail. Thread the tail onto a yarn needle and use it to secure and reinforce both ends to the neck edge, creating a loop.

MAKING THE LINING

- Cut a piece of fabric 17½"/44.5 cm wide at the top, 22½"/57 cm wide at the bottom, and 15½"/39.5 cm long. Sew a ¼"/6 mm seam from top to bottom.
- With wrong sides together, slip the lining onto the dress, placing the seam at the center back and aligning the top with the base of the eyelet border. Hand sew in place with small stitches.

FINISHING

- Weave in all ends. Sew button to back opposite button loop. Steam block.
- Thread ribbon through eyelet round, tie into a bow and trim to desired length.

KNITTING THE HEADBAND

- With smaller needle cast on 10 stitches.
- Maintaining 1 stockinette edge stitch at the beginning and end of each row, work Rows 1–4 of Little Petals Lace until piece measures 12"/30.5 cm.
- Bind off; do not cut yarn.
- With 1 stitch remaining on the needle and RS facing, pick up and knit 61 stitches along edge of headband.

- Purl 1 row, then work Picot bind off on all stitches.
- Pick up and knit 62 stitches along other side of headband and work as for first side.
- Sew cast-on edge to bound-off edge.
- Block. Sew rosette to cover seam if desired.

Notes: This type of silk yarn was designed for weaving and it is very soft and shiny. The NS-28 is a special weight developed by Habu Textiles for knitters, but it is not the easiest yarn to knit with. Because there is virtually no twist in the yarn, the filament tends to get caught in rough hands. But the rich results are worth the extra care.

- Normally we would not recommend that an open lace be used on the skirt for babies — the holes are large enough to let little fingers get caught in them. However, since the dress will be worn for a matter of hours, we think it's worth the risk.

Bell Lace

pattern repeat

Little Petals Lace

4-stitch repeat

	knit on RS, purl on WS
•	purl on RS, knit on WS
•V•	on RS, p1, purlwise open bar inc, p1
⌒	on WS, k3, pass the first st over the other 2 sts

	knit
•	purl
⟋	k2tog
⟍	ssk
⅄	sk2p
ℛ	knit tbl
O	yarnover
⁄.	p2tog
(grey)	no stitch
	see Knitting the Skirt on page 130

Star Baby Bonnet

Designed by Barbara Rottman

This lovely garment is fashioned after many traditional baby bonnets that begin with a circular star motif for the back. The body is knit in a simple lace stitch, and it's finished off with a picot edge and I-cord ties.

SIZE AND FINISHED MEASUREMENTS
To fit 0–3 months: 5½"/14 cm deep, 6½"/16.5 cm tall

YARN
Araucania Ruca Solid, 100% sugar cane, 263 yds (241 m)/3.5 oz (100 g), Color 103 Mauve (3)

NEEDLES
Set of four US 3 (3.25 mm) double-point needles, US 3 (3.25 mm) circular needle 16"/40 cm long, and US 2 (2.75 mm) circular needle 16"/40 cm long (optional) *or size needed to obtain correct gauge* **Note:** Bamboo or wood recommended for knitting with specified yarn

GAUGE
22 stitches and 28 rows = 4"/10 cm in Cell Stitch pattern

OTHER SUPPLIES
Yarn needle

KNITTING THE LACE STAR

- Cast on 7 stitches. Arrange stitches onto 3 double-point needles. Join into a round, being careful not to twist the stitches. Knit 1 round. Follow chart or written instructions below.

- **Round 1:** *Yo, k1; repeat from * to end of round. *You now have* 14 stitches.

- **Round 2 (and all even-numbered rounds):** Knit.

- **Round 3:** *Yo, k2; repeat from * to end of round. *You now have* 21 stitches.

- **Round 5:** *Yo, k3; repeat from * to end of round. *You now have* 28 stitches.

- **Round 7:** *Yo, k4; repeat from * to end of round. *You now have* 35 stitches.

- **Round 9:** *Yo, k5; repeat from * to end of round. *You now have* 42 stitches.

- **Round 11:** *Yo, k6; repeat from * to end of round. *You now have* 49 stitches.

- **Round 13:** *Yo, k5, k2tog; repeat from * to end of round.

- **Round 15:** *K5, k2tog, yo; repeat from * to end of round.

- **Round 17:** *K4, k2tog, yo, k1, yo; repeat from * to end of round. *You now have* 56 stitches.

- **Round 19:** *K3, k2tog, yo, k3, yo; repeat from * to end of round. *You now have* 63 stitches.

- **Round 21:** *K2, k2tog, yo, k5, yo; repeat from * to end of round. *You now have* 70 stitches.

- **Round 23:** *K1, k2tog, yo, k7, yo; repeat from * to end of round. *You now have* 77 stitches.

- **Round 25:** *K2tog, yo, k9, yo; repeat from * to end of round. *You now have* 84 stitches.

- **Round 26:** Knit.

CONTINUING THE BONNET

- Turn work to begin working back and forth in rows.
- **Next Row (WS):** P41, p2tog, p41. *You now have 83 stitches.*

Note: You may need to work a few rows on the double-point needles. When the work is a several rows long, you can switch to a 16"/40 cm circular needle for easier knitting.

- Work Cell Stitch for 2½"/6.5 cm (5"/12.5 cm from center cast on), or desired length, ending with WS row.

KNITTING THE PICOT EDGE

- **Row 1 (RS):** Knit.
- **Row 2:** Purl.
- **Row 3:** Knit.
- **Row 4:** P2tog, p81. *You now have 82 stitches.*
- **Row 5:** *K2tog, yo; repeat from * to last 2 stitches, k2tog. *You now have 81 stitches.*
- For a more elastic edge, change to smaller needle (optional).
- **Rows 6–7:** Repeat Rows 2–3.
- **Row 8:** Purl.
- Cut yarn leaving a tail at least 3 times the width of your knitting. Thread tail onto yarn needle. Remove one stitch at a time and stitch the live stitch to its corresponding stitch on WS of Row 1 of stockinette stitch. Alternatively, bind off all stitches, fold edge to WS along Row 5, and hem stitch to WS of Row 1 of stockinette stitch.

FINISHING

- Use the 3-stitch I-cord method (see page 277) to make two ties, each 6"/15 cm long. **Note:** The photographed sample used a longer I-cord ties. However, we recommend keeping ties on items for young children to 6" or less.
- Attach I-cord ties to each corner.
- Weave in ends. Block. **Note:** Do not use heat with specified yarn. Cold block only.

Pattern Essentials

CELL STITCH
(multiple of 4 stitches plus 3)

Row 1 (RS): K2; *yo, sk2p, yo, k1; repeat from * to last stitch, k1.

Row 2: Purl.

Row 3: K1, k2tog, yo, k1, *yo, sk2p, yo, k1; repeat from *to last 3 stitches, yo, ssk, k1.

Row 4: Purl.

Repeat Rows 1–4 for pattern.

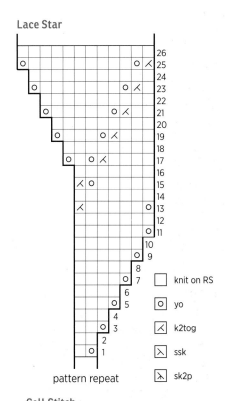

Lace Star

pattern repeat

□ knit on RS

○ yo

╱ k2tog

╲ ssk

⅄ sk2p

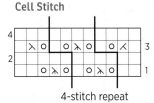

Cell Stitch

4-stitch repeat

Screw Top Hat

Designed by Jenise Reid

This spiraling stitch pattern is surprisingly easy to knit and to memorize. It is knit from the bottom up and the pattern is written for four sizes, from newborn through two-to-five years.

SIZES AND FINISHED MEASUREMENTS
To fit newborn (3 months, 6–12 months, 2–5 years): 12 (14, 16, 18)"/30.5 (35.5, 40.5, 45.5) cm

YARN
Knit Picks Wool of the Andes Superwash, 100% superwash wool, 110 yds (101 m)/1.75 oz (50 g), Fjord Heather (4)

NEEDLES
Set of four or five US 5 (3.75 mm) double-point needles *or size needed to obtain correct gauge*

GAUGE
22 stitches and 32 rows = 4"/10 cm in stockinette stitch, blocked

OTHER SUPPLIES
Yarn needle

SPECIAL ABBREVIATIONS
M1T (make 1 twist)
 Bring yarn between needles to the back, then wrap yarn over right needle from back to front. On the next round, knit through the front of the stitch to twist it.

KNITTING THE HAT

- Cast on 60 (70, 80, 90) stitches, and join into a round, being careful not to twist the stitches.
- **Rounds 1–7:** *P1, (k2, p1) 3 times; repeat from * around.
- **Round 8:** *P1, M1T, k8, p1; repeat from * around. *You now have 66 (77, 88, 99) stitches.*
- **Round 9:** *P1, M1T, k7, p2tog, p1; repeat from * around.
- Repeat round 9 until hat measures 3 (4, 4½, 5½)"/7.5 (10, 11.5, 14) cm.

Decreasing for the Crown

- **Round 1:** *P1, k7, p2tog, p1; repeat from * around. *You now have 60 (70, 80, 90) stitches.*
- **Rounds 2–4:** *P1, M1T, k6, p2tog, p1; repeat from * around.
- **Round 5:** *P1, k6, p2tog, p1; repeat from * around. *You now have 54 (63, 72, 81) stitches.*
- **Rounds 6 and 7:** *P1, M1T, k5, p2tog, p1; repeat from * around.
- **Round 8:** *P1, k5, p2tog, p1; repeat from * around. *You now have 48 (56, 64, 72) stitches.*
- **Round 9:** *P1, M1T, k4, p2tog, p1; repeat from * around.
- **Round 10:** *P1, k4, p2tog, p1; repeat from * around. *You now have 42 (49, 56, 63) stitches.*
- **Round 11:** *P1, M1T, k3, p2tog, p1; repeat from * around.
- **Round 12:** *P1, k3, p2tog, p1; repeat from * around. *You now have 36 (42, 48, 54) stitches.*
- **Round 13:** *P1, M1T, k2, p2tog, p1; repeat from * around.
- **Round 14:** *P1, k2, p2tog, p1; repeat from * around. *You now have 30 (35, 40, 45) stitches.*
- **Round 15:** *P1, k1, p2tog, p1; repeat from * around. *You now have 24 (28, 32, 36) stitches.*
- **Round 16:** *P1, p2tog, p1; repeat from * around. *You now have 18 (21, 24, 27) stitches.*
- **Round 17:** *P2tog, p1; repeat from * around. *You now have 12 (14, 16, 18) stitches.*
- **Round 18:** (P2tog) around. *You now have 6 (7, 8, 9) stitches.*

Baby Bud Bonnet

Designed by Barbara Rottman

This vintage style hat starts first with a ruffled brim. The crown is worked in Bud Lace pattern, with a simple shaped back and sewn side seams. Ribbon ties are embellished with easy-to-make ribbon roses.

SIZE AND FINISHED MEASUREMENTS
To fit newborn, 5"/12.5 cm deep, 5"/12.5 cm tall

YARN
Debbie Bliss Ecobaby, 100% organic cotton, 137 yds (125 m)/1.75 oz (50 g), Color 006 Pea Green (2)

NEEDLES
US 3 (3.25 mm) straight needles *or size needed to obtain correct gauge*

GAUGE
23 stitches = 4"/10 cm in stockinette stitch

OTHER SUPPLIES
Stitch holder, two ⅜"/10 mm buttons, 14"/35.5 cm of 1"/2.5 cm ribbon, embroidery floss to match ribbon, sewing needle, yarn needle
Note: The photographed sample used more ribbon for longer ties. However, we recommend keeping ties on items for young children to 6" or less.

FINISHING

- Cut yarn leaving an 8"/20.5 cm tail. Thread tail onto yarn needle and draw through remaining stitches. Pull up snug and weave in ends.

- Block lightly.

Pattern Essentials

FLOWER BUD LACE
(multiple of 8 stitches plus 5)

Row 1: K3, *yo, k2, p3tog, k2, yo, k1; repeat from * to last 2 stitches, k2.

Row 2: Purl.

Rows 3–6: Repeat rows 1 and 2 twice.

Row 7: K2, p2tog, *k2, yo, k1, yo, k2, p3tog; repeat from * to last 9 stitches, k2, yo, k1, yo, k2, p2tog, k2.

Row 8: Purl.

Rows 9–12: Repeat rows 7 and 8 twice.

Repeat Rows 1–12 for pattern.

· ·

RUFFLE
(multiple of 9 stitches plus 1)

Row 1: P2, *k6, p3; repeat from * to last 8 stitches, k6, p2.

Row 2: K2, *p6, k3; repeat from * to last 8 stitches, p6, k2.

Row 3: P2, *k4, k2tog, p3; repeat from * to last 2 stitches, p2.

Row 4: K2, *p2tog, p3, k3; repeat from * to last 2 stitches, k2.

Row 5: P2, *k2, k2tog, p3; repeat from * to last 2 stitches, p2.

Row 6: K2, *p2tog, p1, k3; repeat from * to last 2 stitches, k2.

Row 7: P2, *k2tog, p3, repeat from * to last 4 stitches, k2tog, p2.

Row 8: Purl.

Work Rows 1–8 for pattern.

KNITTING THE BRIM

- Cast on 136 stitches. Work Rows 1 through 8 of Ruffle pattern. *You now have* 61 stitches.

KNITTING THE BONNET

- Repeat Rows 1 through 12 of Flower Bud pattern until piece measures approximately 4¼"/11 cm from cast-on edge, ending with Row 6 or 12.

- Maintaining pattern, bind off 20 stitches at the beginning of next 2 rows. Work even in pattern on center 21 stitches until section measures the same length as the bound-off edges. Place stitches on a holder.

SEWING THE SEAMS

- Stitch the bound-off edges to the sides of the center (crown) section.

KNITTING THE RIBBING

- With right side facing, beginning at edge of ruffle, pick up and knit 21 stitches along front left edge of bonnet to held stitches, knit held center 21 stitches, pick up and knit 21 stitches to end of ruffle. *You now have* 63 stitches.

- **Row 1:** *K1, p1; repeat from * to last stitch, k1.

- **Row 2:** *P1, k1; repeat from * to last stitch, p1.
- Repeat Rows 1 and 2 three more times. Bind off in pattern.

FINISHING

- Cut two 7"/18 cm pieces of ribbon for ties and attach them at each side of bonnet. Sew ribbon rose (see below) over join.

Making a Ribbon Rose (make 2)

- Cut two 15–24"/38–61 cm strands of ribbon, depending on size flower desired.
- Thread a needle with all 6 strands of embroidery floss and sew a running stitch along one edge of the ribbon, leaving tails at each end.
- Bring the floss tails together, drawing up and gathering the edge. Knot the tails.
- Twist ribbon into flower shape, bring tails to back, and sew across back of rose to secure. Trim with button or other embellishment.

Greenleaf Hat

Designed by Evelyn Uyemura

This simple yet charming hat can be knit in a day, and a 100-gram skein of worsted weight yarn should yield three hats. Make one in each of the three sizes given and they'll grow along with baby!

SIZES AND FINISHED MEASUREMENTS
To fit 0–3 (3–6, 6–12) months: 14 (16, 18)"/35.5 (40.5, 45.5) cm circumference
Note: Hat has negative ease.

YARN
Malabrigo Rios, 100% superwash merino wool, 210 yds (192 m)/3.5 oz (100 g), Color 037 Lettuce 【3】

NEEDLES
US 8 (5 mm) circular needle 32"/80 cm long or set of five US 8 (5 mm) double-point needles *or size needed to obtain correct gauge*

GAUGE
21 stitches and 30 rounds = 4"/10 cm in stockinette stitch

OTHER SUPPLIES
Yarn needle, stitch marker

KNITTING THE HAT

Note: Use long circular needle for Magic Loop method (see page 280), or use double-point needles.

- Cast on 64 (72, 80) stitches, pm, and join into a round, being careful not to twist the stitches.
- Work even in stockinette stitch until piece measures 5 (5½, 6)"/12.5 (14, 15) cm.

Decreasing for the Crown

- *For 6–12 month size*: *K8, k2tog; repeat from * to end of round. *You now have* 72 stitches. Knit 1 round, then continue as for 3–6 month size.

- *For 3–6 month size:* *K7, k2tog; repeat from * to end of round. *You now have* 64 stitches. Knit 1 round, then continue as for 0–3 month size.

- *For 0–3 month size:* Work decrease rounds as follows.

- **Round 1:** *K6, k2tog; repeat from * to end of round. *You now have* 56 stitches.

- **Rounds 2, 4, 6, 8, 10, 12 and 14:** Knit.

- **Round 3:** *K5, k2tog; repeat from * to end of round. *You now have* 48 stitches.

- **Round 5:** *K4, k2tog; repeat from * to end of round. *You now have* 40 stitches.

- **Round 7:** *K3, k2tog; repeat from * to end of round. *You now have* 32 stitches.

- **Round 9:** *K2, k2tog; repeat from * to end of round. *You now have* 24 stitches.

- **Round 11:** *K1, k2tog; repeat from * to end of round. *You now have* 16 stitches.

- **Round 13:** *K2tog; repeat from * to end of round. *You now have* 8 stitches.

- **Round 15:** *K2tog; repeat from * to end of round. *You now have* 4 stitches.

- **Round 16:** K2, k2tog. *You now have* 3 stitches.

- Work 3-stitch I-cord (see page 277) for 1"/2.5 cm.

The Leaf

Note: Make all increases with the M1R or M1L methods (see page 280). The leaf is knit back and forth in rows.

- **Row 1:** K1, M1R, k1, M1L, k1. *You now have 5 stitches.*

- **Row 2 and all even-numbered WS rows:** Purl.

- **Row 3:** K2, M1R, k1, M1L, k2. *You now have 7 stitches.*

- **Row 5:** K3, M1R, k1, M1L, k3. *You now have 9 stitches.*

- **Row 7:** K4, M1R, k1, M1L, k4. *You now have 11 stitches.*

- **Row 9:** K3, ssk, k1, k2tog, k3. *You now have 9 stitches.*

- **Row 11:** K2, ssk, k1, k2tog, k2. *You now have 7 stitches.*

- **Row 13:** K1, ssk, k1, k2tog, k1. *You now have 5 stitches.*

- **Row 15:** Ssk, k1, k2tog. *You now have 3 stitches.*

- **Row 17:** K1, k2tog. *You now have 2 stitches.*

- **Row 19:** K2tog. Cut yarn and pull through last stitch.

- Weave in ends.

Spring Colors Baby Bonnet

Designed by Tamara Del Sonno

This cute and stretchy baby bonnet begins with the ruffle and is knit to the back, then stitches are picked up along the lower edge and finished with a rib. Tack the ruffle down at the lower edges, forming little "buttonholes" to thread the ribbon ties through.

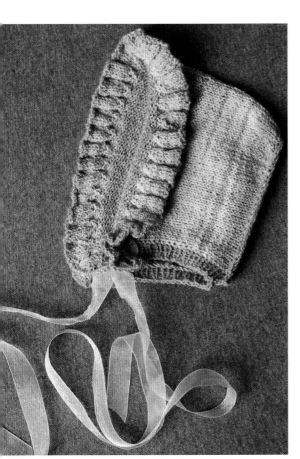

SIZES AND FINISHED MEASUREMENTS
To fit 6 (12, 18) months: 15 (16, 18)"/38 (40.5, 45.5) cm circumference

YARN
Patons Stretch Socks, 41% cotton/39% wool/13% nylon/7% elastic, 239 yds (219 m)/1.75 oz (50 g), Color 31134 Fruit Slices 🆑

NEEDLES
US 3 (3.25 mm) straight needles, US 2 (2.75 mm) straight needles, and two US 1 (2.25 mm) double-point needles *or size needed to obtain correct gauge*

GAUGE
26 stitches and 38 rows= 4"/10 cm in stockinette stitch

OTHER SUPPLIES
2 removable stitch markers, 14"/35.5 cm of ½"/13 mm ribbon, yarn needle, sewing needle and coordinating thread
Note: The photographed sample used more ribbon for longer ties. However, we recommend keeping ties on items for young children to 6" or less.

KNITTING THE BONNET

- With larger needle, cast on 200 (248, 296) stitches. Knit 1 row.

The Ruffle

- **Set-Up Row (WS):** Knit.

- **Row 1 (RS):** Slip 1, k2, p2, *k6, p2; repeat from * to last 3 stitches, k3.

- **Row 2:** Slip 1, p2, k2, *p6, k2; repeat from * to last 3 stitches, p3.

- **Rows 3 and 4:** Repeat Rows 1 and 2.

- **Row 5:** Slip 1, k2, p2 *ssk, k2, k2tog, p2; repeat from * to last 3 stitches, k3. *You now have* 152 (188, 224) stitches.

- **Row 6:** Slip 1, p2, k2, *p4, k2; repeat from * to last 3 stitches, p3.

- **Row 7:** Slip 1, k2, p2, *ssk, k2tog, p2; repeat from * to last 3 stitches, k3. *You now have* 104 (128, 152) stitches.

- **Row 8:** Slip 1, *p2, k2; repeat from * to last 3 stitches, p3.
- **Row 9:** Slip 1, k2tog, p2, *k2tog, p2, (k2tog, p2tog) twice; repeat from * to last 3 stitches, ssk, k1. *You now have 62 (76, 90) stitches.*

Note: As you work the following rows, the ruffle will flip back toward the cap. You'll work from the wrong side of the ruffle into the right side of the cap.

The Cap

- **Row 1 (RS):** With smaller needle, bind off 5, knit to end.
- **Row 2:** Bind off 5, purl to end. *You now have 52 (66, 80) stitches.*
- With larger needles, work even in established stockinette stitch, slipping the first st of every row, until cap measures 3 (4, 5)"/7.5 (10, 12.5) cm from ruffle, ending with a RS row.
- **Next Row (WS):** P17 (22, 26), pm, p18 (22, 28), pm, purl to end of row.
- Using double-point needles cast on 3 stitches at beginning of row using the cable cast on method (see page 276).
- Work 3-stitch I-cord bind off (see page 277) to marker but do not bind off; slip remaining I-cord stitches to left needle; *k2, sk2p; slip these 3 stitches back to left-hand needle; repeat from * to next marker; continue 3-stitch I-cord bind off until 3 stitches remain. K3tog, fasten off.

Finishing

- Fold piece in half with wrong sides (purl sides) together. With right side facing and smaller straight needle, pick up and knit 1 stitch from each slipped stitch along entire neck edge of cap. This joins the cap at the bottom of the I-cord bind off opening.
- Work 6 rows of knit 1, purl 1 rib along the neck edge.
- Bind off in pattern.
- Fold each end of ruffle toward the back and tack it to the neck ribbing, creating a "buttonhole" between the ribbing and the ruffle. Weave in ends.
- Cut two 7"/18 cm pieces of ribbon. Insert one end of each ribbon into "buttonhole" and tack in place under ruffle with needle and thread.

Faux Seams Toque

Designed by Jenise Reid

Evenly spaced slipped stitches form what looks like seams around this delightful little toque. The abutting sections lean in opposite directions, taking full advantage of the subtly variegated yarn.

KNITTING THE TOQUE

- Cast on 72 (84, 96) stitches and join into a round, being careful not to twist the stitches.

- **Round 1:** *K1, p1, s1ip 1, p1; repeat from * to end of round.

- **Round 2:** *Slip 1, p1, k1, p1; repeat from * to end of round.

- **Rounds 3–6:** Repeat rounds 1 and 2 twice.

- **Round 7:** *K1, p1; repeat from * to end of round.

- **Round 8:** *K1, yo, k11, yo; repeat from * to end of round. *You now have* 84 (98, 112) stitches.

- **Rounds 9 and 10:** *Slip 1, k6; repeat from * to end of round.

- **Round 11:** *K1, yo, k5, s2kp, k5, yo; repeat from * to end of round.

- **Rounds 12–13:** Repeat round 9.

- Repeat rounds 11–13 nine (twelve, fifteen, seventeen) times.

Shaping the Crown

- **Round 1:** *K6, s2kp, k5; repeat from * to end of round. *You now have* 72 (84, 96) stitches.

- **Rounds 2–3:** *S1, k5; repeat from * to end of round.

- **Round 4:** *K1, yo, k4, s2kp, k4, yo; repeat from * to end of round.

- **Rounds 5–6:** *S1, k5; repeat from * to end of round.

- **Round 7:** *K5, s2kp, k4; repeat from * to end of round. *You now have* 60 (70, 80) stitches.

- **Rounds 8–9:** *S1, k4; repeat from * to end of round.

....
SIZES AND FINISHED MEASUREMENTS
To fit newborn (3-6 months, 1-2 years): 12 (14, 16)"/30.5 (35.5, 40.5) cm circumference, unstretched
....
YARN
Knit Picks Stroll Fingering, 75% superwash merino wool/ 25% nylon, 462 yds (422 m)/3.5 oz (100 g), Deep Waters Tonal (1)
....
NEEDLES
Set of five US 1 (2.25 mm) double-point needles *or size needed to obtain correct gauge*
....
GAUGE
26 stitches and 44 rows = 4"/10 cm in stockinette stitch
....
OTHER SUPPLIES
Yarn needle

- **Round 10:** *K1, yo, k3, s2kp, k3, yo; repeat from * to end of round.

- **Rounds 11–12:** *S1, k4; repeat from * to end of round.

- **Round 13:** *K4, s2kp, k3; repeat from * to end of round. *You now have* 48 (56, 64) stitches.

- **Rounds 14–15:** *S1, k3; repeat from * to end of round.

- **Round 16:** *K3, s2kp, k2; repeat from * to end of round. *You now have* 36 (42, 48) stitches.

- **Rounds 17–18:** *S1, k2; repeat from * to end of round.

- **Round 19:** *K2, s2kp, k1; repeat from * to end of round. *You now have* 24 (28, 32) stitches.

- **Round 20:** *S1, k1; repeat from * to end of round.

- **Round 21:** *K1, s2kp; repeat from * to end of round. *You now have* 12 (14, 16) stitches.

- **Round 22:** Knit.

- **Round 23:** *K2tog; repeat from * to end of round. *You now have* 6 (7, 8) stitches.

FINISHING

- Cut yarn leaving an 8"/20.5 cm tail. Thread tail onto yarn needle and draw through remaining stitches. Pull up snug and weave in ends.

- Block lightly.

Cutie Pie Baby Hat

Designed by Anita Grahn

This little cutie will keep your cutie warm outdoors! The garter-stitch brim covers the ears, and it ties securely under the chin. The top of the hat is shaped like a crown, with the finishing tail at the center folded into a loop.

SIZES AND FINISHED MEASUREMENTS
To fit 0–6 months (6–12 months): 15½ (17¾)"/39.5 (45) cm circumference

YARN
Zitron Nimbus, 100% organic merino wool, 109 yds (100 m)/1.75 oz (50 g), Color 20 (**4**)

NEEDLES
US 8 (5 mm) circular needle 16"/40 cm long and set of four US 8 (5 mm) double-point needles *or size needed to obtain correct gauge*

GAUGE
18 stitches and 25 rounds = 4"/10 cm in stockinette stitch

OTHER SUPPLIES
Yarn needle, scrap yarn and crochet hook for cast on, stitch marker

KNITTING THE BRIM

- Using two double-point needles and a provisional method (see page 281), cast on 12 (14) stitches.

The First Side

- **Row 1:** Knit.
- **Row 2:** Slip 3 wyif, knit to end of row.
- **Repeat Rows 1 and 2 fourteen (sixteen) more times.**

The Front

- **Row 1:** Knit to end of row, put last 4 stitches back onto left needle, k2tog, k2.
- **Row 2:** Slip 3 wyif, knit to end of row.
- **Repeat Rows 1 and 2 three more times.** *You now have 8 (10) stitches.*

- Work Rows 1 and 2 as for first side 30 (34) times.
- **Next Row:** Knit to last 4 stitches, kfb, k3, put 3 stitches back on left needle, k3.
- **Next Row:** Slip 3 wyif, knit to end of row.
- Work last two rows three more times. *You now have 12 (14) stitches.*

The Second Side

- Work Rows 1 and 2 as for first side 14 (16) times, then work Row 1 once more.
- Undo the provisional cast on and place the 12 (14) stitches on a double-point needle. Join the center back seam with three-needle bind off (see page 282). *Do not cut yarn.*

KNITTING THE CROWN

- With circular needle, RS facing, and beginning at center back, pick up and knit 69 (79) stitches from straight edge of brim. *You now have 70 (80) stitches.* Place a marker and begin working in the round.
- **Rounds 1 and 2:** Knit.
- **Round 3:** K4 *M1, knit 7 (8); repeat from * to last 3 (4) stitches, M1, k3 (4). *You now have 80 (90) stitches.*
- **Rounds 4–6:** Knit.
- **Round 7:** K1 *M1, knit 8 (9); repeat from * to last 7 (8) stitches, M1, k7 (8). *You now have 90 (100) stitches.*
- **Rounds 8–10:** Knit.
- **Round 11:** K7 *M1, knit 9 (10) repeat from * to last 2 (3) stitches, M1, k2 (3). *You now have 100 (110) stitches total.*
- **Rounds 12–14:** Knit.
- **Round 15:** K3 *M1, knit 10 (11); repeat from * to last 7 (8) stitches, M1, k7 (8). *You now have 110 (120) stitches total.*
- **Rounds 16–18:** Knit.
- **Round 19:** K6 *M1, knit 11 (12); repeat from * to last 5 (6) stitches, M1, k5 (6). *You now have 120 (130) stitches.*

KNITTING THE TOP OF THE HAT

- Knit to last 2 stitches.
- **First corner:** K2tog, remove marker, ssk, (put 3 stitches back on left needle, k2tog, ssk) 10 (11) times. **Note:** Use one or more double-point needles to rearrange your stitches if necessary to work comfortably.
- **Second corner:** K10 (11), k2tog, ssk, (put 3 stitches back on left needle, k2tog, ssk) 10 (11) times.
- Repeat second corner three more times. *You now have 10 stitches.*

The Top Loop

- **Next Row:** K1, (k2tog) 4 times, k1. *You now have 6 stitches.* Arrange the stitches on three double-point needles to work comfortably.
- Knit in the round until tail measures 3"/7.5 cm. Cut yarn and pull the end through the remaining stitches.

FINISHING

- Sew the top tail down to form a loop. Weave in all ends.
- Cut 2 yds/2 m of yarn and fold it in half. Pull the folded end through the tip of one of the ear covers so that the hat is in the center of the doubled yarn. Maintaining tension on the yarn, twist the doubled yarn from both ends until it is tightly twisted. Bring the ends of the twisted yarn together with the hat hanging in the center. Hold the ends and allow the hat to spin around until the strands of the tie are sufficiently twisted. Trim tie to 6"/15 cm and tie ends in an overhand knot. Repeat for second tie for the other ear cover. **Note:** Sample used longer ties, but we recommend short ties for baby items.
- Steam the hat lightly and leave to dry.

Cabled Baby Hat

Designed by Cathy Campbell

Here's a triple cable hat with a self-rolling brim and a top knot. Any toddler will be proud to don this one, in any color you want to knit!

SIZE AND FINISHED MEASUREMENTS
To fit 6–12 months: 14"/35.5 cm circumference

YARN
Crystal Palace Merino 5, 100% superwash merino wool, 110 yds (101 m)/1.75 oz (50 g), Color 5209 Sky Blue (4)

NEEDLES
US 7 (4.5 mm) circular needle 12"/30 cm long and set of four or five US 7 (4.5 mm) double-point needles *or size needed to obtain correct gauge*

GAUGE
23 stitches and 28 rounds = 4"/10 cm in stockinette stitch

OTHER SUPPLIES
Stitch marker, cable needle, yarn needle

SPECIAL ABBREVIATIONS
2/1 LPC
 Slip 2 stitches to cable needle and hold in front, purl 1 from left needle, knit 2 from cable needle
2/1 RPC
 Slip 1 stitch to cable needle and hold in back, knit 2 from left needle, purl 1 from cable needle
2/2 LC
 Slip 2 stitches to cable needle and hold in front, knit 2 from left needle, knit 2 from cable needle

Pattern Essentials

CABLE PANEL
(worked on 24 stitches)

Round 1: P2, (k4, p4) twice, k4, p2.

Round 2: P2, k4, p4, 2/2 LC, p4, k4, p2.

Round 3: Repeat Round 1.

Round 4: P2, k4, p3, 2/1 RPC, 2/1 LPC, p3, k4, p2.

Round 5: P2, k4, p3, k2, p2, k2, p3, k4, p2.

Round 6: P2, 2/2 LC, p2, 2/1 RPC, p2, 2/1 LPC, p2, 2/2 LC, p2.

Rounds 7–9: P2, k4, p2, k2, p4, k2, p2, k4, p2.

Round 10: P2, k4, p2, 2/1 LPC, p2, 2/1 RPC, p2, k4, p2.

Round 11: Repeat Round 5.

Round 12: P2, 2/2 LC, p3, 2/1 LPC, 2/1 RPC, p3, 2/2 LC, p2.

Repeat Rounds 1–12 for Cable Panel.

KNITTING THE HAT

- With circular needle, cast on 72 stitches. Place marker and join into a round, being careful not to twist the stitches.

- **Rounds 1–11:** Knit.

- **Round 12:** *K4, M1L; repeat from * to end of round. *You now have 90 stitches.*

The Cable Pattern

- **Round 1:** (K21, pm, work Round 1 of Cable Panel on next 24 stitches, following the written instructions or the chart) two times.

- **Round 2:** (K21, work Round 2 of Cable Panel as established) two times.

- **Rounds 3–28:** Work in pattern as established.

Decreasing for the Crown

- Work Rounds 29 through 41 as described below, changing to double-point needles when necessary.

- **Round 29:** [(K5, k2tog) 3 times, work established cable panel] twice. *You now have* 84 *stitches.*

- **Round 30:** (Knit to marker, work cable panel) twice.

- **Round 31:** [(K4, k2tog) 3 times, work cable panel] twice. *You now have* 78 *stitches.*

- **Round 32:** Repeat Round 30.

- **Round 33:** [(K3, k2tog) 3 times, work cable panel] twice. *You now have* 72 *stitches.*

- **Round 34:** Repeat Round 30.

- **Round 35:** [(K2, k2tog) 3 times, p1, k2tog, k2, ssk, (p2, k2) twice, p2, k2tog, k2, ssk, p1] twice. *You now have* 58 *stitches.*

- **Round 36:** (Knit to marker, p1, 2/2 LC, p2, 2/1 LPC, 2/1 RPC, p2, 2/2 LC, p1) twice.

- **Round 37:** [(K1, k2tog) 3 times, k2tog, k2, ssk, p2, k4, p2, k2tog, k2, ssk] twice. *You now have* 44 *stitches.*

- **Round 38:** (K10, p2, 2/2 LC, p2, k4) twice.

- **Round 39:** [(K2tog) 3 times, k3, ssk, k2tog, k2, ssk, k2tog, k3] twice. *You now have* 30 *stitches.*

- **Round 40:** (K1, k2tog) around. *You now have* 20 *stitches.*

- **Round 41:** (K2tog) around. *You now have* 10 *stitches.*

Cable Panel

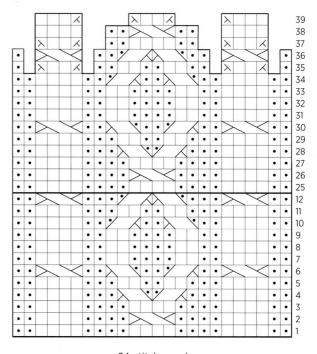

24-stitch panel

	knit
•	purl
⋏	k2tog
⋋	ssk
	2/2 LC
	2/1 LPC
	2/1 RPC

The Cord

• Knit remaining 10 stitches even in the round for 3"/7.5 cm. Cut yarn, leaving a 6"/15 cm tail. Thread tail onto yarn needle and draw through remaining 10 stitches. Pull up snug and fasten off. Tie cord in knot. Weave in all ends.

Happy Hat

Designed by Robin Allen, A Texas Girl Knits

This unique and easy-to-knit pattern looks like a collection of smiles. Make some kids in your life happy today — you can knit two hats from one skein of yarn.

SIZES AND FINISHED MEASUREMENTS

To fit 3–6 (12–36) months: 13¾ (17)"/35 (43) cm circumference, stretches to fit 15 (18)"/38 (45.5) cm

YARN

Berroco Comfort, 50% super fine nylon/50% super fine acrylic, 210 yds (193 m)/3.5 oz (100 g), Color 9738 Kidz Green (**4**)

NEEDLES

Set of five US 7 (4.5 mm) double-point needles, US 7 (4.5 mm) circular needle 16"/40 cm long for larger size *or size needed to obtain correct gauge*

GAUGE

21 stitches and 32 rounds = 4"/10 cm in pattern stitch

OTHER SUPPLIES

Stitch marker, yarn needle

KNITTING THE HAT

- Using double-point (circular) needles, loosely cast on 72 (90) stitches. Place marker and join into a round, being careful not to twist the stitches. Following chart (see next page) or line-by-line instructions, work Rounds 1–14 of Happy Stitch pattern 2 (3) times, then work Rounds 1–11 (1–4) once more.

Decreasing for the Crown

- Work crown decreases as follows.

- **Round 1:** *P3, k2tog, k4; repeat from * to end of round. *You now have* 64 (80) stitches.

- **Rounds 2, 4, 6, 8, and 10:** Knit the knits and purl the purls (see page 279).

- **Round 3:** *P2, k2tog, k4; repeat from * to end of round. *You now have* 56 (70) stitches.

- **Round 5:** *P1, k2tog, k4; repeat from * to end of round. *You now have* 48 (60) stitches.

- **Round 7:** *K2tog, k4; repeat from * to end of round. *You now have* 40 (50) stitches.

- **Round 9:** *K2tog, k3; repeat from * to end of round. *You now have* 32 (40) stitches.

- **Round 11:** P4, k5, p4, k5; repeat from * to end of round. *You now have* 24 (30) stitches.

- **Round 12:** Knit.

- **Round 13:** *K2tog; repeat from * to end of round. *You now have* 12 (15) stitches.

- **Round 15:** *K1, k2tog; repeat from * to end of round. *You now have* 8 (10) stitches.

- Cut yarn, leaving a 12"/30.5 cm tail. Thread tail onto yarn needle and draw through remaining stitches, pull snug and fasten off.

- Weave in ends.

Pattern Essentials

HAPPY STITCH
(multiple of 18 stitches)

Round 1: *K3, p7, k8; repeat from * to end of round.

Round 2: *K2, p9, k7; repeat from * to end of round.

Round 3: *K1, p11, k6; repeat from * to end of round.

Round 4: *P4, k5, p4, k5; repeat from * to end of round.

Round 5: *P3, k7, p3, k5; repeat from * to end of round.

Round 6: *P2, k9, p2, k5; repeat from * to end of round.

Round 7: *P1, k11, p1, k5; repeat from * to end of round.

Round 8: *P1, k11, p6; repeat from * to end of round.

Round 9: *P2, k9, p7; repeat from * to end of round.

Round 10: *P3, k7, p8; repeat from * to end of round.

Round 11: *P4, k5, p9; repeat from * to end of round.

Round 12: *K1, p3, k5, p3, k6; repeat from * to end of round.

Round 13: *K2, p2, k5, p2, k7; repeat from * to end of round.

Round 14: *K3, p1, k5, p1, k8; repeat from * to end of round.

Repeat Rounds 1 through 14 for pattern.

Happy Stitch

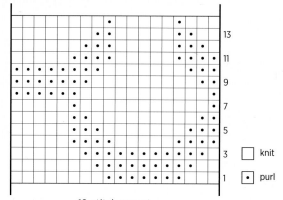

18-stitch repeat

Daisy Hat

Designed by Andrea Wong, Andrea Wong Knits

Andrea was inspired to knit this hat when she discovered the daisy stitch. The stitch is easy to work yet has a striking appearance. The earflaps will keep your baby girl warm while she charms her admirers.

SIZE AND FINISHED MEASUREMENTS
To fit 3–12 months: 16"/40.5 cm circumference

YARN
Sirdar Sublime Organic Merino Wool DK, 100% organic merino wool, 113 yds (105 m)/1.75 oz (50 g), Color 0116 Pink ③

NEEDLES
Set of five US 5 (4 mm) double-point needles *or size needed to obtain correct gauge*

GAUGE
20 stitches and 32 rounds = 4"/10 cm in pattern

OTHER SUPPLIES
Yarn needle

SPECIAL ABBREVIATIONS
Ds (daisy stitch)
  Insert needle into stitch 3 rows below the 2nd stitch on left needle, yarn over needle and draw up a loop, k2, draw 2nd loop through same stitch 3 rows below, k2, draw 3rd loop through same stitch 3 rows below.

Pattern Essentials

DAISY STITCH PATTERN
(multiple of 10 stitches)

Rounds 1–6: Knit.

Round 7: *K1, Ds, k5; repeat from * to end of round.

Round 8: (K2tog, k1) twice, k2tog, k5; repeat from * to end of round.

Rounds 9–14: Knit.

Round 15: *K5, Ds, k1; repeat from * to end of round.

Round 16: *K4, (k2tog, k1) three times; repeat from * to end of round.

Repeat Rounds 1–16 for pattern.

KNITTING THE HAT

- Cast on 80 stitches. Divide stitches evenly onto 4 double-point needles and join into a round, being careful not to twist the stitches.

153

- **Rounds 1–5:** Purl.
- **Round 6 (turning ridge):** Knit.
- Following the chart or line-by-line instructions, work Rounds 1–16 of the Daisy Stitch pattern once, then work Rounds 1–8 once more.
- Knit all rounds for 1"/2.5 cm.

Decreasing for the Crown

- **Round 1:** *K8, ssk; repeat from * to end of round. *You now have* 72 stitches.
- **Round 2:** *K7, ssk; repeat from * to end of round. *You now have* 64 stitches.
- **Round 3:** *K6, ssk; repeat from * to end of round. *You now have* 56 stitches.
- **Round 4:** *K5, ssk; repeat from * to end of round. *You now have* 48 stitches.
- **Round 5:** *K4, ssk; repeat from * to end of round. *You now have* 40 stitches.
- **Round 6:** *K3, ssk; repeat from * to end of round. *You now have* 32 stitches.
- **Round 7:** *K2, ssk; repeat from * to end of round. *You now have* 24 stitches.
- **Round 8:** *K1, ssk; repeat from * to end of round. *You now have* 16 stitches.
- **Round 9:** *Ssk; repeat from * to end of round. *You now have* 8 stitches.
- Cut yarn leaving an 8"/20.5 cm tail. Thread tail onto yarn needle, draw through remaining stitches, pull up snug, and fasten off. Weave in ends.

The Ear Flaps

- Fold hat in half and measure about 2"/5 cm from fold line. With RS facing and beginning at this point, pick up and knit 14 stitches through loops of turning ridge on the inside of the hat.
- **Row 1 (WS):** Knit.
- **Row 2:** Ssk, knit to last 2 stitches, k2tog.
- Repeat Rows 1 and 2 until you have 4 stitches.

- **Next Row:** K1, k2tog, k1. *You now have* 3 stitches.
- Work 3-stitch I-cord (see page 277) for 4½"/11.5 cm. Make a second ear flap on opposite side of hat.
- Weave in ends.

Daisy Stitch

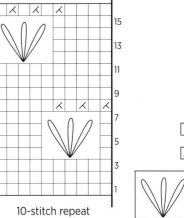

10-stitch repeat

	knit
⋌	k2tog
	daisy stitch

The Pat Hat

Designed by Kathleen Day

All three of these hats came from one 100-gram skein of yarn. But since we all knit a little differently, you may need a little more yarn for all three. For sure you can knit two!

SIZES AND FINISHED MEASUREMENTS

To fit 18"/45.5 cm doll (0–6 months, 1–2 years): 3 (4, 5¼)"/7.5 (10, 13.5) cm deep at lower edge, 4 (4½, 6)"/10 (11.5, 15) cm high at front edge, relaxed

Note: Hat stretches considerably to allow for a good fit on a variety of head sizes.

YARN

Lion Brand Sock Ease, 75% superwash wool/24% nylon, 438 yds (400 m)/3.5 oz (100 g), Color 100 Marshmallow ❶

NEEDLES

US 2 (2.75 mm) straight needles *or size needed to obtain correct gauge*

GAUGE

28 stitches and 40 rows = 4"/10 cm in pattern

OTHER SUPPLIES

A few yards of contrasting yarn for edging (optional), yarn needle

KNITTING THE HAT

- Loosely cast on 82 (102, 122) stitches. **Note:** Use contrasting yarn if desired for cast on and Rows 1 through 3.

- **Row 1 (RS):** *K2, p2; repeat from * to last 2 stitches, k2.

- **Row 2:** *P2, k2; repeat from * to last 2 stitches, p2.
- **Row 3:** Repeat Row 1.
- **Row 4:** K4, *p2, k2; repeat from * to last 6 stitches, p2, k4.
- **Rows 5 and 6:** Knit the knits and purl the purls (see page 279).
- **Row 7:** K6, *p2, k2; repeat from * to last 8 stitches, p2, k6.
- **Rows 8 and 9:** Knit the knits and purl the purls.
- **Row 10:** K8, *p2, k2; repeat from * to last 10 stitches, p2, k8.
- **Rows 11 and 12:** Knit the knits and purl the purls.
- **Row 13:** K10, *p2, k2; repeat from * to last 12 stitches, p2, k10.
- **Rows 14 and 15:** Knit the knits and purl the purls.
- **Row 16:** K12. *p2, k2; repeat from * to last 14 stitches, p2, k12.
- **Row 17 and 18:** Knit the knits and purl the purls.
- **Row 19:** K14, *p2, k2; repeat from* to last 16 stitches, p2, k14.
- **Row 20 and 21:** Knit the knits and purl the purls.
- Continue in this manner, knitting 2 more stitches in stockinette/reverse stockinette stitch every 3rd row, followed by 2 rows of knit the knits and purl the purls, until you work k40 (50, 60), p2, k40 (50, 60).

Note: The p2 bar runs down the inside center of the top of the hat.

- Slip 41 (51, 61) stitches back onto the empty needle, turn the hat inside out and graft the live stitches for the center back seam together with Kitchener stitch (see page 278) or join with three-needle bind off (see page 282).

KNITTING THE TIE

- Cast on 5 (6, 10) stitches. Work kl, p1 rib for 21 (24, 32)"/53.5 (61, 81.5) cm. Bind off.
- Turn back the front edge of the hat ½"/13 mm each side and sew the center 7 (8, 10)"/18 (20.5, 25.5) cm of the tie to the bottom edge, leaving the ends free to tie under the chin. Weave in the ends.

Faux Bow Hat

Designed by Ruth Roland

This cute hat has a self-rolling brim and a sweet "faux" bow. It works well in solid colors as well as variegated and hand-dyed yarns.

KNITTING THE HAT

- Cast on 54 (63, 72, 81, 90, 99) stitches. Divide evenly onto 3 double-point needles. Place marker and join into a round, being careful not to twist the stitches.
- Work in stockinette stitch (knit every round) until piece measures 4½ (5, 5½, 6, 7, 8)"/11.5 (12.5, 14, 15, 18, 20.5) cm from cast-on edge.
- **Next Round:** *K6 (7, 8, 9, 10, 11), pm; repeat from * to end of round.

Decreasing for the Crown

- **Decrease Round:** Knit to 2 stitches from marker, k2tog; repeat from * to end of round. *You now have* 45 (54, 63, 72, 81, 90) stitches.
- Repeat Decrease Round until 18 stitches remain (2 stitches between each marker).
- **Next Round:** *K2tog, k1, ssk, k1, removing markers; repeat from * to end of round. *You now have* 12 stitches.

The Bow

First Bow Tail

- Work 3-stitch I-cord (see page 277) for 3"/7.5 cm, leaving remaining

SIZES AND FINISHED MEASUREMENTS
To fit preemie (0–3 mos, 3–6 mos, 6–18 mos, 18–24 mos, 3–5 yrs): 9¾ (11½, 13, 14¾, 16½, 18)"/25 (29, 33, 37.5, 42, 45.5) cm circumference
Shown in 3–6 mos (pink) and 6–18 mos (blue)

YARN
Willow Yarns Daily DK, 100% superwash wool, 248 yds (260 m)/3.5 oz (100 g), Color 0022 Blossom (**3**); or The Unique Sheep Green Sheep Sport, 100% superfine organic merino wool, 330 yds (302 m)/3.5 oz (100 g), Tide Pool (**2**)

NEEDLES
Set of four US 3 (3.25 mm) double-point needles *or size needed to obtain correct gauge*

GAUGE
22 stitches and 32 rounds = 4"/10 cm in stockinette stitch

OTHER SUPPLIES
Stitch markers, yarn needle

SPECIAL ABBREVIATIONS
yo-b
   Yarn over needle from back to front

stitches unworked. Cut yarn leaving a 4"/10 cm tail. Thread tail on yarn needle and draw through remaining stitches. Weave in end.

First Faux Loop

- Attach yarn leaving an 8"/20.5 cm tail and continue work on next 3 stitches.
- **Row 1:** *Kfb; repeat from * to end of row. *You now have 6 stitches.*
- **Row 2:** *K1, slip 1 wyif; repeat from * to end of row.
- **Row 3:** [K1, slip 1 wyif, bring yarn between needles, (yo-b) twice] 2 times, k1, slip 1 with yarn in front. *You now have 10 stitches.*
- **Row 4:** *K1, slip 1 wyif, k1 in front loop of next yo, slip following yo wyif; repeat from *, k1, slip 1 wyif.
- Repeat Row 2 until piece measures 1½"/4 cm.
- Bind off as follows: K1, (k2tog, slip first stitch worked over second stitch to bind off) 4 times, k1, bind off 1; cut yarn and pull through last stitch.

Second Faux Loop

- Work as for First Faux Loop over next 3 stitches but without the 8"/20.5 cm tail.

Second Bow Tail

- Work as for First Bow Tail over next 3 stitches.

FINISHING

- Thread yarn needle with the 8"/20.5 cm tail and draw through the 12 stitches at the base of the bow; pull up snugly and fasten off.
- Tie two I-cord pieces in a knot.
- Weave in ends. Block.

Infant Crown

Designed by Marcia J. Sommerkamp, Sommerkamp Designs

Your baby will love to play Queen or King for the Day with this adorable crown. You can knit crowns for the whole neighborhood with one skein of yarn. This is a photo op waiting to happen.

SIZE AND FINISHED MEASUREMENTS
To fit newborn: 13"/33 cm circumference
Note: For safety, don't leave baby unattended while wearing a crown.

YARN
SRK On Your Toes Sock Yarn, 75% superwash wool/25% nylon, 390 yds (360 m)/3.5 oz (100 g), Color 3824 sunset print (1)

NEEDLES
US 2 (2.75 mm) straight needles, US 2 (2.75 mm) circular needle 16"/40 cm long *or size needed to obtain correct gauge*

GAUGE
28 stitches = 4"/10 cm in stockinette stitch

OTHER SUPPLIES
20"/51 cm of ¼"/6 mm ribbon, yarn needle

KNITTING THE CROWN

- With straight needles, cast on 17 stitches.
- **Row 1:** Knit.
- **Row 2:** K2 tog, knit to last 2 stitches, ssk. *You now have* 15 stitches.
- Repeat Row 2 until 3 stitches remain.
- **Last row:** Sk2p.
- Fasten off. Make 4 additional triangles.

KNITTING THE BASE

- Using circular needle to accommodate large number of stitches, pick up and knit 17 stitches along base of each triangle. *You now have* 85 stitches.
- **Row 1 (WS):** Knit.
- **Row 2:** Knit.
- **Row 3:** Purl.
- **Row 4 (eyelet row):** *K1, yo, k2tog; repeat from * to last stitch, k1.
- **Row 6:** Purl.
- **Rows 7–11:** Knit.
- Bind off.

Hootenanny Hat of Owls

Designed by Anna Smegal

This bottom-up seamless cap is a quick knit in worsted weight yarn with minimal patterning. Simple cables and tiny buttons become little owls in the fashion of the popular Penny Straker patterns.

FINISHING

• Sew ends together to a form circle. Thread ribbon through eyelets and tie a bow in front.

Hat Sizing

When in doubt, make a baby hat larger than you think ideal rather than smaller. A hat that's too big can be grown into, but one that's too small is useless. In general, you can estimate one to two inches of negative ease, meaning that a hat with a finished measurement of 14 inches will fit a 15-to-16-inch head — some stitch patterns and yarn will have more negative ease, some will have less.

Pattern Essentials

OWL
(multiple of 11 stitches)

Round 1: *P4, k2, p5; repeat from * to end of round.

Round 2: *P1, 1/3 RC, 1/3 LC, p2; repeat from * to end of round.

Rounds 3-11: *P1, k8, p2; repeat from * to end of round.

Round 12: *P1, 2/2 RPC, 2/2 LPC, p2; repeat from * to end of round.

Round 13: P1, 1/1 RPC, p4, 1/1 LPC, p2; repeat from * to end of round.

Works Rounds 1-13 for pattern.

SIZES AND FINISHED MEASUREMENTS

To fit 0–3 months (3–6 months, 6–12 months, 1–3 years, 3–5 years): 12 (14, 16, 18, 20)"/30.5 (35.5, 40.5, 45.5, 51) cm

YARN

Knit Picks Wool of the Andes Tweed, 80% Peruvian Highland wool/20% Donegal tweed, 110 yds (101 m)/1.75 oz (50 g), Dill Heather (4)

NEEDLES

Set of four or five US 4 (3.5 mm) double-point needles and set of four or five US 6 (4 mm) double-point needles *or size needed to obtain correct gauge*

GAUGE

22 stitches and 28 rounds = 4"/10 cm in stockinette stitch on larger needles

OTHER SUPPLIES

Stitch markers, cable needle, yarn needle, 12 (14, 16, 18, 20) ¼"/6 mm buttons, sewing needle and coordinating thread

SPECIAL ABBREVIATIONS

1/3 RC
  Slip 3 stitches onto cable needle and hold in back, k1 from left needle, k3 from cable needle

1/3 LC
  Slip 1 stitch to cable needle and hold in front, k3 from left needle, k1 from cable needle

2/2 RPC
  Slip 2 stitches onto cable needle and hold in back, k2 from left needle, p2 from cable needle

2/2 LPC
  Slip 2 stitches onto cable needle and hold in front, p2 from left needle, k2 from cable needle

1/1 RPC
  Slip 1 stitch onto cable needle and hold in back, k1 from left needle, p1 from cable needle

1/1 LPC
  Slip 1 stitch onto cable needle and hold in front, p1 from left needle, k1 from cable needle

M1P (make 1 purlwise)
  Insert the left-hand needle from back to front under the strand of yarn running between the stitches on the left- and right-hand needles, lift this strand onto the left-hand needle and purl it through the front loop

KNITTING THE HAT

- With smaller needles, cast on 60 (70, 80, 90, 100) stitches. Divide evenly onto double-point needles and join into a round, being careful not to twist the stitches.

- Knit 3 (3, 4, 4, 5) rounds.

- **Increase Round:** *P10, M1P, pm; repeat from * to end of round. *You now have 66 (77, 88, 99, 110) stitches.*

- Purl 0 (0, 1, 1, 2) rounds.

- Change to larger needles. Working from chart or line-by-line instructions, work Rounds 1 through 13 of Owl pattern, working 6 (7, 8, 9, 10) repeats in each round.

- Work in reverse stockinette stitch (purl every round) until piece measures 2½ (3, 4, 4½, 5)"/6.5 (7.5, 10, 11.5, 12.5) cm from bottom edge.

Decreasing for the Crown

- **Round 1:** *Purl to 2 stitches before marker, k2tog; repeat from * to end of row. *You now have 60 (70, 80, 90, 100) stitches.*

- **Round 2:** *Purl to 1 stitch before marker, k1; repeat from * to end of row.

- Repeat Rounds 1 and 2 until you have 4 stitches between each pair of markers, 24 (28, 32, 36, 40) stitches total.

- **Next Round:** *P2, k2tog; repeat from * to end of round. *You now have 18 (21, 24, 27, 30) stitches.*

- **Next Round:** *P1, k2tog; repeat from * to end of round. *You now have 12 (14, 16, 18, 20) stitches.*

- **Last Round:** *K2tog; repeat from * to end of round. *You now have 6 (7, 8, 9, 10)*
- Cut yarn leaving a 6"/15 cm tail. Thread tail onto yarn needle and draw through remaining stitches. Pull up snug and fasten off.

FINISHING

- Weave in ends. Wet block, pinning flat to keep owls in a straight line. Sew on 2 buttons for each owl, just below cable Round 12.

Owl Chart

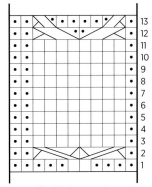

11-stitch repeat

	knit
•	purl
	1/1 RPC
	1/1 L PC
	1/3 RC
	1/3 LC
	2/2 RPC
	2/2 LPC

Cool Dude Cap

Designed by Tamara Del Sonno

Strangers on the street will marvel at the cuteness of your little boy when he's sporting the Cool Dude Cap. And it's written in three sizes, so the look can stay with him as he grows.

SIZES AND FINISHED MEASUREMENTS
To fit newborn (6 months, 12 months): 13¾ (15½, 17)"/35 cm (39.5 cm, 43 cm) circumference

YARN
Patons Stretch Socks, 41% cotton/39% wool/13% nylon/7% elastic, 239 yds (219 m)/1.75 oz (50 g), Color 31135 Mineral ①

NEEDLES
Sets of four or five US 1 (2.25 mm) and US 3 (3.25 mm) double-point needles *or size needed to obtain correct gauge*

GAUGE
28 stitches = 4"/10 cm in stockinette stitch using larger needle

OTHER SUPPLIES
7 stitch markers (one in a unique color), yarn needle, one ⅜" (10 mm) button

SPECIAL ABBREVIATIONS
p-inc (purlwise open bar increase)
   Purl 1 into the strand between the stitch on the right needle and the stitch on the left needle.

KNITTING THE CAP

- With smaller needles, cast on 96 (108, 120) stitches. Place unique color marker and join into a round, being careful not to twist the stitches.
- **Rounds 1–5:** Knit.
- **Round 6 (turning ridge):** Purl.
- **Rounds 7–12:** Knit.
- Change to larger needles.

- **Round 13:** *K7 (8, 9), p-inc, pm for increase, k1, p-inc, k7 (8, 9), p-inc, k1, p-inc; repeat from * to end of round. *You now have* 120 (132, 144) stitches.

- **Round 14:** Knit.

- **Round 15:** *Knit to increase marker, p-inc, sm, k1, p-inc; repeat from * to end of round. *You now have* 132 (144, 156) stitches.

- **Round 16:** Knit.

- Repeat Rounds 15 and 16 three more times. *You now have* 168 (180, 192) stitches.

- **Next Round:** *Knit to 1 st before marker, p1, sm, k1, p1; repeat from * to end of round.

- **Next Round:** Knit.

- Repeat these last 2 rounds 4 (5, 6) more times.

Decreasing for the Crown

- **Round 1:** *Knit to 2 stitches before marker, p2tog, sm, k1, p2tog; repeat from * to end of round. *You now have* 156 (168, 180) stitches.

- **Round 2:** Knit.

- **Round 3:** *Knit to 1 st before marker, p1, sm, k1, p1; repeat from * to end of round.

- **Round 4:** Knit.

- Repeat Rounds 1–4 twelve (thirteen, fourteen) times. *You now have* 12 stitches.

- **Next Round:** *K2tog; repeat from * to end of round. *You now have* 6 stitches.

- Cut yarn, thread through remaining stitches, pull up snug, and fasten off.

Finishing

- Sew button to top of cap.

- Fold up brim and sew to the inside.

- Weave in ends.

Claire, a Baby Hat

Designed by Sarah Grieve

This cute hat is fairly simple to knit and you can create it in three sizes. It is knit from the bottom up, and the ruffle is worked separately and sewn to the hat.

SIZES AND FINISHED MEASUREMENTS
To fit 3 months (6 months, 12+ months): 13¾" (15½, 17)"/35 (39.5, 43) cm in circumference

YARN
Skacel Collection HiKoo Simplicity, 55% superwash merino wool/28% acrylic/17% nylon, 117 yds (107 m)/1.75 oz (50 g), Color 003 Natural (4)

NEEDLES
US 4 (3.25 mm) circular needle 16"/40 cm long, US 5 (3.75 mm) circular needle 16"/40 cm long, and set of four US 5 (3.75 mm) double-point needles *or size needed to obtain correct gauge*

GAUGE
22 stitches and 30 rounds = 4"/10 cm in stockinette stitch on larger needle

OTHER SUPPLIES
Stitch marker, yarn needle, five ½"/13 mm buttons

KNITTING THE HAT

- With smaller needle, cast on 82 (90, 100) stitches. Place marker and join into a round, being careful not to twist the stitches.
- **Rounds 1–3:** Knit.
- **Rounds 4–6:** *K1, p1; repeat from * to end of round, decreasing 1 (0, 1) st on last round. *You now have 81 (90, 99) stitches.*
- Change to larger needle.
- Work even in stockinette stitch (knit every round) until piece measures 4½ (5, 5½)"/11.5 (12.5, 14) cm.

Shaping the Crown

Note: Change to double-point needles when necessary.

- **Round 1:** *K7 (8, 9), k2tog; repeat from * to end of round. *You now have 72 (81, 90) stitches.*
- **Round 2:** *K6 (7, 8), k2tog; repeat from * to end of round. *You now have 63 (72, 81) stitches.*
- **Round 3:** *K5 (6, 7), k2tog; repeat from * to end of round. *You now have 54 (63, 72) stitches.*
- **Round 4:** *K4 (5, 6), k2tog; repeat from * to end of round. *You now have 45 (54, 63) stitches.*
- Continue to decrease 9 stitches each round in this manner, knitting 1 fewer stitch between the

decreases on each round, until 9 stitches remain.

- Cut yarn leaving a 6"/15 cm tail. Thread tail onto yarn needle, draw through remaining stitches, pull up snug, and fasten off.

The Ruffle

- With larger needle, cast on 40 stitches.
- **Rows 1 and 3:** Knit.
- **Rows 2 and 4:** Purl.
- **Row 5:** *K1, M1; repeat from * to last stitch, k1. _You now have_ 79 stitches.
- **Row 6:** Purl.
- Bind off.
- Fold ruffle in half lengthwise, with cast-on edges aligned and right sides facing. Use mattress stitch to sew the edges together.

FINISHING

- Weave in all ends. Sew ruffle to hat, lining the flat edge up with the first row of ribbing. Sew buttons down center of ruffle. Block lightly.

Circus Rings Baby Hat

Designed by Cathy Campbell

This fun hat uses alternating bands of stockinette and reverse stockinette stitches to create the horizontal ribbing, or rings, and decreases form a virtually flat top. The remaining stitches are worked into a cord and tied into a knot.

SIZE AND FINISHED MEASUREMENTS
To fit 6–12 months: 14"/35.5 cm circumference

YARN
Crystal Palace Mini Mochi, 80% merino wool/20% nylon, 195 yds (180 m)/ 1.75 oz (50 g), Color 101 Intense Rainbow **1**

NEEDLES
US 3 (3.25 mm) circular needle 12"/30 cm long and/or set of four US 3 (3.25 mm) double-point needles _or size needed to obtain correct gauge_

GAUGE
26 stitches and 32 rows = 4"/10 cm in stockinette stitch

OTHER SUPPLIES
Stitch marker, yarn needle

KNITTING THE HAT

- With circular or double-point needles, cast on 90 stitches. Place marker and join into a round, being careful not to twist the stitches.
- **Rounds 1–10:** Knit.
- **Rounds 11-16:** Purl.
- **Rounds 17–22:** Knit.
- Repeat Rounds 11 through 22 six more times, then work Rounds 11 through 16 once more.

Decreasing for the Crown

Note: If using a circular needle, change to double-point needles when necessary.

- **Round 1**: Knit.
- **Round 2**: *K7, k2tog; repeat from * to end of round. *You now have 80 stitches.*
- **Round 3**: Knit.
- **Round 4**: *K6, k2tog; repeat from * to end of round. *You now have 70 stitches.*
- **Round 5**: Knit.
- **Round 6**: *K5, k2tog; repeat from * to end of round. *You now have 60 stitches.*
- **Round 7**: Knit.
- **Round 8**: *K4, k2tog; repeat from * to end of round. *You now have 50 stitches.*
- **Round 9**: Knit.
- **Round 10**: *K3, k2tog; repeat from * to end of round. *You now have 40 stitches.*
- **Round 11**: Knit.
- **Round 12**: *K2, k2tog; repeat from * to end of round. *You now have 30 stitches.*
- **Round 13**: Knit.
- **Round 14**: *K1, k2tog; repeat from * to end of round. *You now have 20 stitches.*
- **Round 15**: Knit.
- **Round 16**: *K2tog; repeat from * to end of round. *You now have 10 stitches.*
- Knit even on remaining stitches for 3"/7.5 cm. Cut yarn, leaving a 6"/15 cm tail. Thread tail onto yarn needle and draw yarn through remaining 10 stitches. Weave in ends. Tie cord in a knot.

Lily Pad Hood

Designed by Margaret Radcliffe

This sweet hood project is worked from the top down, beginning at the center of hood and working flat. After the hood is completed, the neckband and collar are worked circularly. Decorative triangular points finish off the outer edge.

KNITTING THE HOOD

- Cast on 68 (72, 76) stitches using Judy's Magic Cast On (see page 278) and both circular needles. There will be 34 (36, 38) stitches on each needle. *Options:* If you prefer, you may use a provisional cast on or cast on conventionally, then sew the top of the hood together when the project has been completed.

Note: As you work the hood, you'll first knit the stitches from one needle onto that same needle. Then you'll knit across the other side of the hood, knitting the stitches on the second needle onto itself. This is similar to working in the round on two circular needles, except that you will not be working circularly — you'll be working back and forth throughout the hood section.

- **Row 1 (RS):** Slip 1 knitwise, knit to last stitch, p1.
- **Row 2 (WS):** Slip 1 knitwise, k3, purl to last 4 stitches, k3, p1.
- Repeat rows 1 and 2 until hood measures 6½ (7, 7¼)"/16.5 (18, 18.5) cm from cast on, ending with a WS row.

JOIN FOR NECKBAND

- With right side facing, slip 4 stitches from the end of the needle where the working yarn is not attached onto a cable needle. Hold these 4 stitches behind the first 4 stitches of the round (where the working yarn is attached) so that the beginning of the round overlaps with the end of the round.
- Knit the two layers together and join in a round as follows.
- Using needle #2 (the one where the working yarn is not attached), knit the first stitch from the front needle together with the first stitch from the cable needle, then knit the next stitch from each needle together.
- Using needle #1 (the other needle), knit the next two pairs of stitches together. *You now have 64 (68, 72) stitches, 32 (34, 36) stitches on each of the two needles.*

SIZES AND FINISHED MEASUREMENTS
To fit 6 (12, 18) months: 6½ (7, 7¼)"/16.5 (18, 18.5) cm hood height, 41 (44, 46)"/104 (112, 117) cm outer edge of collar circumference

YARN
Tess Designer Yarns Superwash Merino Worsted, 100% superwash merino wool, 285 yds (261 m)/4 oz (114 g), Bahama Bay (4)

NEEDLES
Two US 8 (5 mm) circular needles 16"/40 cm or longer *or size needed to obtain correct gauge*

GAUGE
21 stitches and 29 rows = 4"/10 cm in stockinette stitch

OTHER SUPPLIES
Cable needle, yarn needle, 8 stitch markers, 4"/10 cm square of cardboard to make tassel

- You have already knitted the first two stitches of the round. (P2, k2) to last 2 stitches, p2.
- Work even in k2, p2 rib as established for 1", ending last round at the end of needle 1 (center back of hood). This will be the beginning of round as you work the collar.
- Knit one round increasing 0 (4, 0) stitches evenly spaced around. *You now have 64 (72, 72) stitches.*

KNITTING THE COLLAR

- Place 3 markers on each needle, one at the center of each needle and two more spaced halfway between the center and the ends of the needles. This will divide the stitches on each needle into 4 equal sections of 8 (9, 9) stitches each.

- **Rounds 1, 3, 5, and 7:** Purl.
- **Round 2:** In each of the 8 sections, knit 1, kfb, knit to end of section. *You now have* 72 (80, 80) stitches.
- **Round 4:** In each of the 8 sections, knit halfway across, kfb, knit to end of section. *You now have* 80 (88, 88) stitches.
- **Round 6:** In each of the 8 sections, knit three-quarters of the way across, kfb, knit to end of section. *You now have* 88 (96, 96) stitches.
- **Round 8:** In each of the 8 sections, knit one-quarter of the way across, kfb, knit to end of section *You now have* 96 (104, 104) stitches.
- Repeat these 8 rounds until there are 184 (192, 192) stitches. When the collar is large enough to work comfortably on one needle, you may shift all of the stitches onto one needle, adding two more markers to identify the beginning of round and the halfway point. End after completing a purl round.
- Knit the following round, increasing 1 (3, 8) stitches evenly spaced around. 185 (195, 200) stitches.

KNITTING THE POINTED EDGING

- Turn work so the wrong side is facing you.
- **Set-Up Row:** K5, turn.
- **Row 1:** Slip 1 knitwise, k4, turn.
- **Row 2:** K4, turn.
- **Row 3:** Slip 1 knitwise, k3, turn.
- **Row 4:** K3, turn.
- **Row 5:** Slip 1 knitwise, k2, turn.
- **Row 6:** Bind off 5, k4, turn. (Note that to bind off 5 stitches you must work one stitch past the end of the triangle in order to pass the fifth stitch over it. When you knit the additional 4 stitches on Row 6 you'll have 5 stitches on your working needle, ready to begin working the following triangle.)
- Repeat Rows 1 through 6 until all stitches have been bound off.

FINISHING

- Cut yarn leaving a 6"/15 cm tail. Use the tail to neatly join the end of the final triangle to the beginning of the first triangle, and then weave this tail in on the wrong side. Weave the cast-on tail in on the wrong side of the hood.
- Use the leftover yarn to make a tassel (see page 282) and attach it to point of hood. Tassel shown was made by wrapping the yarn around a 4"/10 cm piece of cardboard 30 times.

Little

SOCKS & BOOTIES

Sideways Baby Socks

Designed by Andrea Wong

Simple garter-stitch socks are knit sideways on two needles. Because you can knit these up in a couple of hours, baby can have some in every color! When baby grows, consider hanging the socks on your Christmas tree.

SIZE AND FINISHED MEASUREMENTS
To fit 0–6 months: 3½"/9 cm from heel to toe, 5"/12.5 cm circumference

YARN
Reynolds Cottontail, 60% cotton/40% microfiber, 116 yds (106 m)/1.75 oz (50 g), Color 3611 (3)

NEEDLES
US 4 (3.5 mm) straight needles *or size needed to obtain correct gauge*

GAUGE
24 stitches and 40 rows = 4"/10 cm in garter stitch

OTHER SUPPLIES
Stitch markers, yarn needle, US E-4 (3.5 mm) crochet hook (optional)

KNITTING THE SOCKS

- Using a provisional cast on method (see page 281), cast on 46 stitches, marking stitch 12 and 24.

- **Row 1:** P22, (M1RP, p1, M1LP, p11) twice. *You now have* 50 stitches.

- **Row 2 and all even rows:** Purl.

- **Row 3:** P23, M1RP, p1, M1LP, p13, M1PR, p1, M1PL, p12. *You now have* 54 stitches.

- **Row 5:** P24, M1RP, p1, M1LP, p15, M1RP, p1, M1LP, p13. *You now have* 58 stitches.

- **Row 7:** P25, M1RP, p1, M1LP, p17, M1RP, p1, M1LP, p14. *You now have 62 stitches.*

- **Rows 8–15:** Purl.

- **Row 16:** P25, sp2p, p17, sp2p, p14.

- Repeat decreases on marked stitches every other row until you have 46 stitches left.

FINISHING

- Graft the sides of the sock together with Kitchener stitch (see page 278). Weave in ends.

- *Optional:* With crochet hook, chain 14, leaving a 1"/2.5 cm tail. With RS facing, single crochet around top of sock (1 sc for each garter ridge), chain 14. Fasten off, leaving a 1"/2.5 5 cm tail. Tie chains into a knot.

Lizzie Janes

Designed by Debbie Haymark, iPurl

A classic Mary Jane shoe is knit using Judy's Magic Cast On, and the Magic Loop circular knitting technique requires absolutely no seaming to finish. When the knitting is complete, simply weave in the ends and sew on buttons and flowers. Simply beautiful!

SIZES AND FINISHED MEASUREMENTS
To fit newborn (3-6 months): 3½"(3¾)/9 (9.5) cm long

YARN
Cascade Fixation, 98.3% cotton/1.7% elastic, 100 yds (91 m)/1.75 oz (50 g), Color 8001 Opulent White (3)

NEEDLES
US 1 (2.25 mm) circular needle 24"/60 cm long *or size needed to obtain correct gauge*

GAUGE
32 stitches and 44 rows = 4"/10 cm in stockinette stitch

OTHER SUPPLIES
Stitch markers, two ⁵⁄₁₆"/8 mm buttons, small amount of crochet cotton in two colors of choice (DMC Cebelia 10 shown in sample) for flower embellishment or purchased embellishment, crochet hook size C-2 (2.75 mm) for crocheting flower, yarn needle, sewing needle and coordinating thread

KNITTING THE BOOTEE (make 2)

- Using Judy's Magic Cast On method (see page 278), cast on 30 (34) stitches, 15 (17) on each needle end.

- **Round 1:** Knit.

- **Round 2:** On needle 1, kfb, k13 (15), pm, M1R, k1; on needle 2, k1, M1L, pm, knit to last stitch, kfb. *You now have 34 (38) stitches.*

- **Round 3:** Knit.

- **Round 4:** On needle 1, kfb, knit to marker, sm, (M1R, k1) twice; on second needle, (k1, M1L) twice, sm, knit to last stitch, kfb. *You now have* 40 (44) stitches.

- **Round 5:** Knit.

- **Round 6:** On needle 1, kfb, knit to marker, sm, (M1R, k1) four times; on needle 2, (k1, M1L) four times, sm, knit to last stitch, kfb. *You now have* 50 (54) stitches.

- **Round 7:** Knit.

- **Round 8:** On needle 1, kfb, knit to marker, sm, M1R, k1, M1R, k7; on needle 2, k7, M1L, k1, M1L, sm, knit to last stitch, kfb. *You now have* 56 (60) stitches.

- **Rounds 9 and 10:** Knit.

- **Round 11:** Purl.

Note: Sole ends with Round 11.

- **Rounds 12–19:** Knit.

- **Round 20:** On needle 1, knit to marker, sm, ssk 5 times; on needle 2, k2tog 5 times, sm, knit to end of round. *You now have* 46 (50) stitches.

- **Rounds 21 and 22:** Knit.

- **Round 23:** On needle 1, knit to marker, ssk twice, move remaining stitch to needle 2; on needle 2, k2tog 3 times, sm, knit to end of round. *You now have* 41 (45) stitches.

- **Round 24:** Knit.

The Straps

Right Foot Strap

- Arranging stitches on needles as necessary, k10, bind off 21, knit to end of round, then knit 10 (12) from needle 1. *You now have* 20 (24) stitches. Move all stitches onto one needle to work back and forth in rows.

- Cast on 13 using the cable cast on method (see page 276).

- **Row 1:** P2, bind off 2, purl to last 11 stitches, p2tog, p9.

- **Row 2:** Knit to last 2 stitches, cast on 1, k2tog.

- Bind off all stitches knitwise.

Left Foot Strap

- Arranging stitches on needles as necessary, k10, bind off 21. *You now have* 20 (24) stitches. Move all stitches onto one needle to work back and forth in rows.

- Cast on 13 stitches using the purlwise cable cast on method.

- **Row 1:** K2, bind off 2, knit to last 11 stitches, k2tog, k9.

- **Row 2:** Purl to last 2 stitches, cast on 1, p2tog.

- Bind off all stitches purlwise.

Montana Moccasins

Designed by Ann Faith

This comfy slipper is knit flat in garter and stockinette stitches and is shaped with simple increases and decreases. Pink yarn with purple ribbon would make an oh-too-cute pair for the little girl in your life.

Crocheting the Flowers

- With crochet hook and first color crochet thread, chain 3 (see page 276), join with slip stitch to form a ring.

- **Round 1:** Ch 1, 6 sc in ring; with second color, slip stitch in back loop of first sc to join. Cut first color.

- **Round 2:** Working into back loops only throughout, (ch 8, slip stitch in same stitch, ch 8, slip stitch in next sc) around, ending slip stitch in first sc.

- **Round 3:** Working into front loops of Round 1 throughout, (ch 6, slip stitch in same stitch, ch 6, slip stitch in next sc) around, ending slip stitch in first sc. Fasten off.

FINISHING

- Weave in ends. Sew on buttons with needle and thread for straps. Sew on embellishment. Block if necessary.

173

SIZES AND FINISHED MEASUREMENTS
To fit 2–3 (4–5) years: 4½ (6)"/11.5 (15) cm length

YARN
Patons Shetland Chunky, 75% acrylic/25% wool, 121 yds (110 m)/3.5 oz (100 g), Color 03022 **⑤**

NEEDLES
US 9 (5.5 mm) straight needles *or size needed to obtain correct gauge*

GAUGE
16 stitches and 34 rows = 4"/10 cm in garter stitch

OTHER SUPPLIES
2 locking stitch markers, two 12"/30.5 cm leather ties or shoelaces

SPECIAL ABBREVIATIONS
skp (slip, knit, pass)
> Slip 1 stitch to right needle, k1, pass the slipped stitch over the knit stitch.

KNITTING THE MOCCASINS (make 2)

- Cast on 20 (22) stitches.

The Sole

- Row 1 (RS): Knit.

- Row 2: Knit.

- Repeat Rows 1 and 2 until piece measures 3 (4½)"/7.5 (11.5) cm, ending with a WS row.

Shaping the Sides

- Row 1: K1, skp, k14 (16), k2tog, k1. *You now have* 18 (20) stitches.

- Rows 2–4: Knit.

- Work Rows 1 through 4 three more times. *You now have* 12 (14) stitches.

- Place locking marker at beginning and end of next row to indicate fold line for toe seaming.

- Work Rows 1 through 4 once more. *You now have* 10 (12) stitches and piece measures approximately 5 (6½)"/12.5 (16.5) cm.

The Front Flap

- Rows 1, 3, 5, and 7: Knit.

- Row 2: Knit.

- Row 4: K3, p4 (6), k3.

- Row 6: K2, p6 (8), k2.

- Row 8: K1, p8 (10), k1.

- Row 9: K1, kfb, k6 (8), kfb, k1. *You now have* 12 (14) stitches.

- Row 10: K1, p10 (12), k1.

- Row 11: Knit.

- Row 12: K1, p10 (12), k1.

- Repeat Rows 11 and 12 once (twice) more.

Decreasing the Flap

- Row 1: K1, skp, k6 (8), k2tog, k1. *You now have* 10 (12) stitches.

- Row 2: K1, p8 (10), k1.

- Row 3: K1, skp, k4 (6), k2tog, k1. *You now have* 8 (10) stitches.

- Bind off purlwise.

Finishing

- Form the heel at the cast-on edge as follows. Fold cast-on edge in half. Starting at top, join edges and seam for 1"/2.5 cm. Flatten bottom and stitch perpendicular to 1" seam, forming T-shaped seam and heel pocket.

- Assemble the toe at the other end as follows: At locking markers, fold front flap toward heel and stitch sides to flap.

- Thread leather tie or shoelace through center front flap and tie bow.

- For non-skid sole, apply grip stop fabric, Slipper Gripper, or puff paint to bottom of slipper.

Easy Baby Bootees

Designed by Andrea Wong

These delightful bootees are knit back and forth and seamed along the bottom of the foot and up the back. Worked in stockinette and reverse stockinette stitches, you can whip up several pairs in no time!

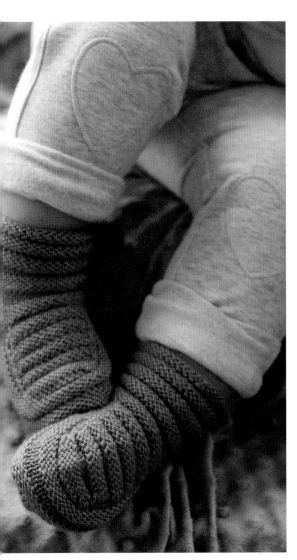

SIZE AND FINISHED MEASUREMENTS
To fit 6–12 months: approximately 4"/10 cm from heel to toe

YARN
Dale of Norway Baby Ull, 100% superwash wool, 180 yds (165 m)/1.75 oz (50 g), Color 0020 Hot Pink ❶

NEEDLES
US 2 (2.75 mm) straight needles *or size needed to obtain correct gauge*

GAUGE
28 stitches and 36 rows = 4"/10 cm in pattern stitch

OTHER SUPPLIES
Yarn needle

KNITTING THE CUFFS (make 2)

- Using the long-tail method (see page 279), cast on 36 stitches.

- Row 1 (RS): Purl.

- Row 2: Knit.

- Row 3: Purl.

- Rows 4 and 5: Knit.

- Row 6: Purl.

- Row 7: Knit.

- Row 8: Purl.

- Repeat Rows 1–8 three more times, then work Rows 1–4 once more.

KNITTING THE INSTEP

- **Next Row:** K24, turn, p12, turn.

- Leaving remaining stitches on each end of the needle on holder and working center 12 stitches only, work Rows 7 and 8 once. Work Rows 1–8 four times, then work Rows 1–4 once more. Cut yarn and transfer all stitches to left needle.

KNITTING THE FOOT

- **Next Row (RS):** K12, pick up and knit 12 stitches along right side of instep panel, knit 12 instep stitches, pick up and knit 12 stitches along left side of instep panel, k12. *You now have 60 stitches.*

- **Next Row:** Purl.

- Work Rows 1–8 of pattern twice.

- **Next Row:** Knit.

- **Next Row:** Purl.

- Continue in stockinette stitch for 6 more rows.

- Bind off. Fold piece in half and sew back seam and sole.

- Weave in ends. Block.

Lacy Cuff Baby Socks

Designed by Terry Liann Morris, The Sailing Knitter

These sweet little socks for baby have ribbing to snuggle the ankles underneath a folded lacy cuff. The ribbing continues down the top of the foot for a close fit.

KNITTING THE CUFF (make 2)

- With larger needles, loosely cast on 55 stitches. Divide stitches evenly onto 3 needles and join into a round, being careful not to twist the stitches. Purl 1 round.

- Following the chart on the next page or line-by-line instructions, work Rounds 1–4 of the Lacy Cuff pattern 5 times (20 rounds).

KNITTING THE RIBBING

- **Round 1:** *P2tog, p7, p2tog; repeat from * to end of round. *You now have* 45 stitches.

- **Round 2:** P2tog, purl to end of round. *You now have* 44 stitches.

- Turn cuff inside out. What was on the outside of your work will now be on the inside. You will be reversing the direction of your knitting.

- Change to smaller needles, reverse the direction of your knitting and work k2, p2 ribbing for 1½"/4 cm.

KNITTING THE HEEL FLAP

- Knit the next 22 stitches onto one needle for the heel flap. Evenly divide the remaining stitches onto the remaining 2 needles and keep them on holder for the instep stitches. Turn and work back and forth in rows as follows.

- **Row 1:** Slip 1 purlwise, purl to end of row.

- **Row 2:** Slip 1 knitwise, knit to end of row.

- Repeat Rows 1 and 2 until heel flap measures 1¼"/3 cm ending with Row 1.

SIZE AND FINISHED MEASUREMENTS
To fit 6–12 months: 4"/10 cm from heel to toe

YARN
Red Heart Heart & Sole, 70% superwash wool/30% nylon, 213 yds (195 m)/1.76 oz (50 g), Color 3115 Ivory (**1**)

NEEDLES
Set of four US 1 (2.25 mm) double-point needles and set of four US 2 (2.75 mm) double-point needles *or size needed to obtain correct gauge*

GAUGE
34 stitches and 44 rows = 4"/10 cm in stockinette stitch

OTHER SUPPLIES
Yarn needle

Pattern Essentials

LACY CUFF
(multiple of 11 stitches)

Round 1: *K2tog twice, (yo, k1) three times, yo, ssk twice; repeat from * to end of round.

Round 2: Purl.

Rounds 3 and 4: Knit.

Repeat Rounds 1–4 for pattern.

TURNING THE HEEL

Note: Slip all stitches purlwise.

- **Row 1:** Slip 1, k13, ssk, k1, turn. You will leave 5 unworked stitches.

- **Row 2:** Slip 1, p7, p2tog, p1, turn.

- **Row 3:** Slip 1, k8, ssk, k1, turn.

- **Row 4:** Slip 1, p9, p2tog, p1, turn.

- **Row 5:** Slip 1, k10, ssk, k1, turn.

- **Row 6:** Slip 1, p11, p2tog, p1, turn.

- **Row 7:** Slip 1, k12, ssk, turn.

- **Row 8:** Slip 1, p12, p2tog, turn.

- Knit the remaining 14 heel stitches.

- Round 2 (decrease round): Knit to last 3 stitches on Needle 1, k2tog, k1; on Needle 2, work in rib as established; on Needle 3, k1, ssk, knit to end of round.

- Repeat Rounds 1 and 2 three more times. *You now have* 44 stitches.

KNITTING THE FOOT

- Work even in patterns as established until foot measures 3¼"/8.5 cm.

Shaping the Toe

- Round 1: Knit to last 3 stitches on Needle 1, k2tog, k1; on Needle 2, k1, ssk, knit to last 3 stitches, k2tog, k1; on Needle 3, k1, ssk, knit to end of round. *You now have* 40 stitches.

- Round 2: Knit.

- Repeat Rounds 1 and 2 four more times. *You now have* 24 stitches.

- Work Round 1 twice more. *You now have* 16 stitches.

- Knit 4 stitches from Needle 1 onto Needle 3.

KNITTING THE GUSSETS

- With right side facing and using needle that holds heel stitches (Needle 1), pick up and knit (see page 281) 8 stitches along side of heel flap. Beginning with a p2, work 22 held instep stitches in pattern as established onto Needle 2. With Needle 4, pick up and knit 8 stitches down other side of heel flap, knit 7 heel stitches from Needle 1. The round begins at the center of the sole.

- *You now have* 52 stitches: 15 stitches each on Needles 1 and 3 and 22 stitches on Needle 2.

- Round 1: On Needle 1, knit; on Needle 2, work in rib as established; on Needle 3, knit.

FINISHING

- Use Kitchener stitch (see page 278) to graft the two sets of 8 stitches together. Weave in ends. Block. Fold lace cuff down over the rib section.

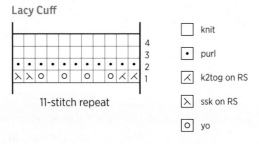

Lacy Cuff

11-stitch repeat

knit

• purl

╱ k2tog on RS

╲ ssk on RS

O yo

Little Ballerina Slippers

Designed by Grace Akhrem

These darling slippers are knit back-and-forth and circularly, all in one piece — no seams to sew! Simple I-cord laces crisscross up baby's legs and tie at the top.

....
SIZE AND FINISHED MEASUREMENTS
To fit 0–3 months: 3¼"/8.5 cm from heel to toe
....
YARN
Pagewood Farm Yukon, 70% superwash merino wool/20% bamboo/10% nylon, 450 yds (411 m)/4 oz (113 g), Color S16 Cotton Candy ❶
....
NEEDLES
Set of five US 2 (2.75 mm) double-point needles *or size needed to obtain correct gauge*
....
GAUGE
29 stitches and 36 rows = 4 inches/10 cm in stockinette stitch
....
OTHER SUPPLIES
1 locking stitch marker, yarn needle, 6 silk or rayon rosettes, sewing needle and coordinating thread

KNITTING THE SOLE (make 2)

- Cast on 10 stitches. Work back and forth on two needles as follows.

- **Rows 1, 3, and 5:** Slip 1 purlwise wyif, knit to end of row.

- **Row 2:** Slip 1 purlwise wyif, M1R, k to last stitch, M1L, k1. *You now have* 12 stitches.

- **Row 4:** Repeat Row 2. *You now have* 14 stitches.

- **Row 6:** Repeat Row 2. *You now have* 16 stitches.

- **Rows 7–34:** Slip 1 purlwise wyif, knit to end of row.

- **Row 35:** Slip 1 purlwise wyif, ssk, knit to last 3 stitches, k2tog, k1. *You now have* 14 stitches.

- **Row 36:** Repeat Row 1.

- **Row 37:** Repeat Row 35. *You now have* 12 stitches.

- **Row 38:** Repeat Row 1.
- **Row 39:** Repeat Row 35. *You now have 10 stitches.*
- **Row 40:** Slip 1 purlwise wyif, knit to end of row. Place marker, do not turn work.
- On needle 2, pick up and knit 19 stitches from long edge, on needle 3 pick up and knit 8 stitches from cast-on edge, on needle 4 pick up and knit 19 stitches from remaining long edge. *You now have 56 stitches.*

KNITTING THE FOOT

- Work in rounds as follows.
- **Rounds 1 and 3:** Purl.
- **Round 2:** Knit.
- **Rounds 4–8:** Knit.

The Instep

- Work back and forth as follows.
- **Row 1:** K9, ssk, turn.
- **Row 2:** Slip 1 purlwise wyif, k8, k2tog, turn.
- Repeat Row 2 fourteen more times. *You now have 40 stitches.*
- **Rows 3–4:** Slip 1 purlwise wyif, k8, k2tog, WT. (See WT, wrap and turn, on page 282.) *You will have 38 stitches at the end of Row 4.*

The Cuff

- Work in Rounds as follows.
- **Round 1:** Knit all stitches, picking up wraps and working them together with the stitch they wrap.
- **Round 2:** Purl.

- **Round 3:** Knit.
- **Round 4:** Purl.
- Bind off 21 stitches, k6, bind off 11 stitches. *You now have 6 stitches at the center back heel.*

KNITTING THE STRAPS

- Split the remaining stitches onto 2 needles, 3 stitches on each needle. Work 3-stitch I-cord (see page 277) on each set of stitches for 15"/38 cm or longer if desired. Bind off all stitches.

FINISHING

- Weave in all ends. Block the slippers to shape. Using needle and thread, sew one rosette to the end of each I-cord and at the top center of the instep.

Little

ACCESSORIES

Poseidon Mitts

Designed by Angela Myers

These fingerless mitts are knit in the round from the fingers to the cuff in an allover lace design. Sized for mom and toddler, you may go up in needle size and use the toddler pattern to accommodate a larger child. One mom and toddler set uses less than 2 ounces (57 grams) of fingering yarn.

SIZES AND FINISHED MEASUREMENTS
To fit Toddler (Mom): 5 (7)"/12.5 (18) cm circumference

YARN
Yarn Love Amy March Fingering, 100% superwash merino wool, 555 yds (507 m)/4 oz (113 g), Rosy Cheeks 1

NEEDLES
Set of five US 3 (3.25 mm) double-point needles *or size needed to obtain correct gauge*
Note: Try size US 4 (3.5 mm) for larger child

GAUGE
28 stitches and 30 rows = 4"/10 cm in stockinette stitch
32 stitches and 48 rounds = 4"/10 cm in lace pattern, relaxed

OTHER SUPPLIES
Scrap yarn for holders, yarn needle

Pattern Essentials

LACE
(multiple of 11 stitches)

Round 1: *K1, yo, k3, sk2p, k3, yo, k1; repeat from * to end of round.

Round 2 and all even-numbered rounds: Knit.

Round 3: *K2, yo, k2, sk2p, k2, yo, k2; repeat from * to end of round.

Round 5: *K3, yo, k1, sk2p, k1, yo, k3; repeat from * to end of round.

Round 7: *K4, yo, sk2p, yo, k4; repeat from * to end of round.

Round 8: Knit.

Repeat Rounds 1–8 for pattern.

KNITTING THE THUMB (make 2)

- Cast on 12 (16) stitches. Join into a round, being careful not to twist the stitches.

- **Rounds 1–4:** *K2, p2; repeat from * to end of round.

- Knit all rows until thumb measures 1 (1½)"/2.5 (4) cm

- Place stitches on scrap yarn to hold.

KNITTING THE HANDS

- Cast on 32 (44) stitches, Join into a round.

- **Rounds 1–4:** *K2, p2; repeat from * to end of round.

- Following the chart or written instructions, work Row 1 of Lace pattern, increasing 1 (0) stitch. *You now have* 33 (44) stitches. **Note:** Chart will be worked 3 (4) times in each round.

- Work Rounds 1–8 of Lace pattern 1 (2) times, then work Rounds 1–7 once more.

JOINING THE THUMBS

- Knit 9 hand stitches, place the next 4 stitches on hold; place the first 4 stitches of thumb on hold; pick up and knit (see page 281) 1 stitch on the right side of thumb, knit 1 thumb stitch, pm, knit 6 (10) thumb stitches, pm, knit 1 thumb stitch, pick up and knit 1 stitch from thumb; knit to end of round on hand. *You now have* 39 (54) stitches.

- Continue in pattern, beginning again with Round 1, as follows.

- **Odd-numbered rounds:** Work even in pattern to marker, sm, knit to next marker, sm, work even in pattern to end of round.

- **Rounds 2 and 6:** Knit to marker, sm, ssk, knit to two stitches before marker, k2tog, sm, knit to end of round.

- **Rounds 4 and 8:** Knit.

- Repeat rounds 1–8 for adult size only. *You now have* 2 stitches between markers.

- **Next round:** Work even in established pattern (round 1).

- **Next round:** Knit to one stitch before marker, remove marker, ssk, k2tog, removing marker, knit to end of round. *You now have* 33 (44) stitches.

KNITTING THE CUFFS

- Work Rounds 3–8 of pattern once, then Rounds 1–8 two (five) more times, working the pattern repeat 3 (4) times in each round, and decreasing 1 (0) stitch in the last round. *You now have* 32 (44) stitches.

- **Next 4 Rounds:** *K2, p2; repeat from * to end of round.

- Bind off loosely, or with your favorite stretchy bind off.

FINISHING

- Graft thumb stitches and held hand stitches. Close holes and weave in ends.

Lace Pattern

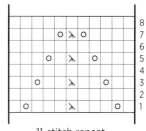

11-stitch repeat

- ☐ knit on RS
- ⊙ yo
- ⧄ k2tog
- ⧅ ssk
- ⧊ sk2p

Pop-Top Mittens

Designed by Joan Beebe, SSKnits

These fun convertible mittens are a quick knit and a great stash buster. Sizes are given for ages 2 through 10 years, but measure your child's hand before beginning. The palm circumference is most important, and places to customize are indicated in the instructions.

SIZES AND FINISHED MEASUREMENTS

To fit 2 (4, 6, 8, 10) years: 5¼ (5½, 6, 6½, 6¾)"/13.5 (14, 15, 16.5, 17) cm palm circumference
Sample shown is size 4 years

YARN

Malabrigo Rios, 100% superwash merino wool, 210 yds (192 m)/3.5 oz (100 g), Color 030 Purple Mystery (4)
Note: Smaller sizes can be made with a fifty-gram ball of many yarns.

NEEDLES

Set of four US 5 (3.75 mm) double-point needles and set of US 7 (4.5 mm) double-point needles *or size needed to obtain correct gauge*

GAUGE

20 stitches and 26 rounds = 4"/10 cm in stockinette stitch

OTHER SUPPLIES

Scrap yarn for stitch holders, markers, two ¾"/19 mm buttons (optional), sewing needle and coordinating thread (optional), crochet hook size G-6 (4 mm) (optional), yarn needle

KNITTING THE RIGHT MITTEN

The Cuff

- With larger needles, cast on 24 (26, 26, 28, 30) stitches. Divide evenly onto 3 needles and join into a round, being careful not to twist the stitches.
- Change to smaller needles.
- **Round 1:** *K1, p1; repeat from * to end of round.
- Repeat Round 1 until cuff measures 2 (2¼, 2½, 2½, 2¾)"/5 (5.5, 6.5, 6.5, 7) cm.

The Thumb Gusset

- Change to larger needles.
- **Round 1:** Knit, increasing 2 (2, 4, 4, 4) stitches evenly spaced. *You now have 26 (28, 30, 32, 34) stitches.*
- **Round 2:** Knit.
- **Round 3:** K12 (13, 14, 15, 16), pm, M1R, k2, M1L, pm, k12 (13, 14, 15, 16). *You now have 28 (30, 32, 34, 36) stitches.*
- **Round 4:** Knit.
- **Round 5:** Knit to marker, sm, M1R, knit to marker, M1L, sm, knit to end of round. *You now have 30 (32, 34, 36, 38) stitches.*
- Repeat these last 2 rounds 1 (1, 2, 2, 3) times. *You now have 32 (34, 38, 40, 44) stitches.*
- Work even in stockinette stitch until piece measures 3¼ (3¾, 4, 4¼, 4¾)"/8.5 (9.5, 10, 11, 12) cm from cast-on edge.

The Hand

- **Round 1:** Knit to 1 stitch before marker, M1R, k1, place next 8 (8, 10, 10, 12) stitches on holder, k1, M1L, knit to end of round. *You now have 26 (28, 30, 32, 34) stitches.*
- Knit 1 (2, 2, 2, 3) rounds.

* to marker, sm; with larger needles, knit to end of round.

- With larger needles, knit in the round until piece measures 4¾ (5¼, 6, 6, 7)"/12 (13.5, 15, 15, 18) cm from cast-on edge or ¾ (¾, ¾, 1, 1)"/2 (2, 2, 2.5, 2.5) cm less than desired finished length.

Shaping the Top

- **Round 1:** K1, ssk, k7 (8, 9, 10, 11), k2tog, k2, ssk, k7 (8, 9, 10, 11), k2tog, k1. *You now have 22 (24, 26, 28, 30) stitches.*

- **Round 2:** Knit.

- **Round 3:** K1, ssk, k5 (6, 7, 8, 9), k2tog, k2, ssk, k5 (6, 7, 8, 9), k2tog, k1. *You now have 18 (20, 22, 24, 26) stitches.*

- **Round 4:** Knit.

- **Round 5:** K1, ssk, k3 (4, 5, 6, 7), k2tog, k2, ssk, k3 (4, 5, 6, 7), k2tog, k1. *You now have 14 (16, 18, 20, 22) stitches.*

- *For sizes 8 and 10 only:*

- **Round 6:** Knit.

- **Round 7:** K1, ssk, k4 (5), k2tog, k2, ssk, k4 (5), k2tog, k1. *You now have 16 (18) stitches.*

- *For all sizes:* Slip first 7 (8, 9, 8, 9) stitches onto one needle and remaining stitches onto second needle. Graft the stitches together with Kitchener stitch (see page 278).

The Thumb

- With larger needles and RS facing, pick up and knit 1 stitch in the base before the held stitches, knit held stitches, pick up and knit 1 stitch in the base after the held stitches. *You now have 10 (10, 12, 12, 14) stitches.*

- Divide stitches evenly onto double-point needles.

- **Round 1:** Knit.

- **Round 2:** Ssk, knit to last 2 stitches, k2tog. *You now have 8 (8, 10, 10, 12) stitches.*

- Knit even until thumb measures 1¼ (1¼, 1½, 1¾, 2)"/3 (3, 4, 4.5, 5) cm or desired length.

- **Next Round:** P13 (14, 15, 16, 17), k13 (14, 15, 16, 17).

- Knit 2 (3, 4, 4, 5) rounds.

- Change to smaller needles.

- **Next Round:** *K1, p1; repeat from * to end of round.

- Repeat this round 3 more times.

- With larger needle, bind off in pattern.

The Pop Top

- With larger needle, cast on 13 (14, 15, 16, 17) stitches, pm; holding cuff toward you, pick up and knit (see page 281) 1 stitch in each upper loop of the purl ridge on the back of hand; pm, join into a round. *You now have 26 (28, 30, 32, 34) stitches.*

- **Rounds 1–4:** With smaller needles, k1 (0, 1, 0, 1), *p1, k1; repeat from

- **Last Round:** *K2tog; repeat from * to end of round. *You now have* 4 (4, 5, 5, 6) *stitches.*
- Cut yarn leaving a 6"/15 cm tail. Thread tail onto yarn needle, draw through remaining stitches, pull up snug, and fasten off.

KNITTING THE LEFT MITTEN

- Work as for Right Mitten through Knitting the Thumb Gusset.

The Hand

- **Round 1:** Knit to 1 stitch before marker, M1R, k1, place next 8 (8, 10, 10, 12) stitches on holder, k1, M1L, knit to end of round. *You now have* 26 (28, 30, 32, 34) stitches.
- Knit 1 (2, 2, 2, 3) rounds.
- **Next Round:** K13 (14, 15, 16, 17), p13 (14, 15, 16, 17).
- Knit 2 (3, 4, 4, 5) rounds.
- Change to smaller needles and complete as for Right Mitten.

FINISHING

- The button and button closure are optional and not recommended for children for whom this may pose a choking hazard.
- Fold pop top back and attach button to cuff where it meets the top.
- With crochet hook and RS of pop top facing and working in grafted row, join yarn with slip stitch 1 stitch right of center, chain 6, join with slip stitch 1 stitch left of center, fasten off.
- Weave in ends.

Katrina's Angora Mitts

Designed by Diana Foster

These warm and fuzzy mitts will make any young girl smile. Mitts are knit in the round and can be worked traditionally on four or five double-point needles, on two medium-length circular needles, or with Magic Loop technique on one long circular needle — knitter's choice.

SIZE AND FINISHED MEASUREMENTS
To fit 5-year-old: 5¾"/14.5 cm circumference, 5"/12.5 cm long

YARN
Schulana Angora Fashion, 80% angora/20% nylon, 122 yds (112 m)/0.88 oz (25 g), Color 1 White **(3)**

NEEDLES
Set of five US 5 (3.5 mm) double-point needles, US 5 (3.5 mm) circular needle 40"/100 cm long (for Magic Loop), or two US 5 (3.5 mm) circular needles 24"/60 cm long (knitting on two circulars) *or size needed to obtain correct gauge*

GAUGE
26 stitches and 36 rounds = 4"/10 cm in stockinette stitch

OTHER SUPPLIES
Stitch markers, stitch holder, yarn needle

SPECIAL ABBREVIATIONS
Tw2 (twist 2)
    Knit 2 stitches together and leave stitches on needle, knit the first stitch again, and drop both stitches from needle.

Pattern Essentials

TWISTED RIB
(multiple of 4 stitches)

Rounds 1–3: *K2, p2; repeat from * to end of round.

Round 4: *Tw2, p2; repeat from * to end of round.

Repeat Rounds 1 through 4 for pattern.

KNITTING THE MITTS (make 2)

- Loosely cast on 36 stitches. Place marker and join into a round, being careful not to twist the stitches.

- Work Rounds 1 through 4 of Twisted Rib pattern four times.

Making the Gusset

- **Round 1:** K18, pm, M1L, k1, M1R, pm, knit to end of round. *You now have 38 stitches.*

- **Round 2:** Knit.

- **Round 3:** Knit to marker, sm, M1R, knit to marker, M1L, sm, knit to end of round.

- **Round 4:** Knit.

- Repeat Rounds 3 and 4 until there are 13 stitches between the markers for the thumb.

- **Next Round:** Knit to marker, place 13 thumb stitches on hold, cast on 3 stitches, knit to end of round. *You now have 38 stitches.*

Finishing the Hand

- Work even in stockinette stitch for 2"/5 cm, decreasing 2 stitches evenly spaced on the last round. *You now have 36 stitches.*

- Work Rounds 1 through 4 of Twisted Rib pattern.

- Bind off in pattern.

The Thumb

- Place 13 held stitches on needles and pick up 1 stitch in each of the 3 cast-on stitches. *You now have 16 stitches. Join for working in the round.*

- Work Rounds 1 through 4 of Twisted Rib pattern.

- Bind off in pattern.

FINISHING

- Weave in ends.

Kitty Kat's Leg Warmers

Designed by Diana Foster

Your child will be stylish and warm while walking about with these colorful leg warmers. Knit from the bottom up in stockinette and reverse stockinette stitches, they are easy to make.

SIZE AND FINISHED MEASUREMENTS
To fit 4-6 years: 11"/28 cm long and 7"/18 cm around

YARN
Great Adirondack Bloomin' Colors, 100% Bluefaced Leicester, 210 yds (192 m)/3.5 oz (100 g), Color DL2 Rainbow (🧶3)

NEEDLES
Set of four or five US 5 (3.75 mm) double-point needles *or size needed to obtain correct gauge*

GAUGE
25 stitches and 32 rounds = 4"/10 cm in stockinette stitch

OTHER SUPPLIES
Stitch marker, yarn needle

KNITTING THE LEG WARMERS (make 2)

- Loosely cast on 34 stitches. Divide onto 3 needles and join into a round, being careful not to twist the stitches.

- Rounds 1–5: Knit.

- Round 6: *K1, p1; repeat from * to end of round.

- Repeat Round 6 until ribbing measures 1½"/4 cm, increasing 10 stitches evenly spaced on last round. *You now have* 44 stitches.

- Next 8 Rounds: Knit.

- Next 8 Rounds: Purl.

- Repeat these 16 rounds 4 more times.

- Work Round 6 for 1½"/4 cm.

- Bind off loosely in pattern.

- Weave in ends.

Snow Baby Leg Warmers

Designed by Gina House, Sleepy Eyes Knits

These super soft and cozy leg warmers are knit in the round from the bottom up. The ankle is ribbed for a snug fit, and the leg has a spiral pattern that finishes with lacy hearts and seed stitch at the top.

Pattern Essentials

SPIRAL RIBBING (multiple of 6 stitches)

Round 1: *P1, k3, p2; repeat from * to end of round.

Round 2: *P2, k3, p1; repeat from * to end of round.

Round 3: *P3, k3; repeat from * to end of round.

Round 4: *K1, p3, k2; repeat from * to end of round.

Round 5: *K2, p3, k1; repeat from * to end of round.

Round 6: *K3, p3; repeat from * to end of round.

Repeat Rounds 1–6 for pattern.

HEART LACE
(multiple of 7 stitches)

Round 1: *K1, k2tog, yo, k1, yo, ssk, k1; repeat from * to end of round.

Round 2: *K2tog, yo, k3, yo, ssk; repeat from * to end of round.

Round 3: *K1, yo, k2tog, yo, sk2p, yo, k1; repeat from * to end of round.

Round 4: *K1, yo, k2tog, k1, ssk, yo, k1; repeat from * to end of round.

Round 5: *K2, yo, sk2p, yo, k2; repeat from * to end of round.

Work Rounds 1–5 for pattern.

SEED STITCH
(odd number of stitches)

Round 1: *K1, p1; repeat from * to the last stitch, k1.

Round 2: *P1, k1; repeat from * to the last stitch, p1.

Repeat Rounds 1 and 2 for pattern.

SIZE AND FINISHED MEASUREMENTS
To fit 0–3 months: 6¾"/17 cm long and 7"/18 cm circumference at widest point

YARN
Elsebeth Lavold Cool Wool, 50% wool/50% cotton, 109 yds (100 m)/1.75 oz (50 g), 06 White ❨4❩

NEEDLES
Set of four US 5 (3.75 mm) double-point needles *or size needed to obtain correct gauge*

GAUGE
22 stitches and 32 rounds = 4"/10 cm in spiral rib stitch

OTHER SUPPLIES
Stitch markers, yarn needle

KNITTING THE LEG WARMERS (make 2)

- Cast on 30 stitches. Divide onto 3 double-point needles and join into a round, being careful not to twist the stitches.

- **Rounds 1–7:** *K3, p3; repeat from * to end of round.

- Following chart on next page or line-by-line instructions, work Rounds 1–6 of Spiral Ribbing pattern 6 times.

- **Next Round:** *K6, M1L; repeat from *
  to end of round. *You now have* 35 stitches.

- Following chart below or line-by-line instructions,
  work Rounds 1–5 of Heart Lace pattern.

- Work 4 rounds in Seed Stitch.

- Bind off loosely in pattern. Weave in ends.

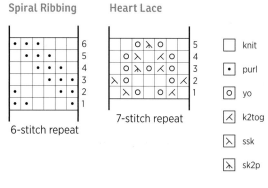

Spiral Ribbing

•	•	•				6
	•	•	•			5
		•	•	•		4
			•	•	•	3
•				•	•	2
•	•				•	1

6-stitch repeat

Heart Lace

	o	⅄	o			5
o		⅄		⅄	o	4
o		⅄	o	⅄	o	3
⅄	o			o	⅄	2
	⅄	o		o	⅄	1

7-stitch repeat

☐	knit
•	purl
o	yo
⅄	k2tog
⅄	ssk
⅄	sk2p

A Pair of Curly Headbands

Designed by Kirsten Avent,
Clickity Sticks

Cute headbands will dress up
your little girl's head for all
occasions. Quick to knit, so you
can make one in every color of
the rainbow.

Pattern Essentials

SEED STITCH
(odd number of stitches)

Row 1: *K1, p1, repeat from * to last stitch, k1.

Repeat Row 1 for pattern.

KNITTING THE CURLY CURLY HEADBAND

- Place slip knot on crochet hook, leaving the loop on the hook large (about the size of a nickel). This loop will serve as the center of the curls; do not tighten until directed to do so. *Ch 16, 3 sc in 2nd ch from hook, 3 sc in each ch across to loop, slip st in loop; repeat from * until you have 15 curls.

The Headband

- Pick up 4 stitches as follows: *Yarn over hook, insert hook into center loop and pull up a stitch, pass the yarnover over the pulled up stitch. Repeat from * 3 more times. *You now have* 5 stitches. Transfer the stitches to a knitting needle and pull the center loop tight.

- Work in Seed Stitch until band measures 1½"/4 cm less than desired finished length.

- Now work a buttonhole in the band as follows.

- **Row 1:** K2, bind off 1, knit to end.

- **Row 2:** K2, yo, k2.

- **Row 3:** K2, k1 tbl, k2.

- Bind off.

- Weave in ends. Pull the headband all the way through the headband hole.

FINISHED MEASUREMENTS
To fit 4–6 years: Curly Curly, 18"/45.5 cm circumference; Bow, 16"/40.5 cm circumference

YARN
Fibra Natura Mermaid, 42% cotton/35% superwash merino wool/12% silk/11% seacell, 125 yds (114 m)/1.75 oz (50 g), White (4)

NEEDLES
US 6 (4 mm) straight needles and US E-4 (3.5 mm) crochet hook *or size needed to obtain correct gauge*

GAUGE
20 stitches and 28 rows = 4"/10 cm in stockinette stitch

OTHER SUPPLIES
Yarn needle

KNITTING THE WINTERY BOW HEADBAND

- Place slip knot on crochet hook, leaving the loop large (about the size of a nickel). Do not tighten until directed to do so. Ch 20, 3 sc in 2nd ch from hook, 3 sc in each ch across, slip st in large loop.

- **Next Row:** (Yo, insert hook into large loop and pull up a stitch) two times. *You now have* 5 stitches.

- Transfer the stitches to a knitting needle and pull the center loop tight.

The Back of the Bow

- **Rows 1–8:** Work in Seed Stitch.

- **Rows 9 and 10:** *Kfb; repeat from * to end of row. *You now have* 20 stitches.

- **Row 11:** Slip 1, *k1, slip 1 wyif; repeat from * to last stitch, k1.

- Repeat Row 11 until piece measures 8"/20.5 cm.

- **Next 2 Rows:** *K2tog; repeat from * to end of row. *You now have* 5 stitches.

The Bow Band

- **Row 1:** Work in Seed Stitch.

- **Row 2:** *Kfb; repeat from * to end of row. *You now have* 10 stitches.

191

The Headband

- **Row 1:** Slip 1, *k1, slip 1 wyif; repeat from * to last stitch, k1.
- Repeat Row 1 until band is 1½"/4 cm less than desired finished length.
- Now work a buttonhole in the band as follows.
- **Row 1:** Slip 1, k2, bind off 4, k3.
- **Row 2:** Slip 1, k2, cast on 4 using the backward loop cast on method (see page 276), k3.
- **Row 3:** *K2tog; repeat from * to end of row. *You now have* 5 stitches.
- **Row 4:** K2tog, sk2p. *You now have* 2 stitches.
- **Row 5:** K2tog. *You now have* 1 stitch.
- Transfer the last stitch to the crochet hook. Ch 20, 3 sc in 2nd ch from hook, 3 sc in each ch across, slip st in last knit st. Fasten off leaving a 15"/38 cm tail.

Making the Bow

- Lay the bow piece flat with the headband to the right and the first curl on the left.
- Fold the left portion of the bow rectangle to the middle of the rectangle with bow back and first curl hanging down from the center of the bow rectangle.
- Fold the other side of the bow rectangle to meet in the middle, crossing the bow band over the bow back and down.
- Wrap the bow band down under, up around the center, and over the top of the bow into the original position.
- Pull the headband portion through the middle of the folded bottom right bow rectangle until the headband portion is all the way through.
- Pull second curl and the buttonhole through the knot on the back of the bow. Then grab the headband through the buttonhole and pull it through.
- Pull the first curl through the buttonhole and then pull it through the knot on the back of the bow. Weave in ends.

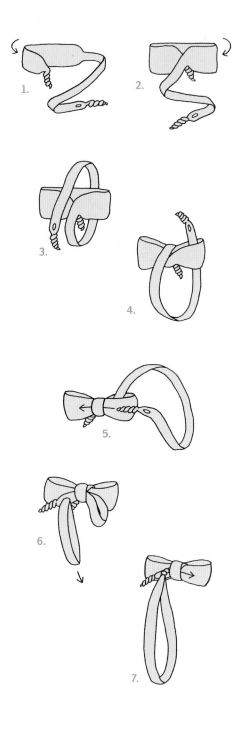

Lace Edged Baby Bibs

Designed by Faith Schmidt

These bibs make a great last-minute gift. Each bib begins with one of two easy-to-knit lace edgings. The remainder of the bib is in stockinette stitch, providing coverage where it's most needed. The straps are knitted with I-cord. You can knit two bibs from one 50-gram ball.

FINISHED MEASUREMENTS
Each bib is 7"/18 cm wide and 6½"/16.5 cm tall

YARN
Knit Picks Comfy Worsted, 75% pima cotton/25% acrylic, 109 yds (100 m)/1.75 oz (50 g), Color 8062 Silver Sage (4)

NEEDLES
US 7 (4.5 mm) straight and double-point needles *or size needed to obtain correct gauge*

GAUGE
18 stitches and 26 rows = 4"/10 cm in stockinette stitch

OTHER SUPPLIES
Stitch holder, yarn needle

Pattern Essentials

FEATHER AND FAN
(multiple of 12 + 8 stitches)

Row 1 (RS): Knit.

Row 2: K4, p to last 4 stitches, k4.

Row 3: K4, *(k2tog) twice, (yo, k1) 4 times, (k2tog) twice; repeat from * to last 4 stitches, k4.

Row 4: Knit.

Repeat Rows 1–4 of pattern.

WAVE LACE
(multiple of 12 + 9 stitches)

Row 1 (RS): K5, *(k2tog) twice, (yo, k1) 3 times, yo, (ssk) twice, k1; repeat from * to last 4 stitches, k4.

Row 2: K4, p to last 4 stitches, k4.

Repeat Rows 1–2 for pattern.

KNITTING THE FEATHER AND FAN BIB

- Cast on 32 stitches.
- Knit 4 rows (2 garter ridges).
- Work Rows 1–4 of Feather and Fan pattern 3 times.
- Keeping the first and last 4 stitches in garter stitch (knit every row), continue in stockinette stitch until piece measures 6"/15 cm at the longest point, ending with a WS row.
- Knit 4 rows (2 garter ridges).
- **Next Row (RS):** Ssk, k8, place these 9 stitches on a holder, bind off 12 stitches, knit to last 2 stitches, k2tog. *You now have* 9 stitches.
- Knit 1 row.

The Strap

- **Row 1 (RS):** Ssk, knit to last 2 stitches, k2tog. *You now have* 7 stitches.
- **Row 2:** Knit.

Feather and Fan

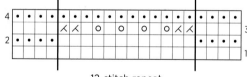

12-stitch repeat

Wave Lace

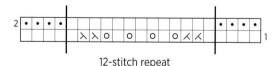

12-stitch repeat

☐ knit on RS, purl on WS

☐ yo

☐ k2tog

☐ ssk

☐ purl

- Repeat Rows 1 and 2 once, then work Row 1 once more. *You now have* 3 stitches.
- Work a 3 stitch I-cord (see page 277) for 10"/25.5 cm. On final row, k2tog, k1, then lift the 2nd stitch on the right hand needle over the 1st stitch and off the needle. Cut the yarn and pull it through the last stitch on the needle.
- Place stitches from holder onto a needle. Reattach yarn to the WS and knit 1 row.
- Repeat instructions for first strap.

Finishing

- Weave in ends and block lightly, if desired.

KNITTING THE WAVE BIB

- Cast on 33 stitches.
- Knit 4 rows (2 garter ridges).
- Work Rows 1 and 2 of Wave Lace pattern five times.
- Keeping the first and last 4 stitches in garter stitch (knit every row), continue in stockinette stitch until piece measures 6"/15 cm at the longest point, ending with a WS row.
- Knit 4 rows (2 garter ridges).
- **Next Row (RS):** Ssk, k8, place these 9 stitches on holder, bind off 13 stitches, knit to the last 2 stitches, k2tog. *You now have* 9 stitches.
- Knit 1 row.
- Work straps and finish as for Feather and Fan Bib.

Blue Sky Cotton Baby Bibs

Designed by Lynn M. Wilson, Lynn Wilson Designs

An easy-to-work bib in two sizes uses a slip-stitch pattern to create interesting texture and fluted edges. Great last-minute gift idea.

SIZES AND FINISHED MEASUREMENTS
To fit 3–6 (6–12) months: Each bib is 6½ (8)"/16.5 (20.5) cm wide and 6½ (7½)"/16.5 (19 cm) tall

YARN
Small Bib: Blue Sky Multi Cotton, 100% organic cotton, 100 yds (91 m)/2 oz (67 g), Color 6804 Limeade (4)
Large Bib: Blue Sky Cotton, 100% organic cotton, 150 yds (137 m)/3.5 oz (100 g), Color 627 Flamingo (4)

NEEDLES
US 8 (5 mm) straight needles and set of two US 8 (5 mm) double-point needles *or size needed to obtain correct gauge*

GAUGE
18 stitches = 4"/10 cm in pattern

OTHER SUPPLIES
Stitch holder, yarn needle

Pattern Essentials

SLIP-STITCH
(multiple of 6 stitches)

Rows 1, 3 and 5 (WS): K2, *slip 2 wyif, k4; repeat from * to last 4 stitches, slip 2 wyif, k2.

Rows 2 and 4: K2, slip 2 wyib, * k4, slip 2 wyib; repeat from * to last 2 stitches, k2.

Row 6: Knit.

Rows 7, 9 and 11: K5, *slip 2 wyif, k4; repeat from * to last stitch, k1.

Rows 8 and 10: K5, *slip 2 wyib, k4; repeat from * to last stitch, k1.

Row 12: Knit.

Repeat Rows 1–12 for pattern.

KNITTING THE BIB

- Cast on 24 (30) stitches.

- **Set-Up Row (RS):** Knit.

- **Row 1 (WS):** K2, slip 2 wyif, *k4, slip 2 wyif; repeat from * to last 2 stitches, k2.

- **Row 2:** K1, M1, k1, slip 2 wyib, *k4, slip 2 wyib; repeat from * to last 2 stitches, k1, M1, k1. *You now have 26 (32) stitches.*

- **Row 3:** K3, slip 2 wyif, *k4, slip 2 wyif; repeat from * to last 3 stitches, k3.

- **Row 4:** K1, M1, k2, slip 2 wyib, *k4, slip 2 wyib; repeat from * to last 3 stitches, k2, M1, k1. *You now have 28 (34) stitches.*

- **Row 5:** K4, slip 2 wyif, *k4, slip 2 wyif; repeat from * to last 4 stitches, k4.

- **Row 6:** K1, M1, knit to last stitch, M1, k1. *You now have 30 (36) stitches.*

- Work Rows 1 through 12 of Slip-Stitch pattern 4 (5) times, then work Rows 1 through 5 (11) once more.

Shaping the Neck

- **Next Row (RS):** K12 (15) stitches and place on holder; bind off next 6 stitches purlwise; knit to end of row.

- Work 12 (15) stitches in Right Neck Shaping chart for appropriate size.

- Slip remaining 3 stitches onto a double-point needle for Right Tie. Work 3-stitch I-cord (see page 277) until tie measures approximately 9 (10)"/23 (25.5) cm. Cut yarn and fasten off.

- Slip 12 (15) left neck stitches from holder onto needle. Rejoin yarn and work 12 (15) in Left Neck Shaping chart for appropriate size.

- Slip remaining 3 stitches onto a double-point needle and work tie as for Right Tie. Cut yarn and fasten off. Weave in ends.

Size Large, Left Neck Shaping

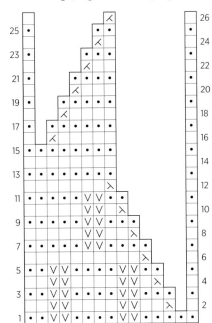

Size Large, Right Neck Shaping

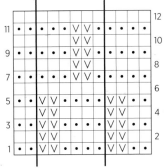

Slip-Stitch Pattern

6-stitch repeat

Size Small, Left Neck Shaping

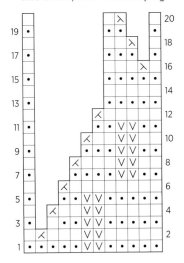

Size Small, Right Neck Shaping

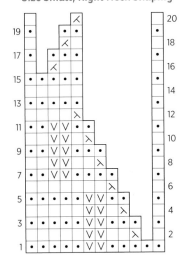

	knit on RS, purl on WS
•	p on RS, k on WS
⟋	k2tog
⟍	ssk
V	slip 1 pwise with yarn on WS

The Perfect Baby Bib

Designed by Debbie Haymark, iPurl

Designed in quality cotton, this over-the-head bib is perfect for a teething baby. Consider including a couple with every baby gift.

SIZES AND FINISHED MEASUREMENTS
To fit 6 (12) months: 7"/18 cm wide and 5½"/14 cm long
Note: The sizing difference is in the length of the strap

YARN
The Sassy Skein Karibbean Kotton Kollection, 100% mercerized cotton, 107 yds (98 m)/1.75 oz (50 g), Color 108 Island Waters, 112 Banana, or 130 Bubble Gum **(3)**

NEEDLES
US 5 (3.75 mm) and US 7 (4.5 mm) circular needles 12"/30 cm long *or size needed to obtain correct gauge*

GAUGE
24 stitches and 32 rows = 4"/10 cm in stockinette stitch on larger needle

OTHER SUPPLIES
Stitch marker, US 10 (6 mm) double-point needle for bind off, yarn needle

KNITTING THE BIB

The Strap

- With smaller needle, cast on 76 (80) stitches. Place marker and join into a round, being careful not to twist the stitches.
- Work k2, p2 ribbing for 1"/2.5 cm.
- Using a size 10 double-point needle, bind off 38 (40) stitches, slipping the last stitch back to the left needle. *You now have 38 (40) stitches.*

The Body

- Change to larger needle. You will now work back and forth in rows.
- Row 1 (RS): K5, pm, knit to last 5 stitches, pm, k5.
- Row 2: K5, purl to marker, k5.
- Repeat Rows 1 and 2 for 4"/10 cm.
- Knit in garter stitch (knit all rows) for 1"/2.5 cm, ending with a WS row.
- Bind off.
- Weave in ends.

Tutti Frutti Bib

Designed by Tonia Barry

This cute little bib is knit in stockinette stitch with pockets of garter stitch at the bottom. Have fun searching for the perfect button.

SIZE AND FINISHED MEASUREMENTS
To fit 0–9 months: 6½"/16.5 cm wide and 9"/23 cm long

YARN
Classic Elite Verde Collection Seedling, 100% organic cotton, 110 yds (100 m)/1.75 oz (50 g), Color HP 4526 Lava (4)

NEEDLES
US 7 (4.5 mm) straight needles *or size needed to obtain correct gauge*

GAUGE
20 stitches and 29 rows = 4"/10 cm in stockinette stitch

OTHER SUPPLIES
Stitch holder, yarn needle, 1"/25 mm button

KNITTING THE BIB

- Cast on 32 stitches.

The Tie

- Rows 1–8: Knit.
- Row 9 (RS): Knit 5 stitches and place them on hold, bind off 22 stitches, knit 5.
- Knit 9 rows on these 5 stitches.

The Body

- Row 1: K5, turn. Cast on 27 stitches for front neck using the cable cast on method (see page 276). *You now have 32 stitches.*
- Rows 2–4: Knit.
- Row 5 (WS): K3, p26, k3.
- Repeat Rows 4 and 5 until piece measures 9"/23 cm from neck cast on, ending with a WS row.

The Pocket

- **Next Row (RS):** *K4, m1; repeat from * to last 4 stitches, k4. *You now have 39 stitches.*
- Work even in garter stitch (knit every row) for 2"/5 cm, ending with a RS row.
- Bind off using the 3-stitch I-cord bind off method (see page 277).

The Button Strap

- With wrong side facing, knit 5 stitches from holder. Knit 14 rows.
- **Next row (buttonhole row):** K2, yo, k2tog, k1.
- Knit 5 rows. Bind off.

FINISHING

- With RS facing, fold pocket at increase row, sew center of pocket through pocket and bib. Sew side seams of each pocket, allowing pocket to puff. Sew button to upper corner of bib. Weave in ends. Block to measurements.

Little

Blankets

Tuck Me In

Designed by Reyna Thera Lorele, YIYO Designs

Closely woven blanket stitch ensures that tiny fingers and toes don't get tangled up. The cozy, quilt-like texture of this blanket fits the bill perfectly. This is an easy pattern that even a confident beginner can knit.

FINISHED MEASUREMENTS
Approximately 19" x 21"/48 x 53.5 cm

YARN
James C. Brett Marble Chunky, 100% acrylic, 341 yds (312 m)/7.3 oz (200 g), Color MC17 Pink (5)

NEEDLES
US 10 (6 mm) circular needle 24"/60 cm long *or size needed to obtain correct gauge*

GAUGE
13 stitches and 25 rows = 4"/10 cm in pattern

OTHER SUPPLIES
Yarn needle

Pattern Essentials

Tuck Wyib, insert right needle through the center of the stitch 2 rows below the next stitch; knit the stitch by pulling a loop through to the front and dropping the stitch above from the needle.

BLANKET STITCH
(multiple of 4 plus 3)

Row 1 (RS): Purl.

Row 2 and all even-numbered WS rows: Knit.

Row 3: *P3, tuck; repeat from * to last 3 stitches, p3.

Row 5: Purl.

Row 7: P1, *tuck, p3; repeat from * to last 2 stitches, tuck, p1.

Row 8: Knit.

Repeat Rows 1 through 8 for pattern.

KNITTING THE BLANKET

- Cast on 65 stitches. Knit 4 rows.

- Knitting the first 3 and last 3 stitches of every row to form a garter stitch border, work Rows 1 through 8 of Blanket Stitch pattern over center 59 stitches until blanket is desired length (20½"/52 cm).

- Knit 4 rows.

- Bind off. Weave in ends. Block.

Falling Leaves Baby Blankie

Designed by Myrna A.I. Stahman, Rocking Chair Press

This "blankie," knit circularly from the center out using a simple eight-round lace leaf motif, is just the right size for cuddling and rocking a baby.

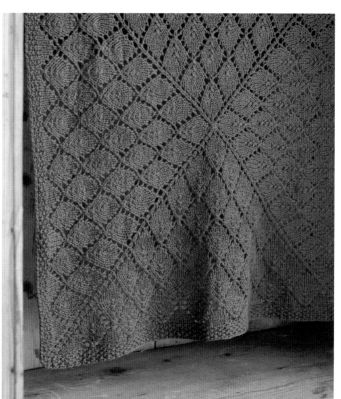

Blanket Stitch

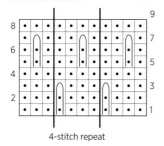

4-stitch repeat

knit

• p on RS, k on WS

tuck stitch

Pattern Essentials

SEED STITCH
(in the round; odd number of stitches)

Follow the chart for Seed Stitch on the next page, working the repeat to the next corner marker.

FINISHED MEASUREMENTS
Approximately 25"/63.5 cm square

YARN
Imperial Stock Ranch Tracie Too, 100% wool, 395 yds (361 m)/4 oz (113 g), Color 341 Sweet Plum **2**

NEEDLES
Set of five US 2.5 (3 mm) double-point needles and US 2.5 (3 mm) circular needle 24"/60 cm long *or size needed to obtain correct gauge*

GAUGE
19 stitches and 24 rows = 4"/10 cm in lace pattern, washed and blocked

OTHER SUPPLIES
Stitch markers, yarn needle

KNITTING THE BLANKET

- With double-point needles and using the cast on and divide circular cast on method (see page 276), cast on 8 stitches. Divide stitches evenly onto 4 double-point needles and join into a round, being careful not to twist the stitches.

- Work Rounds 1a through 8e (because even rounds are not charted, 8e does not show on chart, but it's the all-knit round following 7e) of the chart, repeating the chart four times in each round (once on each needle); change to a circular needle when you have enough stitches, placing a marker at the end of each of the four sections. **Note:** Only odd-numbered rounds are charted; knit all even-numbered rounds.

- Work four more 8-round pattern repeats, adding an additional building block for each additional repeat.

KNITTING THE BORDER

- **Round 1:** *Yo, work in seed stitch to last st before marker, yo, k1; repeat from * to end of round.

- **Round 2:** *Work in established seed stitch pattern to last st before marker, k1; repeat from * to end of round.

- Repeat Rounds 1 and 2 twice more.

- Bind off.

FINISHING

- Weave in all ends. Block.

Falling Leaves Pattern

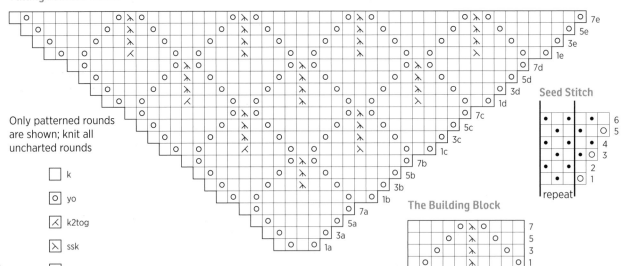

Only patterned rounds are shown; knit all uncharted rounds

☐ k

ⓞ yo

⊠ k2tog

⊠ ssk

⊠ sk2p

• purl

Only patterned rounds are shown; knit all uncharted rounds

Four-Squared Stroller Blanket

Designed by Liz Nields

Simple garter stitch squares are joined together as you knit to create this handy stroller blanket. The blanket has sixteen squares and a garter stitch edge that is picked up and knit when the squares are completed. If you choose a yarn with a long color-change length, you'll produce different colored squares.

FINISHED MEASUREMENTS
19¾"/50 cm square

YARN
Cascade Pinwheel, 100% acrylic, 440 yds (400 m)/ 7 oz (200 g), Color 10 (4)

NEEDLES
US 8 (5 mm) straight needles and US 8 (5 mm) circular needle 40"/100 cm long *or size needed to obtain correct gauge*

GAUGE
17 stitches and 34 rows = 4"/10 cm in garter stitch

OTHER SUPPLIES
Stitch marker, scrap yarn or double-point needles with stoppers for stitch holders, yarn needle

KNITTING THE BLANKET

Square 1

- Cast on 20 stitches. Knit every row for 38 rows. Place a marker on square 1: it will help to mark your place as you progress.

- Place stitches on hold.

- Pick up and knit (see page 281) 20 stitches along left edge of square 1.

Square 2

- Knit every row for 38 rows, ending with a RS row. Place stitches on hold. Pick up and knit 20 stitches along left edge of square 2.

Square 3

- Knit every row for 38 rows, ending with a RS row. Place stitches on hold. Pick up and knit 20 stitches along left edge of square 3.

Square 4

- Knit 1 stitch from cast on edge of square 1, pass 2nd stitch on right needle over 1st stitch and off the needle. Turn.
- Next Row (WS): Slip 1 purlwise, knit to end of row.
- Next Row (RS): K19, slip 1, pick up 1 from cast on edge, psso. Turn.
- Repeat these 2 rows until all cast-on stitches have been joined, ending with a RS row. Place stitches on hold. Pick up and knit 20 stitches along right edge of square 1.

Square 5

- Knit every row for 38 rows, ending with a RS row. Place stitches on hold. Pick up and knit 20 stitches along left edge of square 5.

Square 6

- Knit every row for 38 rows, ending with a RS row. Place stitches on hold. Pick up and knit 20 stitches along left edge of square 6.

Square 7

- Knit 1 held stitch from square 1, pass 2nd stitch over 1st stitch and off the needle. Turn.
- Next Row (WS): Slip 1 purlwise, knit to end of row.
- Next Row (RS): Knit 19, slip 1, knit 1 from holder, psso. Turn.
- Repeat these 2 rows until all held stitches are worked, ending with a RS joining row. Knit 2 rows. Pick up and knit 20 stitches along right edge of square 2. Turn.

Square 8

- Next Row (WS): Knit 19, slip 1, knit 1 from holder, psso. Turn.
- Next Row (RS): Slip 2 purlwise, knit to end of row.
- Repeat these 2 rows until all held stitches are worked.
- Knit 1 row. Place all stitches on hold. Pick up and knit 20 stitches along left edge of square 8.

Square 9

- Knit every row for 38 rows, ending with a RS row. Place all stitches on hold. Pick up and knit 20 stitches along left edge of square 9.

Square 10

- Knit 1 held stitch from square 2, pass 2nd stitch over 1st stitch and off the needle. Turn.
- Next Row (WS): Slip 1 purlwise, knit to end of row.
- Next Row (RS): Knit 19, slip 1, knit 1 from holder, psso. Turn.
- Repeat these last 2 rows until all held stitches are worked, ending with a RS row. Place first 19 stitches on hold. Pick up 1 and knit 1 stitch from left edge of square 3, pass 2nd stitch over 1st stitch.
- Pick up and knit 19 stitches along left edge of square 3. Turn.

Square 11

- Next Row (WS): Knit 19, slip 1, knit 1 held stitch from square 10, psso. Turn.
- Next Row (RS): Slip 1 purlwise, knit to end of row. Turn.
- Repeat these 2 rows until all held stitches are worked, ending with a RS row. Place stitches on hold. Pick up 20 stitches along left edge of square 11.

Square 12

- Knit every row for 38 rows, ending with a RS row. Place stitches on hold. Pick up and knit 20 stitches along left edge of square 12.

Square 13

- **Next Row (WS):** Knit.

- **Next Row (RS):** Knit 19, slip 1, knit 1 held stitch from square 3, psso. Turn.

- Repeat these 2 rows until all held stitches have been worked, ending with a RS row. Place first 19 sts on hold. Pick up and knit 1 stitch from right edge of square 4, pass 2nd stitch over 1st stitch. Pick up and knit 19 more stitches along the right edge of square 4.

Square 14

- **Next Row (WS):** Knit 19, slip 1, knit 1 held stitch from square 13, psso. Turn.

- **Next Row (RS):** Slip 1 purlwise, knit to end of row. Turn.

- Repeat these 2 rows until all held stitches are worked, ending with a RS row. Place stitches on hold. Pick up and knit 20 stitches along left edge of square 14.

- Turn.

Square 15

- Knit 38 rows. Place stitches on hold. Pick up and knit 20 stitches along left edge of square 15, knit 1 held stitch from square 4, pass 2nd stitch over 1st stitch. Turn.

Square 16

- **Next Row (WS):** Slip 1 purlwise, knit to end of row.

- **Next Row (RS):** Knit 19, slip 1, knit 1 held stitch from square 4, psso. Turn. Repeat these 2 rows until all stitches have been worked. Bind off while working last RS row.

- Sew bound off edge of square 16 to right edge of square 5.

The Border

- Beginning in center of any side, knit across held stitches, pick up 20 stitches from next square, pm, pick up 1 stitch in corner, pm, work across next side by knitting across held stitches and picking up 20 stitches from sides of square, placing markers to indicate corner stitches. When all sides have been worked, place a marker to indicate beginning of round. *You now have* 164 stitches, 40 stitches on each side and 4 corner stitches.

- **Next Round:** Purl, slipping markers as you go.

- **Next Round:** *Knit to 1 stitch before corner marker, kfb, k1, sm, kfb; repeat from * to end of round.

- Repeat these 2 rounds 2 times more. Knit 1 round. Bind off next round purlwise.

Finishing

- Weave in ends and block.

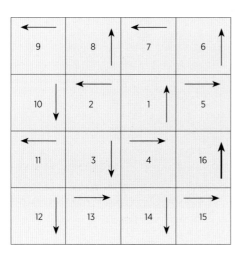

Colorful Carriage Blanket

Designed by Gwen Steege

Multicolor yarns are ideal for working small motifs. It's a constant surprise and delight to watch the colors for the motifs develop, with anywhere from none to three-color shifts in each.

FINISHED MEASUREMENTS
26½"/67.5 cm across; each motif measures 3¾"/9.5 cm

YARN
Wisdom Yarns Poems Socks, 75% superwash wool/25% nylon, 459 yds (420 m)/3.5 oz (100g), Color 963 Girly Girl 1

NEEDLES
Set of four US 3 (3.25 mm) double-point needles *or size needed to obtain correct gauge*

GAUGE
28 stitches = 4"/10 cm in stockinette stitch

OTHER SUPPLIES
Size G-6 (4 mm) crochet hook, yarn needle

KNITTING THE MOTIFS
(make 37)

- Cast on 72 stitches. Divide stitches evenly onto three double-point needles (24 stitches on each needle). Join into a round, being careful not to twist the stitches.

- Round 1: *K3, yo, s2kp twice, yo, k3; repeat from * to end of round. *You now have* 60 stitches; 20 on each needle.

- Round 2: Knit.

- **Round 3:** *K2, yo, s2kp twice, yo, k2; repeat from * to end of round. *You now have* 48 stitches; 16 on each needle.

- **Rounds 4–6:** Knit.

- **Round 7:** *K1, yo, s2kp twice, yo, k1; repeat from * to end of round. *You now have* 36 stitches; 12 on each needle.

- **Round 8:** Knit.

- **Round 9:** *Ssk, k2, k2tog; repeat from * to end of round. *You now have* 24 stitches; 8 on each needle.

- **Round 10:** Knit.

- **Round 11:** *Ssk, k2tog; repeat from * to end of round. *You now have* 12 stitches; 4 on each needle.

- **Round 12:** Knit.

- **Round 13:** Repeat round 11. *You now have* 6 stitches; 2 on each needle.

- Cut yarn, leaving a 6"/15 cm tail. Thread the tail through a yarn needle, draw through remaining stitches, pull up snug, and fasten off. Weave in end.

FINISHING AND ASSEMBLY

- Wet-block all of the motifs, pulling them into hexagon shapes that are 3¾"/9.5 cm across. To encourage six straight edges, place a pin at each corner and another pin in the middle of each side. Allow to dry thoroughly.

- Arrange the motifs according to the assembly diagram, arranging the colors in whatever way you find most pleasing.

- Using project yarn and mattress stitch (see page 281), sew the motifs together along their edges.

- To finish the outer edge, work single crochet (see page 282) all the way around.

Motif

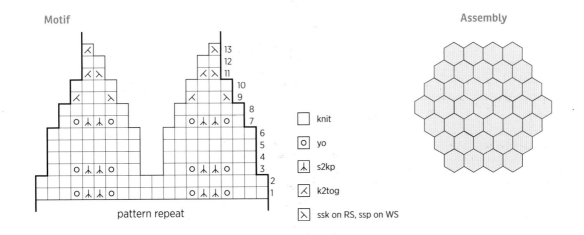

pattern repeat

	knit
O	yo
人	s2kp
人	k2tog
人	ssk on RS, ssp on WS

Assembly

Betula Baby Blanket

Designed by Marina Orry

Betula is a circular baby blanket knit in stockinette stitch with a touch of lace. No purling! The instructions include an innovative bind off using a needle and a hook.

FINISHED MEASUREMENTS
36"/91.5 cm diameter

YARN
Cascade Yarns Eco+, 100% Peruvian Highland wool, 478 yds (437 m)/8.8 oz (250 g), Color 8776 Peony Pink (5)

NEEDLES
7 mm circular and double-point needles *or size needed to obtain correct gauge*

GAUGE
11 stitches and 9 rows = 4"/10 cm in stockinette stitch, blocked

OTHER SUPPLIES
H-8 (5 mm) crochet hook, stitch marker

KNITTING THE BLANKET

- Using double-point needles and the crochet circular cast on (see page 276), cast on 7 stitches. Place marker and join into a round, being careful not to twist the stitches. Knit 1 round.

- Work Rounds 1–87 of the Betula Repeat chart, working the repeat 7 times per round.

- Knit 1 round (Round 88).

- Bind off with crochet hook as follows:

- **Next Round:** *Insert the hook through the next 3 loops on needle and make 1 slip stitch, chain 7; repeat from * to end of round, slip stitch in first slip stitch of round.

- Fasten off. Weave in ends and block.

Betula Repeat

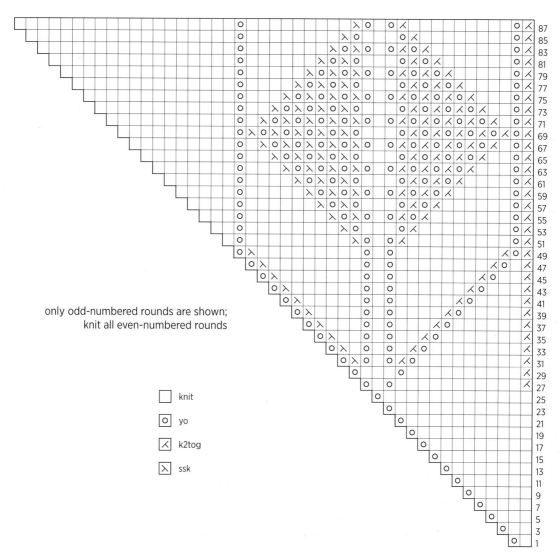

only odd-numbered rounds are shown;
knit all even-numbered rounds

- ☐ knit
- ⊙ yo
- ⟋ k2tog
- ⟍ ssk

Monarch Blanket

Designed by Kim Whelan

A super-sized skein of merino wool becomes a warm and lovely blanket when knit in an easily memorized lace pattern. Use this in the crib, in the stroller, or in the car seat. And machine wash as necessary.

FINISHED MEASUREMENTS
Approximately 28"/71 cm wide, 24"/ 61 cm long

YARN
Miss Babs Yowza! Whatta Skein!, 100% superwash merino wool, 560 yds (512 m)/8 oz (227 g), Dark Oyster

NEEDLES
US 6 (4 mm) circular needle 32"/80 cm long *or size needed to obtain correct gauge*

GAUGE
21 stitches and 28 rows = 4"/10 cm in pattern, blocked

OTHER SUPPLIES
Stitch markers, yarn needle

Pattern Essentials

MONARCH LACE
(multiple of 8 + 7 stitches)

Row 1: K1, *k2tog, yo, k1, yo, skp, k3; repeat from * to last 6 stitches, k2tog, yo, k1, yo, skp, k1.

Row 2: P3, *slip 1, p7; repeat from * to last 4 stitches, slip 1, p3.

Row 3: Repeat Row 1.

Row 4: Repeat Row 2.

Row 5: K5, *k2tog, yo, k1, yo, skp, k3; repeat from * to last 2 stitches, k2.

Row 6: P7, *slip 1, p7; repeat from * to end of row.

Row 7: Repeat Row 5.

Row 8: Repeat Row 6.

Repeat Rows 1–8 for pattern.

KNITTING THE BLANKET

- Cast on 147 stitches, placing a marker after the first 10 stitches and before the last 10 stitches.

The Beginning Border

- Rows 1–16: Knit.

The Body

- Keeping the first and last 10 stitches in garter stitch (knit every row), follow the chart or written instructions to work Rows 1 through 8 of lace pattern between the markers until piece measures approximately 21½/54.5 cm, ending with Row 8.

The Ending Border

- Rows 1–16: Knit.

FINISHING

- Bind off loosely and block, stretching slightly to open the lace pattern.

Monarch Lace

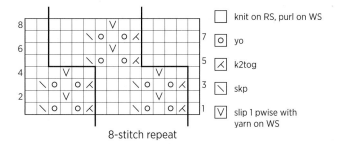

	knit on RS, purl on WS
o	yo
⃭	k2tog
⃮	skp
V	slip 1 pwise with yarn on WS

8-stitch repeat

Tips for Knitting Baby Blankets

Blankets can be used for warmth, for shade, as play or sleep mats, or simply for decoration. They can be used in a stroller, in a car seat, in a crib, or on the floor. Consider the intended use when choosing fiber, weight, and even stitch pattern. A wool blanket is warm, while a cotton blanket can shade the sun and not overheat baby. A heavier weight yarn and waffle-knit pattern may be ideal as a play mat. In any event, the smallest useful size is approximately 24 by 30 inches (61 by 76 cm), which would be fine for a newborn welcome blanket.

Roses and Butterflies Baby Blanket

Designed by Gwen Steege

Pattern rows of butterfly stitch alternate with a simple lace motif that forms a small rosebud. Blocking reveals the interesting butterflies in the midst of a bold lace. The Cascade yarn is not machine-washable, so it must be hand washed.

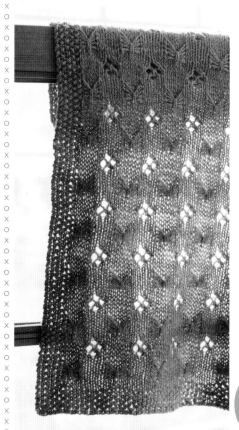

FINISHED MEASUREMENTS

28 x 27"/71 x 68.5 cm

YARN

Cascade Yarns Eco+, 100% Peruvian Highland Wool, 478 yds (437 m)/8.75 oz (250 g), Color 9452 Summer Sky Heather **(5)**

NEEDLES

US 10 (6 mm) circular or straight needles *or size you need to obtain correct gauge*

GAUGE

15 stitches and 18 rows = 4"/10 cm in Butterfly Stitch/Rosebud Pattern

OTHER SUPPLIES

Stitch markers, yarn needle

Pattern Essentials

SEED STITCH (multiple of 2 stitches)

Row 1: * K1, p1; repeat from to end of row.

Repeat Row 1 for pattern.

BUTTERFLY STITCH (multiple of 10 + 5 stitches)

Row 1 (RS): *Slip 5 with yarn in front, k5; repeat from * to last 5 stitches, slip 5 with yarn in front.

Row 2: Purl.

Rows 3–8: Repeat rows 1 and 2.

Row 9: Repeat row 1.

Row 10 (WS): *(P2, insert right-hand needle under the 5 loose strands, lift the strands onto the left-hand needle, and purl them together with the first stitch on the left needle), p7; repeat from * to end of row, ending last repeat p2.

ROSEBUD STITCH (multiple of 10 + 5 stitches)

Row 1 (RS): K5, * k2, yo, ssk, k1; repeat from * to last 5 stitches, k5.

Rows 2 and 4: Purl.

Row 3: K5, * k2tog, yo, k1, yo, ssk; repeat from * to last 5 stitches, k5.

Row 5: K5, * k2, yo, ssk, k1; repeat from * to last 5 stitches, k5.

Row 6: Purl.

KNITTING THE BLANKET

- Cast on 105 stitches. Work Seed Stitch border for 1½"/4 cm.

- **Set-Up Row 1 (RS):** Work in Seed Stitch as established over 5 stitches, pm, knit to last 5 stitches, pm, work in Seed Stitch as established to end of row.

- **Set-Up Row 2:** Work in Seed Stitch as established to marker, purl to next marker, work in Seed Stitch as established to end of row.

- **Rows 1–10:** Maintaining 5 border stitches at each edge in Seed Stitch throughout, work Rows 1–10 of Butterfly Stitch pattern between markers.

- **Rows 11–16:** Work Rows 1–6 of Rosebud Stitch pattern between markers.

- Repeat Rows 1–16 eight more times, then work Rows 1-10 once more.
- **Next Row:** Knit.
- **Next Row:** Purl.
- Work in Seed Stitch for 1½"/4 cm. Bind off. Weave in ends. Wet block.

Rosebud Stitch

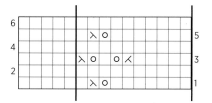

10-stitch repeat

Butterfly Stitch

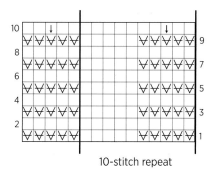

10-stitch repeat

	knit on RS, purl on WS
o	yo
⟋	k2tog
⟍	ssk
⩔	slip 1 pwise with yarn on RS
↓	gather 5 loose strands and purl the together with stitch

Hudson River Fog Blanket

Designed by Gwen Steege

This lightweight blanket would be an ideal gift for a summer baby. The pattern is based on both lace and ribbed motifs. Don't be alarmed if it seems rather narrow when you're knitting. Blocking will stretch and smooth the blanket, revealing its lacy pattern. Even blocked, however, it remains stretchy, a plus when you're wrapping it around the baby.

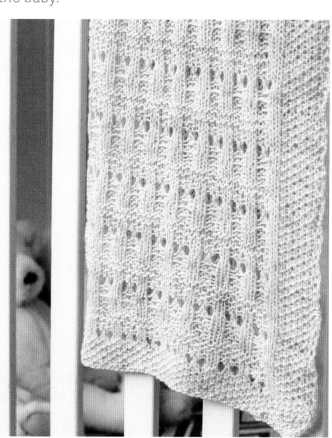

FINISHED MEASUREMENTS

19½ x 27"/49.5 x 68.5 cm

YARN

Madelinetosh Tosh Merino Light, 100% superwash merino wool, 420 yds (384 m)/3.5 oz (100 g), Seasalt 1

NEEDLES

US 7 (4.5 mm) straight or circular needles *or size needed to obtain correct gauge*

GAUGE

20 stitches and 30 rows = 4"/10 cm in pattern stitch, blocked

OTHER SUPPLIES

Yarn needle

KNITTING THE BLANKET

- Cast on 94 stitches. Work in Seed Stitch for 1¼"/3 cm, ending with a WS row.

- **Row 1:** Work in Seed Stitch as established over 7 stitches, pm, work Row 1 of Lacy Rib to last 7 stitches, pm, work in Seed Stitch as established to end of row.

- Maintaining the 7-stitch Seed Stitch border on each edge, continue in Lacy Rib Stitch pattern until 15 full repeats are complete, then work Rows 1–4 once more.

- Work in Seed Stitch for 1¼"/3 cm. Bind off loosely in pattern.

FINISHING

- Weave in any loose ends.

- Wet block, preferably using blocking wires.

Pattern Essentials

SEED STITCH
(even number of stitches)

Row 1: *K1, p1; repeat from to end of row.

Repeat Row 1 for pattern.

LACY RIB (multiple of 5 stitches)

Row 1 (RS): *P1, k1, slip 1 wyib, k1, p1; repeat from * to end of row.

Row 2: *K1, p3, k1; repeat from * to end of row.

Row 3: *P1, yo, s2kp, yo, p1; repeat from * to end of row.

Row 4: Repeat Row 2.

Row 5: Repeat Row 1.

Row 6: Repeat Row 2.

Row 7: *P1, slip 3 wyib, p1; repeat from * to end of row.

Row 8: Repeat Row 2.

Row 9: Repeat Row 1.

Row 10: Repeat Row 2.

Row 11: *K2, slip 1 wyib, k2; repeat from * to end of row.

Row 12: *K2, p1, k2; repeat from * to end of row.

Row 13: Repeat row 11.

Row 14: Repeat Row 12.

Repeat Rows 1–14 for pattern.

Lacy Rib

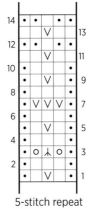

5-stitch repeat

knit on RS, purl on WS

• purl on RS, knit on WS

O yo

V slip 1 pwise with yarn on WS

⅄ s2kp

A Pair of Penguins

Designed by Stana D. Sortor

What child will be able to resist loving this adorable pair of penguins? Knit in the round in stockinette stitch, they require a bit of contrasting scrap yarn for the beaks. This project used only a fraction of the large skein specified; you could knit a whole flock with the rest of the skein.

FINISHED MEASUREMENTS
Approximately 9½"/24 cm circumference and 5"/12.5 cm tall

YARN
Bernat Softee Baby, 100% acrylic, 310 yds (283 m)/4.25 oz (120 g), Color 31201 Prince Pebbles (3)

NEEDLES
Set of four US 3 (3.25 mm) double-point needles *or size needed to obtain correct gauge*

GAUGE
19 stitches and 29 rows = 4"/10 cm in stockinette stitch

OTHER SUPPLIES
Four safety eyes, polyester fiberfill, 5 yds/4.5 m of peach-colored yarn for beak, stitch marker, yarn needle

KNITTING THE PENGUINS (make 2)

- You'll knit the beak first, then the body and head, and finally the wings.

The Beak

- With the peach-colored yarn, cast on 6 stitches. Place 2 stitches on each of 3 double-point needles. Place a marker and join into a round, being careful not to twist the stitches.

- **Round 1 and 2:** Knit.

- **Round 3:** *Ssk; repeat from * to end of round. *You now have 3 stitches.*

- **Round 4:** Knit.

- Cut yarn and thread tail onto yarn needle; draw through remaining stitches, pull up snug, and fasten off.

The Body

- Cast on 6 stitches leaving a 6"/15 cm tail. Place 2 stitches on each of 3 needles. Place a marker and join into a round, being careful not to twist the stitches.

- Round 1: Knit.

- Round 2: *Kfb; repeat from * to end of round. *You now have* 12 stitches.

- Round 3: Knit.

- Round 4: *Kfb; repeat from * to end of round. *You now have* 24 stitches.

- Round 5: Knit.

- Round 6: *Kfb, k1; repeat from * to end of round. *You now have* 36 stitches.

- Round 7: Knit.

- Round 8: *Kfb, k2; repeat from * to end of round. *You now have* 48 stitches.

- Rounds 9–22: Knit.

- Round 23: *Ssk, k6; repeat from * to end of round. *You now have* 42 stitches.

- Rounds 24–26: Knit.

- Round 27: *Ssk, k5; repeat from * to end of round. *You now have* 36 stitches.

- Rounds 28–30: Knit.

- Round 31: *Ssk, k4; repeat from * to end of round. *You now have* 30 stitches.

- Rounds 32–34: Knit.

- Round 35: *Ssk, k1; repeat from * to end of round. *You now have* 20 stitches.

- Thread the tail from cast on onto yarn needle. Draw through all cast-on stitches, pull up snug, and fasten off. Weave in end. Begin filling the body with stuffing.

- Rounds 36–43: Knit.

- Round 44: *Ssk, k2; repeat from * to end of round. *You now have* 15 stitches.

- Round 45: Knit.

- Round 46: *Ssk, k1; repeat from * to end of round. *You now have* 10 stitches.

- Round 47: Knit.

- Using the photo as a guide, attach safety eyes to "face" approximately 1"/2.5 cm down from last row and ½"/13 mm apart. Sew the beak below the eyes.

- Finish stuffing body. Cut yarn, leaving a 6"/15 cm tail. Thread tail onto yarn needle and draw through remaining stitches. Pull up snug and fasten off.

The Wings (make 2)

- Cast on 10 stitches leaving a 10"/25.5 cm tail and place 5 stitches on each of 2 double-point needles. Place a marker on the first stitch and join to knit in the round.

- Round 1: Knit.

- Round 2: *Kfb, k4; repeat from * to end of round. *You now have* 12 stitches.

- Round 3: Knit.

- Round 4: *Kfb, k5; repeat from * to end of round. *You now have* 14 stitches.

- Round 5: Knit.

- Round 6: *Kfb, k6; repeat from * to end of round. *You now have* 16 stitches.

- Round 7: Knit.

- Round 8: *Kfb, k7; repeat from * to end of round. *You now have* 18 stitches.

- Round 9: Knit.

- Round 10: *Kfb, k8; repeat from * to end of round. *You now have* 20 stitches.

- Round 11: *Kfb, k9; repeat from * to end of round. *You now have* 22 stitches.

- Round 12: *Kfb, k10; repeat from * to end of round. *You now have* 24 stitches.

- Round 13: *Kfb, k11; repeat from * to end of round. *You now have* 26 stitches.

- Rounds 14 and 15: Knit.

- Round 16: *Ssk, k11; repeat from * to end of round. *You now have* 24 stitches.

- Round 17: *Ssk, k10; repeat from * to end of round. *You now have* 22 stitches.

- Round 18: *Ssk, k9; repeat from * to end of round. *You now have* 20 stitches.

- Round 19: *Ssk, k8; repeat from * to end of round. *You now have* 18 stitches.

- Round 20: Bind off the 9 front and 9 back stitches together with a three-needle bind off (see page 282). Use the tail from the cast on to sew the wings to the sides of the bodies. Weave in ends.

Toot the Bunny

Designed by Noël Margaret, Wanderlust Knits

This adorable little bunny has jointed arms that are attached to the body with I-cord. The legs are knitted separately and then joined and worked into the body. A simple cable stitch defines the face.

KNITTING THE EARS (make 2)

- Cast on 4 stitches and divide onto three double-point needles. Join into a round, being careful not to twist the stitches.

- Round 1: Knit.

- Round 2: K2, inc-L, inc-R, k2. *You now have* 6 stitches.

- Round 3: Knit.

- Round 4: K3, inc-L, inc-R, k3. *You now have* 8 stitches.

- Round 5: Knit.

- Round 6: K4, inc-L, inc-R, k4. *You now have* 10 stitches.

- Round 7: Knit.

- Round 8: K5, inc-L, inc-R, k5. *You now have* 12 stitches.

- Rounds 9–12: Knit.

- Round 13: Ssk, k8, k2tog. *You now have* 10 stitches.

- Round 14: Knit.

- Round 15: Ssk, k6, k2tog. *You now have* 8 stitches.

- Rounds 16–18: Knit.

- Bind off.

KNITTING THE ARMS (make 2)

- Cast on 6 stitches and divide evenly onto three double-point needles.

- Round 1: Knit.

- Round 2: *Inc-R, k2; repeat from * two more times. *You now have* 9 stitches.

- Round 3: *K3, inc-L; repeat from * two more times. *You now have* 12 stitches.

- Round 4: *Inc-R, k4; repeat from * two more times. *You now have* 15 stitches.

- Round 5: K15, inc-L. *You now have* 16 stitches.

- Round 6: K4, yo, ssk, k4, k2tog, yo, k4.

- Rounds 7–16: Knit.

- Round 17: K6, slip the next four stitches onto one double-point needle and work them as an I-Cord for thumb as follows: k1, k2tog, k1, do not turn, slip stitches

FINISHED MEASUREMENTS
Approximately 6¾"/17 cm long, including ears

YARN
Cascade Yarns Eco Cloud, 70% undyed merino wool/30% undyed baby alpaca, 164 yds (150 m)/3.5 oz (100 g), Color 1803 Fawn ④

NEEDLES
Set of five US 6 (4 mm) double-point needles *or size needed to obtain correct gauge*

GAUGE
24 stitches and 34 rounds = 4"/10 cm in stockinette stitch

OTHER SUPPLIES
Polyester fiberfill, two 6 mm safety eyes, small amount of black yarn for nose, cable needle, stitch holder, removable stitch marker, yarn needle

SPECIAL ABBREVIATIONS
C1L
Cable one left. Place one stitch on cable needle and hold in front, knit one from left needle, knit one from cable needle.
C1R
Cable one right. Place one stitch on cable needle and hold in back, knit one from left needle, knit one from cable needle.
inc-R
Insert right-hand needle from back to front into the stitch below next stitch on left-hand needle and lift this stitch onto the left-hand needle; knit into the stitch to increase 1, then knit next stitch normally.
inc-L
Insert left-hand needle from back to front into the stitch two rows below last stitch on right-hand needle and lift this stitch onto the left-hand needle; knit into the stitch to increase 1, then continue the row.
s2kp
Slip 2 stitches together knitwise, k1, pass the slipped stitches over the knit stitch.

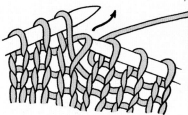

to other end of needle, bring yarn around back of work, k3, do not turn; slip stitches to other end of needle, bring yarn around back of work, k3tog. Cut yarn and pull tail through remaining stitches. Rejoin yarn to the hand at the base of the completed thumb), k6. *You now have* 12 stitches.

- Rounds 18–20: Knit.

- Stuff the arm lightly with fiberfill.

- Round 21: (Ssk, k2, k2tog) twice. *You now have* 8 stitches

- Cut yarn and pull tail through the remaining stitches.

The Arm I-Cord

Note: Leave about a 3"/7.5 cm tail on both ends of the I-Cord and do not weave them in until Finishing the Toy.

- Cast on 3 stitches.

- Knit I-Cord for 27 rows and bind off. Set aside.

KNITTING THE LEGS

The First Leg

- Cast on 6 stitches and divide evenly onto three double-point needles. Join into a round, being careful not to twist the stitches.

- Round 1: Knit.

- Round 2: *K1, inc-L, inc-R, k1; repeat from * two more times. *You now have* 12 stitches.

- Round 2: Knit.

- Round 3: *K2, inc-L, inc-R, k2; repeat from * two more times. *You now have* 18 stitches.

- Rounds 4–14: Knit.

- Cut the yarn, leaving a tail 4"/10 cm or longer for later use.

- Place stitches onto holder and set aside.

The Second Leg

- Make as for first leg through Round 13.

- Round 14: K9, leaving remaining 9 sts unworked.

- Distribute stitches evenly over two double-point needles.

Join the Legs

- Evenly distribute the stitches from the first leg over two double-point needles.

Note: When joining legs, allow the yarn tail from the first leg to dangle between the two legs and on the outside of the work. You can use it later to close any small gap that may form at the join.

- With the working yarn from the second leg, knit the next 9 stitches of the second leg onto Needle 1; knit 9 stitches of the first leg (beginning with the first stitch after the yarn tail) onto Needle 2; knit the remaining 9 stitches of the first leg onto Needle 3; knit the remaining 9 stitches of the second leg onto Needle 4. Place marker in the first stitch of the round. *You now have* 36 stitches.

KNITTING THE BODY

- Rounds 1–9: Knit.

- Round 10: K18, ssk, k14, k2tog. *You now have* 34 stitches.

- Round 11: Knit.

- Round 12: K18, (ssk, k4, k2tog) 2 times. *You now have* 30 stitches.

- Round 13: Knit.

- Stuff the legs firmly with fiberfill.

- Round 14: K18, ssk, k8, k2tog. *You now have* 28 stitches.

- Round 15: Yo, k2tog, k10, ssk, yo, k14.

- Round 16: K15, ssk, k8, k2tog, k1. *You now have* 26 stitches.

- **Round 25:** K4, C1L, k6, C1R, k6, inc-L, k4, inc-R, k2. *You now have* 28 stitches.
- **Round 26:** K5, ssk, k4, k2tog, k15. *You now have* 26 stitches.
- **Round 27:** K5, ssk, k2, k2tog, k15. *You now have* 24 stitches.
- Position safety eyes in desired place on the face and secure according to the manufacturer's instructions. Alternatively, you can use yarn to embroider the eyes after completing the toy (recommended for children 2 years and younger).
- Stuff the body and head firmly with fiberfill.
- **Round 28:** (K2tog, k3, ssk) 2 times, k1, k2tog, k4, ssk, k1. *You now have* 18 stitches.
- **Round 29:** (Ssk, k1, k2tog) 2 times, k1, (s2kp) twice, k1. *You now have* 10 stitches.
- Cut yarn, leaving an 8"/20.5 cm tail. Thread the tail onto yarn needle and draw through the remaining stitches. Pull up snug and fasten off.

FINISHING THE TOY

- Whipstitch (see page 282) the bound off edges of the ears to the top of the head (one on each side).

Note: The mitered increases on the ears face forward.

- To attach the arms using the I-cord, firmly tie a knot at one end of the I-cord and thread the tail on the opposite end of the I-cord onto a yarn needle. Holding the arms so the thumbs face forward, pull the I-cord through the eyelets (yarnovers) of the first arm, the body, and then the second arm. Pull the I-cord tightly and knot the other end.
- Use the I-cord tails to sew the knotted ends onto the arms for extra security (recommended for children 2 years and younger and/or if the toy may be played with roughly).
- Using the yarn tail from the first leg, sew the small gap between the legs closed.
- Use black yarn to embroider the nose.
- Weave in any remaining ends.

- **Round 17:** K20, k2tog, ssk, k2. *You now have* 24 stitches.
- **Round 18:** K7, C1R, C1L, k13.
- **Round 19:** K6, C1R, k2, C1L, k12.
- **Round 20:** K5, C1R, k4, C1L, k11.
- **Round 21:** K4, C1R, k6, C1L, k10.
- **Round 22:** Knit.
- **Round 23:** K18, inc-R, k6, inc-L. *You now have* 26 stitches.
- **Round 24:** Knit.

Graphic Kitty

Designed by Julia Swart

A soft toy for wee ones, this kitty has tabs on the side for carrying or for attaching to a stroller or car seat. The super simple pattern is perfect for beginning knitters and a great quick knit for the more experienced.

....
FINISHED MEASUREMENTS
7"/18 cm wide and 6"/15 cm tall
....
YARN
Fibernymph Dye Works Cozy, 100% superwash merino wool, 220 yds (200 m)/3.5 oz (100 g), Grayscale (4)
....
NEEDLES
US 7 (4.5 mm) straight needles *or size needed to obtain correct gauge*
....
GAUGE
22 stitches and 30 rows = 4"/10 cm in stockinette stitch
....
OTHER SUPPLIES
Two safety eyes, polyester fiber-fill, yarn needle, extra needle for three-needle bind off

KNITTING THE KITTY

• Starting with a black section of yarn in order to begin with a black stripe, cast on 88 stitches using a provisional cast on method (see page 281). Work in stockinette stitch for 15"/38 cm, ending with a RS (knit) row, also a black stripe.

• Place stitches from provisional cast on onto a needle. With right sides facing, use spare needle to join the beginning and ending stitches together with three-needle bind off (see page 282). Cut yarn, leaving a tail for seaming.

The Limbs (make 2)

- Using a gray section of yarn, cast on 9 stitches. Work in stockinette stitch for 20 rows. Bind off. Fold in half with wrong sides facing and sew each limb to the back of one side seam, forming loops approximately 1"/2.5 cm above the bottom seam.

The Tail

- Using a white section of yarn, cast on 9 stitches. Work in stockinette stitch for 12 rows. Bind off. Fold in half with wrong sides facing and sew horizontally to the back, forming a loop approximately 1"/2.5 cm above the bottom seam.

Making the Face

- Using the photograph as a guide, place safety eyes on the front. Use a black section of yarn to embroider the mouth and nose.

FINISHING

- Sew one side seam, drawing through both layers of the limb when you get to it. Sew about three-quarters of the second seam, stuff the kitty with fiberfill to desired density, being sure to poke the stuffing into the top corners to make the ears. Finish the seam and weave in all ends.

Scubaa the Blanket Buddy

Designed by Julie L. Anderson, The Byrd's Nest

This blanket buddy is destined to become baby's best friend. It is knit in a wonderfully squishy garter stitch and has a picot edging. A few scraps of black yarn are all you need to add the personality.

FINISHED MEASUREMENTS
Approximately 12"/30.5 cm square

YARN
Cascade Yarns 220 Superwash, 100% superwash wool, 220 yds (201 m)/3.5 oz (100 g), Color 871 White (4)

NEEDLES
Set of four US 6 (4 mm) double-point needles, set of five US 8 (5 mm) double-point needles, and US 8 (5 mm) circular needle 24"/60 cm long, *or size needed to obtain correct gauge*

GAUGE
20 stitches and 39 rows = 4"/10 cm in garter stitch on larger needles

OTHER SUPPLIES
Stitch markers, polyester fiberfill, yarn needle, small amount of black yarn

KNITTING THE HEAD

- With smaller needle, cast on 9 stitches. Divide evenly onto 3 double-point needles and join into a round, being careful not to twist the stitches. Place a marker on the first stitch to mark beginning of round.

- Round 1: Knit.

- Round 2: *Pfb; repeat from * to end of round. *You now have* 18 stitches.

Pattern Essentials

GARTER STITCH

(in the round)

Round 1: Knit.

Round 2: Purl.

Repeat Rounds 1 and 2 for pattern.

PICOT BIND OFF

Using the cable cast on method (see page 276), *cast on 2 stitches; bind off 4 stitches; slip 1 from right needle back to left; repeat from * until all stitches have been bound off.

- **Round 3:** Knit.
- **Round 4:** Purl.
- **Round 5:** *Kfb; repeat from * to end of round. *You now have* 36 stitches.
- **Round 6:** Purl.
- **Round 7:** Knit.
- **Round 8:** *P2, pfb; repeat from * to end of round. *You now have* 48 stitches.
- **Round 9:** Knit.
- **Round 10:** Purl.
- **Rounds 11–24:** Repeat Rounds 9 and 10 seven times.
- **Round 25:** Knit.
- **Round 26:** Ssk, k12, k2tog, *k2, k2tog; repeat from * to end of round. *You now have* 38 stitches.
- **Round 27:** Knit.
- **Round 28:** Ssk, k10, k2tog, *k1, k2tog; repeat from * to end of round. *You now have* 28 stitches.
- **Rounds 29–34:** Knit.

- **Round 35:** *K2, k2tog; repeat from * to end of round. *You now have* 21 stitches.
- **Round 36:** Knit.
- **Round 37:** (K1, k2tog) three times, k12. *You now have* 18 stitches.
- **Round 38:** *K1, k2tog; repeat from * to end of round. *You now have* 12 stitches.
- Fill the head with fiberfill. Cut yarn, leaving an 8"/20.5 cm tail. Thread tail onto yarn needle and thread through remaining stitches. Add more fiberfill if necessary, pull up taut and fasten off. Sew up hole at back of head. Weave in ends. **Note:** The bottom of the head is the flatter side.

KNITTING THE EARS (make 2)

- With smaller needles, cast on 14 stitches. Divide evenly onto 3 double-point needles and join into a round, being careful not to twist the stitches. Place a marker on the first stitch to mark beginning of round.
- Round 1: Kfb, k12, kfb. *You now have 16 stitches.*
- Round 2: Kfb, k14, kfb. *You now have 18 stitches.*
- Rounds 3–8: Knit.
- Round 9: Ssk, k14, k2tog. *You now have 16 stitches.*
- Round 10: Knit.
- Round 11: Ssk, k12, k2tog. *You now have 14 stitches.*
- Round 12: Knit.
- Round 13: Ssk, k10, k2tog. *You now have 12 stitches.*
- Round 14: Knit.
- Round 15: Ssk, k8, k2tog. *You now have 10 stitches.*
- Round 16: Knit.
- Round 17: Ssk, k6, k2tog. *You now have 8 stitches.*
- Round 18: Ssk, k4, k2tog. *You now have 6 stitches.*
- Round 19: Ssk, k2, k2tog. *You now have 4 stitches.*
- Cut yarn, leaving a 6"/15 cm tail. Thread tail onto yarn needle and thread through remaining stitches, pull up taut and fasten off. Flatten ear. Fold cast on edge together and whipstitch closed (see page 282). Sew to side of head with shaped edge of ear facing down.

KNITTING THE BLANKET BODY

- With larger needles, cast on 8 stitches and divide evenly onto four double-point needles. Join into a round, being careful not to twist the stitches. Place a marker on the first stitch to mark beginning of round. **Note:** When you have enough stitches, you may change to a circular needle.
- Round 1: *K1, kfb; repeat from * to end of round. *You now have 12 stitches.*
- Round 2: *Place marker, p3; repeat from * to end of round.
- Round 3: *Sm, kfb, knit to 1 stitch before marker, kfb; repeat from * to end of round. *You now have 20 stitches.*
- Round 4: Purl.
- Repeat Rounds 3 and 4 until you have 53 stitches between the markers, 212 stitches total, ending on Round 4. Bind off using the Picot bind off (see Pattern Essentials, opposite page).

FINISHING

- Position head over center hole of body blanket and sew head to body. Refer to photograph and use black yarn to embroider eyes and nose. Weave in all ends.

Sunshine

Designed by Judith Durant

Babies love to reach out and grab things, and this solar toy obliges with twelve soft and squishy rays. Baby would also probably enjoy a round of "You Are My Sunshine."

FINISHED MEASUREMENTS
14"/35.5 cm in diameter from point to point

YARN
Anzula Luxury Fibers Milky Way, 80% milk protein/20% superwash merino wool, 500 yds (457 m)/3.5 oz (100 g), Curry **(0)**
Note: Yarn is used double throughout

NEEDLES
Set of four US 4 (3.5 mm) double-point needles *or size needed to obtain correct gauge*

GAUGE
24 stitches = 4"/10 cm in stockinette stitch before stuffing

OTHER SUPPLIES
Polyester fiberfill, yarn needle

KNITTING THE SPHERE

- Cast on 3 stitches. Kfb in each stitch. *You now have* 6 stitches.

- Place 2 stitches on each of 3 needles and join into a round, being careful not to twist the stitches.

Increase Rounds

- Round 1: Kfb in each stitch around. *You now have* 12 stitches.

- Round 2: Knit.

- Round 3: *K1, kfb; repeat from * to end of round. *You now have* 18 stitches.

- Round 4: Knit.

- Round 5: *K2, kfb; repeat from * to end of round. *You now have* 24 stitches.

Pattern Essentials

Yarn is used doubled throughout. Prepare the yarn by winding two equal balls and knitting with one strand from each ball, or wind a center-pull ball and pull from both the inside and the outside of the ball.

- Round 6: Knit.
- Round 7: *K3, kfb; repeat from * to end of round. *You now have* 30 stitches.
- Continue in this manner, working one more stitch between the increases and knitting one round even between increase rounds, until you have 44 stitches on each needle, 132 stitches total.
- Knit 3 rounds even.

Decrease Rounds

Note: When the opening in sphere begins to narrow, stuff the piece with fiberfill. Continue to stuff as you work the ending rounds, making sure the filling is even and the piece is plump.

- Round 1: *Ssk, k20; repeat from * to end of round. *You now have* 126 stitches.
- Round 2: Knit.
- Round 3: *Ssk, k19; repeat from * to end of round. *You now have* 120 stitches.
- Round 4: Knit.
- Round 5: *Ssk, k18; repeat from * to end of round. *You now have* 114 stitches.
- Continue in this manner, working one fewer stitch between the decreases and knitting one round even between the decrease rounds, until you have 4 stitches on each needle, 12 stitches total.
- Next Round: *Ssk; repeat from * to end of round. *You now have* 6 stitches.
- Cut yarn leaving an 8"/20 cm tail. Thread tail onto yarn needle and draw through remaining stitches. Pull up snug and weave in tail.

Note: If the cast-on and bound-off areas protrude slightly, leave a longer tail to thread through the ending stitches and bring the tail through the sphere from bound-off to cast-on stitches, pull in to eliminate bulge, then fasten off and weave in end.

KNITTING THE RAYS (make 12)

- Cast on 24 stitches. Place 8 stitches on each of 3 needles and join into a round, being careful not to twist the stitches.
- Rounds 1–5: Knit.
- Round 6: *Ssk, k6; repeat from * to end of round. *You now have* 21 stitches.
- Rounds 7–9: Knit.
- Round 10: *Ssk, k5; repeat from * to end of round. *You now have* 18 stitches.
- Rounds 11–13: Knit.
- Round 14: *Ssk, k4; repeat from * to end of round. *You now have* 15 stitches.
- Continue in this manner, working one less stitch between decreases and working 3 rounds even between decrease rounds, until you have 2 stitches on each needle, 6 stitches total.
- Next Round: (Ssk) 3 times. *You now have* 3 stitches.
- Cut yarn leaving a 6"/15 cm tail. Thread tail onto yarn needle and draw through remaining stitches. Pull up snug and weave in tail.

FINISHING

- Stuff the rays with fiberfill and sew them along the equator of the sphere, placing two rays into each section between the shaping lines. Fasten off all threads and weave the ends to the inside.

The Hold Me Orb

Designed by Gwen Steege

Each of the six wedges in this little ball is knit separately, making it ideal for a multicolor yarn with long lengths of each color repeat. The wedges also provide an ideal "grabbing" place for tiny hands. The Classic Elite yarn is machine washable and comes in a number of other color combinations that would be great for kids.

FINISHED MEASUREMENTS
3½"/9 cm high; 16"/40.5 in circumference

YARN
Classic Elite Liberty Wool, 100% washable wool, 122 yds (112 m)/ 3.5 oz (50g), Color Print 7870 Rosy Autumn (4)

NEEDLES
Set of four US 7 (4.5 mm) double-point needles *or size you need to obtain correct gauge*

GAUGE
20 stitches and 40 rows = 4"/10 cm in garter stitch

OTHER SUPPLIES
Scrap yarn, polyester fiberfill, yarn needle

KNITTING THE WEDGES
(make 6)

- Using a provisional cast on method (see page 281) and scrap yarn, cast on 40 stitches. Do not join in a round. Knit 1 row with main yarn. Divide the stitches among three needles as follows: Needle 1, 10 stitches; needle 2, 10 stitches; needle 3, 20 stitches. Join, being careful not to twist stitches.

- Round 1: Knit.
- Round 2: Purl.

- Repeat these two rounds three more times. You will have 4 garter ridges.
- Round 9: *K8, ssk; repeat from * to end of round. *You now have* 36 stitches.
- Round 10 and all other even-numbered rounds: Purl.
- Round 11: *K7, ssk; repeat from * to end of round. *You now have* 32 stitches.
- Round 13: *K6, ssk; repeat from * to end of round. *You now have* 28 stitches.
- Round 15: *K5, ssk; repeat from * to end of round. *You now have* 24 stitches.
- Round 17: *K4, ssk; repeat from * to end of round. *You now have* 20 stitches.
- Round 19: *K3, ssk; repeat from * to end of round. *You now have* 16 stitches.
- Round 21: *K2, ssk; repeat from * to end of round. *You now have* 12 stitches.
- Round 23: *K1, ssk; repeat from * to end of round. *You now have* 8 stitches.
- Round 25: *Ssk; repeat from * to end of round. *You now have* 4 stitches.
- Cut yarn leaving a 6"/15 cm tail. Thread tail onto yarn needle and draw through remaining stitches. Fasten off, and draw tail through to the inside.
- Carefully remove the provisional cast on and divide the 40 stitches evenly between two needles.

- Use three-needle bind off (see page 282) to close the opening; when about 6 stitches remain on each needle, stuff the wedge with polyester fill or yarn scraps. Finish closing the opening.

ASSEMBLING THE BALL

- Holding two wedges with the bound-off edges aligned, use main yarn to whipstitch the edges together from end to end, taking small, firm stitches.
- Attach a third wedge to this pair in the same manner. Continue sewing wedges together along the bound-off edges until all six are attached. You may need to take a few extra stitches at the top and bottom to neaten up the place where the edges line up.

I-CORD LOOPS (make at least 3)

- Knit 3-stitch I-cord (see page 277), leaving an 8"/20.5 cm tail. The toy shown has 7 loops in 8, 5, and 3"/20.5, 12.5, and 7.5 cm lengths.
- Fold the cords in half to form loops, and use the tails to firmly stitch the loops to the top of the ball.

Lovey the Octopus

Designed by Rachel Henry

Clever use of short rows makes lifelike tentacles that are worked sideways, and the reverse stockinette stitch curls back on itself so there's no need to seam them. The head is then worked in the round on picked-up stitches.

FINISHED MEASUREMENTS
10"/25.5 cm long, 2¼"/5.5 cm diameter

YARN
Classic Elite Seedling, 100% organic cotton, 110 yds (101 m)/1.75 oz (50 g), Color HP 4565 Tropical Sea

NEEDLES
US 5 (3.75 mm) straight needles and set of four US 5 (3.75 mm) double-point needles *or size needed to obtain correct gauge*
Note: Use a long circular needle for Magic Loop, if desired.

GAUGE
20 stitches and 28 rows = 4"/10 cm in stockinette stitch.

OTHER SUPPLIES
Two plastic safety eyes, yarn needle, polyester fiberfill

SPECIAL ABBREVIATIONS
sp2p
   Slip 1, purl 2 together, pass slipped stitch over p2tog (2 stitches decreased)

KNITTING THE TENTACLES (make 8)

- With straight needles, cast on 40 stitches.
- **Row 1:** K32, turn.
- **Rows 2, 4, 6, and 8:** Slip 1 purlwise, purl to end of row.
- **Row 3:** K24, turn.
- **Row 5:** K16, turn.
- **Row 7:** K8, turn.
- **Row 9:** K7, ssk, (k6, ssk) 3 times, k7.
- **Row 10:** Bind off as follows: *p2tog, return resulting stitch to left needle; repeat from * until all stitches are bound off. Cut yarn and pull yarn through last stitch.
- Weave in all ends before proceeding.

KNITTING THE LOWER BODY

- With double-point needles, purl side facing and the narrow tips of the tentacles hanging down, leave a 12"/30.5 cm tail for sewing and then pick up and knit 5 stitches from the center top of each tentacle. *You now have* 40 stitches.

- Divide stitches evenly onto 3 needles and join for working in the round. Purl 1 round.

- Round 1: *P1, sp2p, p1; repeat form * to end of round. *You now have* 24 stitches.

- Round 2: Purl.

- Round 3: *P2tog; repeat from * to end of round. *You now have* 12 stitches.

- Rounds 4 and 5: Purl.

- Thread the tail left on one tentacle onto a yarn needle and pass through both top corners of each leg; pull tight to form the base of the lower body.

KNITTING THE UPPER BODY

- Round 1: *Pbf, p1; repeat from * to end of round. *You now have* 18 stitches.

- Rounds 2, 4 and 6: Purl.

- Round 3: *Pbf, p2; repeat from * to end of round. *You now have* 24 stitches.

- Round 5: *Pbf, p3; repeat from * to end of round. *You now have* 30 stitches.

- Round 7: *Pbf, p4; repeat from * to end of round. *You now have* 36 stitches.

- Rounds 8–15: Purl.

- Place safety eyes on the upper body in desired position.

- Round 16: *P2tog, p4; repeat from * to end of round. *You now have* 30 stitches.

- Rounds 17, 19, and 21: Purl.

- Round 18: *P2tog, p3; repeat from * to end of round. *You now have* 24 stitches.

- Round 20: *P2tog, p2; repeat from * to end of round. *You now have* 18 stitches.

- Lightly stuff body.

- Round 22: *P2tog, p1; repeat from * to end of round. *You now have* 12 stitches.

- Round 23: *P2tog; repeat from * to end of round. *You now have* 6 stitches.

- Cut yarn and thread onto yarn needle. Draw through remaining 6 stitches, pull up snug, and fasten off.

- Weave in all ends.

Toy Safety

Toys are made to be held, and babies will put anything they can hold into their mouths. Here are some things to keep in mind.

- We strongly recommend using safety eyes or embroidery techniques to add eyes and other features to baby toys.

- Don't use novelty yarn with sequins or bits of fiber that can easily be separated from the main yarn.

- Stuff toys with fiberfill rather than poly-pellets, which can come out through the knitted stitches.

- Always use secure knots when joining new yarn and hide these knots well inside the toy.

Friendly Lizard

Designed by Sarah Gomez

This cute, quick-to-knit lizard toy features I-cord for legs and tail. One skein of yarn will knit enough creatures to fill a small swamp.

FINISHED MEASUREMENTS
7"/18 cm long, excluding tail

YARN
Red Heart Super Saver, 100% acrylic, 364 yds (333 m)/7 oz (198g), Color 672 Spring Green ❹

NEEDLES
Set of four US 6 (4 mm) double-point needles *or size needed to obtain correct gauge*

GAUGE
19 stitches and 28 rows = 4"/10 cm in stockinette stitch

OTHER SUPPLIES
Polyester fiberfill, scraps of black yarn, yarn needle

KNITTING THE BODY

- Beginning at the tail, cast on 3 stitches and work I-cord (see page 277) for 20 rounds.

- Round 1: Divide stitches onto 3 double-point needles to work in the round, *kfb; repeat from * to end of round. *You now have* 6 stitches.

- Round 2: Knit.

- Round 3: *Kfb; repeat from * to end of round. *You now have* 12 stitches.

- Round 4: Knit.

- Round 5: *Kfb, k1; repeat from * to end of round. *You now have* 18 stitches.

- Round 6: Knit.

- Round 7: *Kfb, k2; repeat from * to end of round. *You now have* 24 stitches.

- Rounds 8–27: Knit.

- Round 28: K2tog, k2; repeat from * to end of round. *You now have* 18 stitches.

- Round 29: Knit.

- Round 30: *K2tog, k1; repeat from * to end of round. *You now have* 12 stitches.

- Round 31: Knit.

- Round 32: *Kfb, k1; repeat from * to end of round. *You now have* 18 stitches.

- Round 33: Knit.

- Round 34: *Kfb, k2; repeat from * to end of round. *You now have* 24 stitches.

- Rounds 35–40: Knit.

- Round 41: *K2tog, k2; repeat from * to end of round. *You now have* 18 stitches.

- Rounds 42 and 43: Knit.

- Round 44: *K2tog, k1; repeat from * to end of round. *You now have* 12 stitches.

- Rounds 45 and 46: Knit.

- Stuff the piece with fiberfill to desired firmness.

- Round 47: *K2tog; repeat from * to end of round. *You now have* 6 stitches.

- Cut yarn leaving a 6"/15 cm tail. Thread tail onto yarn needle and draw through remaining stitches. Pull up snug and fasten off.

KNITTING THE LEGS (make 4)

- Work 10 rows of 3-stitch I-cord. Cut yarn, thread through stitches, pull up snug, and fasten off.

FINISHING

- Weave in ends, sewing kinks for leg joints if desired. Sew legs securely to body. Using scraps of black yarn and the photo as a guide, embroider eyes to each side of the head with satin stitch (see page 282); eyes shown have 5 stitches each.

Circus Balls

Designed by Cathy Campbell

Beginning with a provisional cast on, the balls are knit from the center to the ends with simple decreasing. One skein will yield three balls.

KNITTING THE BALLS (make 3)

- Using a provisional cast on method (see page 281), cast on 64 stitches. Divide stitches evenly over 4 double-point needles and join into a round, being careful not to twist the stitches.

FINISHED MEASUREMENTS
4"/10 cm diameter

YARN
Crystal Palace Mochi Plus, 80% merino wool/20% nylon, 95 yds (87 m)/1.75 oz (50 g), Color 551 Intense Rainbow (4)

NEEDLES
Set of five US 5 (3.75 mm) double-point needles *or size needed to obtain correct gauge*

GAUGE
24 stitches = 4"/10 cm in stockinette stitch

OTHER SUPPLIES
Stitch marker, scrap yarn, yarn needle, polyester fiberfill

The First Half

- Rounds 1–4: Knit.

- Round 2: *K6, k2tog; repeat from * to end of round. *You now have* 56 stitches.

- Rounds 3–5: Knit.

- Round 6: *K5, k2tog; repeat from * to end of round. *You now have* 48 stitches.

- Rounds 7 and 8: Knit.

- Round 9: *K4, k2tog; repeat from * to end of round. *You now have* 40 stitches.

- Round 10: Knit.

- Round 11: *K3, k2tog; repeat from * to end of round. *You now have* 32 stitches.

- Round 12: Knit.

- Round 13: *K2, k2tog; repeat from * to end of round. *You now have* 24 stitches.

- Round 14: *K1, k2tog; repeat from * to end of round. *You now have* 16 stitches.

- Round 15: *K2tog; repeat from * to end of round. *You now have* 8 stitches.

- Cut yarn, leaving a 6"/15 cm tail. Thread tail onto yarn needle and draw through remaining 8 stitches. Pull up snug and fasten off.

The Second Half

Note: If possible, begin the second half with a section of the yarn that is a similar color to the cast-on edge.

- Place 64 provisional cast-on stitches on needles and work as for 1st half until you have 24 stitches.

- Stuff the ball with the fiberfill.

- Continue as for 1st half to Round 15. Add any more fiber fill needed to plump up ball but do not overstuff. Finish as for first half.

- Secure ends and thread yarn tail into center of ball.

Baby Rattles

Designed by Lynn M. Wilson, Lynn Wilson Designs

Included are instructions for three rattles: Pig, Bunny, and Fish. Pig parades medallion knitting and a corkscrew tail; Bunny brandishes paired decreases and a bobble tail; Fish flaunts mitered knitting and a crochet chain tail.

FINISHED MEASUREMENTS
Pig is 4"/10 cm diameter; Bunny is 4¼"/11 cm tall; Fish is 3¼"/8.5 cm square (all excluding features)

YARN
Classic Elite Seedling, 100% organic cotton, 110 yds (101 m)/1.75 oz (50 g), Color 4566 Lei

NEEDLES
US 5 (3.75 mm) straight needles and set of five US 5 (3.75 mm) double-point needles *or size needed to obtain correct gauge*

GAUGE
20 stitches = 4"/10 cm in stockinette stitch

OTHER SUPPLIES
E-4 (3.5 mm) crochet hook, stitch marker, yarn needle, scraps of black yarn for features, polyester fiberfill, 3 small plastic rattle inserts

SPECIAL ABBREVIATIONS
MB (make bobble)
> (K1, p1, k1, p1, k1) into next stitch, turn; p5, turn; k5, turn; p5, turn; k5 then successively slip the first 4 stitches over the 5th stitch.

KNITTING PIG

- Pig's body is knit in the round on double-point needles.

The Body Halves (make 2)

- Cast on 48 stitches and divide evenly onto 4 double-point needles. Place marker and join into a round, being careful not to twist the stitches.

- Round 1: Purl.

- Rounds 2–6: Knit.

- Round 7: *K2tog; repeat from * to end of round. *You now have* 24 stitches.

- **Rounds 8–10:** Knit.

- **Round 11:** *K2tog; repeat from * to end of round. *You now have* 12 stitches.

- **Rounds 12 and 13:** Knit.

- **Round 14:** *K2tog; repeat from * to end of round. *You now have* 6 stitches.

- *Front half only:*

- **Round 15:** Purl.

- **Round 16:** *P2tog; repeat from * to end of round. *You now have* 3 stitches.

- *Both halves:* Cut yarn leaving a 6"/15 cm tail. Thread tail onto yarn needle and draw through remaining stitches, pull up snug, and fasten off.

The Ears (make 2)

- Cast on 5 stitches. Work back and forth as follows.

- **Row 1:** Knit.

- **Row 2:** K1, p3, k1.

- **Row 3:** K2, M1, k1, M1, k2. *You now have* 7 stitches.

- **Rows 4, 6:** K1, p5, k1.

- **Row 5:** Knit.

- **Row 7:** K3, M1, k1, M1, k3. *You now have* 9 stitches.

- **Row 8:** K1, p7, k1.

- **Row 9:** Knit.

- Bind off and cut yarn, leaving a length for sewing.

The Tail

- Cast on 6 stitches *very loosely.* Knit into the front, back, and front again of every stitch. Bind off and cut yarn, leaving a length for sewing.

Finishing

- See General Finishing on facing page.

KNITTING BUNNY

- Bunny is knit back and forth in rows with paired decreases to form the triangle shape.

The Body Halves (make 2)

- Cast on 19 stitches and knit 1 row.

- **Rows 1, 3, 7, 11, 15, 19, 23, and 27 (RS):** Knit.

- **Row 2 and all following WS rows:** K1, purl to last stitch, k1.

- **Rows 5, 9, 13, 17, 21, 25, and 29:** K1, ssk, knit to last 3 stitches, k2tog, k1. This decrease 2 stitches per row. *After Row 29 you have* 5 stitches.

- **Row 31:** K1, s2kp, k1. *You now have* 3 stitches.

- **Row 33:** K3tog.

- Cut yarn and fasten off.

The Ears (make 2)

- Cast on 3 stitches.

- **Row 1 (RS):** Knit.

- **Row 2:** K1, p1, k1.

- **Row 3:** K1, (k1, p1, k1) in next stitch, k1. *You now have* 5 stitches.

- **Row 4:** K1, p3, k1.

- **Row 5:** Knit.
- Repeat Rows 4 and 5 four more times, then repeat Row 4 once more.
- **Next Row:** K1, k3tog, k1.
- Bind off all stitches purlwise. Cut yarn and fasten off.

Finishing

- See General Finishing on this page.

KNITTING FISH

- Fish is knit with the mitered knitting technique, decreasing to form the squares.

The Body Halves (make 2)

- Cast on 15 stitches, pm in last stitch, cast on 14 stitches. *You now have* 29 stitches.
- **Set-Up Row:** Knit.
- **Row 1:** Knit to 1 stitch before marked stitch, s2kp, move marker to this stitch, knit to end of row.
- **Row 2:** Knit.
- Repeat Rows 1 and 2 until 3 stitches remain.
- **Last Row:** K3tog. Cut yarn and fasten off.

Finishing

- See General Finishing on this page.

KNITTING THE HOLDING STRAP

- This strap holds all the rattles together.
- Cast on 25 stitches.
- **Rows 1 and 2:** Knit.

- **Row 3:** K3, yo, k2tog (buttonhole made), knit to last 4 stitches, MB, k3.
- **Rows 4 and 5:** Knit.
- Bind off loosely knitwise. Cut yarn and fasten off.

GENERAL FINISHING INSTRUCTIONS

- Refer to the photographs and diagrams when finishing.

I-Cord Handle (make 1 for each rattle)

- Work 3-stitch I-cord (see page 277) for 5"/12.5 cm. Cut yarn and fasten off.
- Fold each I-Cord handle in half and attach to wrong side of one body piece: refer to schematic for placement. Using black scrap yarn, work French knots (see page 277) to make eyes as indicated. Attach ears for Pig and Bunny. Attach Pig tail to center back of Pig body.
- Seam body pieces together using mattress stitch, whip stitch, or slip stitch crochet, leaving an opening to insert fiberfill and rattle. Fill the body with fiberfill and insert rattle, then complete seam. Weave in ends.
- *For Fish:* Make the Tail as follows.
- **Step 1:** Insert crochet hook into Fish at corner opposite eyes, yarnover and draw up a loop (slip stitch); chain 24.
- **Step 2:** Slip stitch in same point on Fish, chain 20.
- **Step 3:** Slip stitch in same point on Fish; cut yarn and fasten off. Weave in ends.

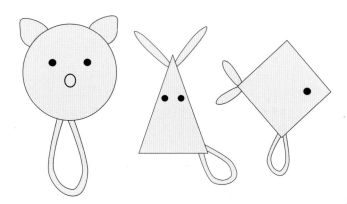

Bloomer Baby Doll

Designed by Gwen Steege

This soft little doll is completely machine washable, and her flapper hat and pinafore bloomers can be easily removed. Hand-embroider the doll's features so that there are no small parts that can be accidentally swallowed.

FINISHED MEASUREMENTS
9"/23 cm tall

YARN
Dale of Norway Baby Ull Dalegarn, 100% superwash merino wool, 180 yds (165 m)/1.75 oz (50 g), Color 2203 Pastel Yellow (1)

NEEDLES
Set of four US 2 (2.75 mm) double-point needles *or size needed to obtain correct gauge*

GAUGE
32 stitches and 40 rounds = 4"/10 cm in stockinette stitch

OTHER SUPPLIES
Polyester fiberfill, 1 yd/1 m of ⅜"/10 mm ribbon, 1 yd/1 m elastic thread, embroidery floss or perle cotton for features, yarn needle, C-2 (2.75 mm) crochet hook

KNITTING THE LEGS (make 2)

- Cast on 6 stitches; place 2 stitches on each of 3 needles and join into a round, being careful not to twist the stitches. Knit 1 round.

- Round 1: *Kfb; repeat from * to end of round. *You now have 12 stitches.*

- Round 2: Knit.

- Rounds 3 and 4: Repeat rounds 1 and 2. *You now have 24 stitches.*

- Round 5: *Kfb, k3; repeat from * to end of round. *You now have 30 stitches.*

- Rounds 6–9: Knit.

- Round 10: *Ssk, k3, k2tog, k3; repeat from * to end of round. *You now have 24 stitches.*

Pattern Essentials

PICOT CAST ON

*Cast on 3 stitches, bind off 1 stitch; repeat from * as needed to cast on required number of stitches.

PICOT BIND OFF

K2, bind off 1, slip stitch from right needle to left needle, cast on 2 stitches using the cable cast on method (see page 276); *bind off 5 stitches, place last stitch from right needle to left needle; repeat from * until all stitches have been bound off.

- Round 11: Knit.

- Round 12: *Ssk, k2, k2tog, k2; repeat from * to end of round. *You now have 18 stitches.*

- Knit 30 more rounds, or until leg measures about 4"/10 cm.

- Stuff the leg lightly with fiberfill. Arrange the stitches so that you have 9 stitches on each needle, and close the opening using the three-needle bind off method (see page 282).

KNITTING THE BODY AND HEAD

Notes: You'll knit the body from the bottom up first, decrease sharply for the neck, then increase and knit the head.

- Leaving a 12"/30.5 cm tail for sewing, pick up and knit 9 stitches from each leg and place all 18 stitches on one needle. Continuing with the same yarn and a new needle, and using the knitted on method (see page 279), cast on 18 stitches and divide these stitches onto two needles. *You now have* 36 stitches. Join to work in the round.

- Rounds 1–25: Knit. Align the cast-on and picked-up edges and use the yarn tail and yarn needle to sew the lower body opening to the legs.

- Round 26: *Ssk three times, k6, k2tog three times; repeat from * to end of round. *You now have* 24 stitches.

- Round 27: Knit. Stuff body with fiberfill.

- Round 28: *Ssk three times, k2tog three times; repeat from * to end of round. *You now have* 12 stitches.

- Round 29: Knit.

- Round 30: *Kfb; repeat from * to end of round. *You now have* 24 stitches.

- Rounds 31–39: Knit.

- Round 40: *K2, M1L; repeat from * to end of round. *You now have* 36 stitches.

- Rounds 41 and 42: Knit.

- Round 43: *Ssk, k1; repeat from * to end of round. *You now have* 24 stitches.

- Rounds 44–50: Knit.

- Round 51: *Ssk, k2; repeat from * to end of round. *You now have* 18 stitches.

- Round 52: *Ssk; repeat from * to end of round. *You now have* 9 stitches.

- Stuff the head with fiberfill.

- Cut yarn, leaving a 6"/15 cm tail. Thread the tail onto a yarn needle and draw through remaining 9 stitches; pull up snug and fasten off.

KNITTING THE LEFT ARM

- Leaving an 8"/20.5 cm tail for sewing and using the long-tail cast on method (see page 279), cast on 6 stitches; with front of doll facing, count down 9 rounds from the neck decrease at side edge and pick up 6 stitches (1 from each row). Arrange the stitches so that the 6 picked-up stitches are on one needle and the 6 cast-on stitches are divided between two needles. *You now have* 12 stitches. Join to work in the round.

- Rounds 1–18: Knit. With yarn tail and yarn needle, sew the arm opening to body.

- Round 19: *K2, M1L; repeat from * to end of round. *You now have* 18 stitches.

- **Round 20:** Knit.
- **Round 21:** *Ssk; repeat from * to end of round. *You now have* 9 stitches.
- **Round 22:** Knit.
- Stuff the arm with fiberfill.
- Cut yarn, leaving a 6"/15 cm tail. Thread the tail through yarn needle and draw through remaining 9 stitches; pull up snug and fasten off.

KNITTING THE RIGHT ARM

- Leaving an 8"/20.5 cm tail for sewing and using the long-tail method, cast on 6 stitches; with front of doll facing, count down 3 rounds from the neck decrease at side edge and pick up 6 stitches (1 from each row). Complete as for Left Arm.

KNITTING THE BLOOMERS

- The bloomers are knit from the top down.
- Use the Picot Cast On (see Pattern Essentials on page 240) to cast on 17 stitches, then cast on 1 more stitch. *You now have* 18 stitches. Join to work in the round.
- **Rounds 1–4:** *K1, p1; repeat from * to end of round.
- **Round 5:** *Kfb, k1; repeat from * to end of round. *You now have* 27 stitches.
- **Round 6:** Purl.
- **Round 7:** *Kfb; repeat from * to end of round. *You now have* 54 stitches.
- **Round 8:** Purl.
- Divide the stitches between two needles to begin working the back

and front separately in rows to create the armholes. *You now have* 27 stitches on each needle. Place one set of stitches on holder and continue work on 27 sts only.

- **Rows 1–10:** Work in stockinette stitch (knit 1 row, purl 1 row).
- **Row 11 (eyelet row):** K1, *k1, yo, k2, yo; repeat from * to last 2 stitches, k2. *You now have* 43 stitches. Place these stitches on hold.
- With RS facing, join yarn and repeat Rows 1–11 on the 27 held stitches.
- To begin again to work in the round, divide the 86 front and back stitches among three double-point needles.
- **Rounds 1–18:** Knit.
- **Rounds 19 and 20:** Purl.
- Use the Picot Bind Off (see Pattern Essentials) to bind off all stitches.
- Weave an 18"/45.5 cm length of ribbon through the eyelets at the waist and tie in a bow. Trim as desired.
- Working on the inside of the bloomers, use running stitch to attach a length of elastic thread through the reverse stockinette stitches at the bottom edge.
- Using project yarn, take several stitches at the front and back middle of the bottom edge to create a crotch.

KNITTING THE HAT

- Cast on 40 stitches and divide onto three double-point needles. Join into a round, being careful not to twist the stitches.
- **Rounds 1 and 2:** *K1, p1; repeat from * to end of round.
- **Round 3:** *K2tog, yo; repeat from * to end of round.
- **Round 4:** *K1, p1; repeat from * to end of round.
- **Rounds 5–9:** Knit.
- **Round 10:** *K3, kfb; repeat from * to end of round. *You now have* 50 stitches.
- **Round 11:** Knit.
- **Round 12:** *K3, ssk; repeat from * to end of round. *You now have* 40 stitches.

- Round 13: Knit.
- Round 14: *K2, ssk; repeat from * to end of round. *You now have* 30 stitches.
- Round 15: Knit.
- Round 16: *K1, ssk; repeat from * to end of round. *You now have* 20 stitches.
- Round 17: Knit.
- Round 18: *Ssk; repeat from * to end of round. *You now have* 10 stitches.
- Round 19: Knit.
- Cut yarn, leaving a 6"/15 cm tail. Thread the tail through yarn needle and draw through remaining 10 stitches; pull up snug and fasten off.
- Weave an 18"/45.5 cm length of ribbon through the eyelets at the edge of the hat and trim as desired.

FINISHING

- Use embroidery floss or perle cotton to embroider the eyes and mouth on the doll's face.
- For the hair, cut 8"/20.5 cm lengths of the project yarn. Fold each strand in half and use a crochet hook to loop it through a stitch at the top of the doll's head (see illustration). Continue to tie strands of hair into the knitted stitches until there is enough to draw into pigtails. Tie pigtails together using a separate length of yarn.

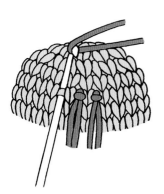

Elephant Blanket Buddy

Designed by Gwen Steege

Knit from the softest of yarns, yet still machine washable, this quirky little toy is bound to become a favorite at naptime. The blanket is hexagonal, shaped by increases at six points around the circumference, starting at the elephant's neck.

243

FINISHED MEASUREMENTS
Blanket, 14"/35.5 cm across; head
and trunk, 3½"/9 cm

YARN
Swans Island, sport weight, 100%
washable merino wool, 175 yds (160
m)/1.75 oz (50 g), Color 106 Sky
Blue **2**

NEEDLES
Set of four US 4 (3.5 mm) double-
point needles and US 4 (3.5 mm)
circular needle 16"/40 cm long *or
size needed to obtain correct gauge*

GAUGE
20 stitches and 30 rounds = 4"/10
cm in stockinette stitch

OTHER SUPPLIES
Stitch marker, small amount of polyester fiberfill, yarn needle, embroidery floss or perle cotton for the eyes

KNITTING THE TRUNK AND HEAD

- Using a double-point needle, cast on 6 stitches. Work 6-stitch I-cord (see page 277) for 17 rounds. Divide the stitches onto three needles (2 stitches on each). Join into a round, being careful not to twist the stitches.

- Round 1: *Kfb; repeat from * to end of round. *You now have* 12 stitches.

- Round 2: Knit.

- Round 3: *Kfb; repeat from * to end of round. *You now have* 24 stitches.

- Rounds 4–7: Knit.

- Round 8: *K2, kfb; repeat from * to end of round. *You now have* 32 stitches.

- Rounds 9 and 10: Knit.

- Round 11: *K1, ssk; repeat from * to last 2 stitches, k2. *You now have* 22 stitches.

- Round 12: Knit.

- Round 13: *Ssk; repeat from * to last 2 stitches, k2. *You now have* 12 stitches.

- Loosely stuff the head with fiberfill.

KNITTING THE BLANKET BODY

- Round 1: Knit.

- Round 2: *Kfb; repeat from * to end of round. *You now have* 24 stitches.

- Divide the stitches evenly onto three needles.

- Round 3: Knit, placing a marker between the 4th and 5th stitches on each needle. **Note:** These markers, along with the ends of each needle, mark the six segments where you will be making the increases.

- Round 4: *K1, M1L, knit to marker, M1R, sm, k1, M1L, knit to end of needle, M1R; repeat from * on needles 2 and 3. *You now have* 36 stitches.

- Rounds 5–7: Knit.

Note: In the following rounds, change to circular needles when appropriate, placing markers at the ends of each double-point needle to mark increase sections.

- Repeat rounds 4–7 fourteen times. *You now have* 204 stitches.

- Next Round: *K2tog, yo; repeat from * to end of round.

- Next Round: Knit.

- Bind off using 3-stitch I-cord bind off (see page 277).

KNITTING THE EARS

- For the left ear, with trunk facing, count down 9 stitches from the center top of the head; pick up and knit 7 stitches along the decrease round on the left side of the face. (There will be 3 stitches on the head between the ears.)

- **Row 1 (WS):** Purl.

- **Row 2:** *Kfb; repeat from * to end of round. *You now have* 14 stitches.

- **Row 3:** Purl.

- **Row 4:** Knit.

- **Row 5:** Purl.

- **Row 6:** K1, ssk, knit to last 3 stitches, k2tog, k1. *You now have* 12 stitches.

- **Rows 7–10:** Repeat rows 5 and 6. *You now have* 8 stitches.

- **Row 11:** Purl.

- **Row 12:** *Ssk; repeat from * to end of round. *You now have* 4 stitches.

- Bind off.

- For the right ear, with trunk facing, skip 3 sts at center top of head, pick up and knit 7 stitches along the decrease round on the other side of the face. Complete as for left ear.

FINISHING

- Cut a 10"/25.5 cm length of yarn and thread onto yarn needle. From the WS, pass through the 12 stitches at the base of the head; pull up snug and fasten off to close the head. Weave in ends. Using embroidery floss or perle cotton and the photo as a guide, make two French knots (see page 277) above the trunk for eyes.

Snowy Owl Blanket Buddy

Designed by Gwen Steege

A wise owl is always a welcome night-time companion. This soft Swans Island yarn is even named "Snowy Owl"! The blanket is hexagonal, shaped by increases at six points around the circumference, starting at the owl's feet.

FINISHED MEASUREMENTS

Blanket, 12"/30.5 cm across; owl, 2½"/6.5 cm tall

YARN

Swans Island, sport weight, 100% washable merino wool, 175 yds (160 m)/1.75 oz (50 g) Color 101 Snowy Owl

2

NEEDLES

Set of four US 3 (3.25 mm) double-point needles and US 3 (3.25 mm) circular needle 16"/40 cm long *or size needed to obtain correct gauge*

GAUGE

24 stitches and 48 rows = 4"/10 cm in garter stitch

OTHER SUPPLIES

Crochet hook for cast on, polyester fiberfill, scraps of lace weight or fingering weight yarn for the owl's features, yarn needle, stitch markers

SPECIAL ABBREVIATIONS

3/3 RC

Slip 3 stitches onto cable needle and hold in back, k3 from left needle, k3 from cable needle

3/3 LC

Slip 3 stitches onto cable needle and hold in front, k3 from left needle, k3 from cable needle

Pattern Essentials

CIRCLE OF BUTTONHOLE STITCH EMBROIDERY

With yarn threaded on yarn needle, bring needle from back to front at the edge of the circle and pull yarn through; pass from front to back through the center of the circle; pass from back to front immediately to the right of the last exit point on the edge; with yarn under the needle tip from left to right, pull yarn through.

KNITTING THE OWL

- Using a provisional cast on method (see page 281), cast on 24 stitches. Divide the stitches onto three needles, with 12 stitches on one needle and 6 on each of the other two. Join into a round, being careful not to twist the stitches.

- Rounds 1–3: Knit.

- Rounds 4 and 5: P8, k8, p8.

- Rounds 6 and 7: P7, k10, p7.

- Rounds 8 and 9: P6, k12, p6.

- Round 10: P6, 3/3 RC, 3/3 LC, p6.

- Rounds 11–20: P6, k12, p6.

- Round 21: Repeat Round 10.

- Rounds 22–26: P6, k12, p6.

- Round 27: Repeat Round 10.

- **Round 28:** Knit.
- Rearrange stitches so that the 12 stitches that hold the owl's front are on one needle and the other 12 stitches are on the other needle. Use the three-needle bind off (see page 282) to bind off the front and back stitches together, leaving a 6"/15 cm tail for sewing. Weave this tail back to center of seam in preparation for sewing ears.

Finishing the Owl's Head

- Following the shape of the smaller cables and using photo as a guide, use scrap yarn to embroider a buttonhole stitch wheel for each of the eyes. Embroider

the beak below the eyes. Stuff the owl's body with fiberfill.

- Use yarn tail at center top to draw the center stitch of the bound-off edge down into the body to create the owl's ears. Secure tail inside body.

KNITTING THE BLANKET BODY

- Carefully remove scrap yarn from the provisional cast on a few stitches at a time, placing the stitches on a needle as you go. Place 8 stitches on each of three needles. Join and purl one round, placing a marker between the 4th and 5th stitch on each needle. These markers along with the ends of each needle, mark the six segments where you will be making the increases.
- **Round 1:** *K1, M1L, knit to marker, M1R, sm, k1, M1L, knit to end of needle, M1R; repeat from * on needles 2 and 3. *You now have 36 stitches.*
- **Round 2:** Purl.
- **Round 3:** Knit.
- **Round 4:** Purl.
- Repeat rounds 1–4 sixteen times. *You now have 228 stitches.*
- Bind off using 3-stitch I-cord bind off (see page 277). Weave in ends.

Fat Kitty

Designed by Jessica Miller

This fat cat is knitted in the round from the bottom up, with no seaming required. Stitches for the tail are picked up at the center back, and the tail is knit as a skinny tube in the round. Finish the look with a simple embroidered face.

FINISHED MEASUREMENTS

6½"/16.5 cm tall

YARN

Catskill Merino Worsted, 100% Saxon merino wool, 140 yds (128 m)/2 oz (57 g), Warm Gray

NEEDLES

Set of four US 6 (4 mm) double-point needles *or size needed to obtain correct gauge*

GAUGE

19 stitches and 28 rows = 4"/10 cm in stockinette stitch

OTHER SUPPLIES

Polyester fiberfill, scrap yarn, yarn needle, embroidery needle, embroidery thread

KNITTING THE BASE

- Cast on 4 stitches. Divide onto 3 needles and join into a round, being careful not to twist the stitches.

- Round 1: *Kfb; repeat from * to end of round. *You now have* 8 stitches.

- Round 2: Repeat Round 1. *You now have* 16 stitches.

- Round 3: Knit.

- Round 4: *Kfb, k1; repeat from * to end of round. *You now have* 24 stitches.

- Round 5: Knit.

- Round 6: *Kfb, k2; repeat from * to end of round. *You now have* 32 stitches.

- Round 7: Knit.

- Round 8: *Kfb, k3; repeat from * to end of round. *You now have* 40 stitches.

- Round 9: Knit.

- Round 10: *Kfb, k4; repeat from * to end of round. *You now have* 48 stitches.

- Round 11: Knit.

- Round 12: *Kfb, k5; repeat from * to end of round. *You now have* 56 stitches.

KNITTING THE BODY

- Knit even for 25 rounds.

KNITTING THE HEAD

- Round 1: *K3, k2tog, k18, ssk, k3; repeat from * once more. *You now have* 52 stitches.

- Round 2: Knit.

- Round 3: *K2, k2tog, k18, ssk, k2; repeat from * once more. *You now have* 48 stitches.

- Round 4: Knit.

- Round 5: *K1, k2tog, k18, ssk, k1; repeat from * once more. *You now have* 44 stitches.

- Round 6: Knit.

- Round 7: *K2tog, k18, ssk; repeat from * once more. *You now have* 40 stitches.

- Stuff body with fiberfill.

Divide for the Ears

- Next Row: K10, put next 20 stitches on scrap yarn to hold, k10. *You now have* 20 stitches.

Right Ear

Note: Stuff the ear as you go.

- Round 1: Knit.

- Round 2: *Ssk, k6, k2tog; repeat from * once more. *You now have* 16 stitches.

- Rounds 3 and 4: Knit.

- Round 5: *Ssk, k4, k2tog; repeat from * once more. *You now have* 12 stitches.

- Rounds 6 and 7: Knit.

- Round 8: *Ssk, k2, k2tog; repeat from * once more. *You now have* 8 stitches.

- Round 9: Knit.

- Round 10: *Ssk, k2tog; repeat from * once more. *You now have* 4 stitches.

- Round 11: K2tog twice.

- With the ear stuffed, cut yarn and draw through the remaining two stitches. Pull yarn to inside and weave in to secure.

Left Ear

- Place 20 held stitches on the needles. Leaving a 6"/12 cm tail for sewing, join yarn at the center of the head, near the base of the right ear. Round starts at center of head. Note: To help close the gap between the ears, when knitting the first stitch of the round, pick up a thread from the base of the right ear and knit it together with the first stitch of the round.

- Knit 1 round even.
- Continue as for right ear, starting with Round 2.

KNITTING THE TAIL

Note: Tail stitches are picked up and worked from a single column of stitches at center back.

- Beginning in body Round 2 at center back, with one double-point needle pick up and knit (see page 281) 1 stitch in each of Rounds 2 through 9, being careful to pick up from the same column of stitches throughout; with a second double-point needle pick up and knit 1 stitch in each of Rounds 9 through 2, working into the other half of the same column of stitches. *You now have* 16 stitches.

- Divide stitches onto three double-point needles and join to work in the round. Knit every round for 6"/15 cm or desired length, stuffing the tail as you go. **Note:** Stuffing loosely and leaving the first ½"/13 mm of tail unstuffed will allow it to curve nicely around the body.

- When the tail is long enough, shape the end as follows.

- Round 1: *K2, k2tog; repeat from * to end of round. *You now have* 12 stitches.

- Round 2: Knit.

- Round 3: *K1, k2tog; repeat from * to end of round. *You now have* 8 stitches.

- Round 4: Knit.

- Round 5: *K2tog; repeat from * to end of round. *You now have* 4 stitches.

- Cut yarn, leaving a 12"/30.5 cm tail. Thread tail onto yarn needle and draw through remaining stitches; pull up snug and fasten off. Thread yarn down into stuffed tail and tack the tail to the body in 2 or 3 spots so it curls cozily around.

- Using the photograph as a guide, embroider a cute face on your kitty.

Little

miscellany

Clean-Up Cloths

Designed by Doreen L. Marquart, Needles 'n Pins Yarn Shoppe

Make bath time extra fun with a bright washcloth and soap sack. Packaged with soap and other bath necessities, these make a perfect shower gift.

FINISHED MEASUREMENTS
Wash cloth: 7"/18 cm square
Soap sack: 3 x 5½"/7.5 x 14 cm

YARN
ONline Linie 2 Supersocke Silk Color, 55% superwash merino wool/20% silk/25% nylon, 219 yds (200 m)/1.75 oz (50 g), Color 0109

NEEDLES
US 2 (2.75 mm) straight needles *or size needed to obtain correct gauge*

GAUGE
32 stitches and 56 rows = 4"/10 cm in Garter Rib pattern

OTHER SUPPLIES
Yarn needle

Pattern Essentials

GARTER RIB
(multiple of 10 + 6 stitches)

Row 1: K6, *p5, k5; repeat from * to end of row.

Repeat Row 1 for pattern.

FANCY RIB
(multiple of 6 stitches)

Row 1 (RS): Knit.

Row 2: P2, k2, *p4, k2; repeat from * to last 2 stitches, p2.

Repeat Rows 1 and 2 for pattern.

KNITTING THE WASH CLOTH

- Cast on 56 stitches. Work in Garter Rib pattern until piece measures 7"/18 cm.

- Bind off.

- Weave in ends.

KNITTING THE SOAP SACK

- Cast on 42 stitches. Work in Fancy Rib until piece measures 4½"/11.5 cm, ending with Row 2.

- **Eyelet Row (RS):** *K1, ssk, yo twice, k2tog, k1; repeat from * to end of row.

- **Next Row:** *P2, (k1, k1 tbl) into double yarnover, p2; repeat from * to end of row.

- Work 4 rows in Fancy Rib pattern.

- Bind off loosely in pattern.

The Drawstring

- Cast on 76 stitches.

- Knit 1 row.

- Bind off loosely.

Finishing

- Fold sack in half and sew side and bottom seams. Weave in all ends.

- Thread drawstring through eyelet holes. Knot ends of drawstring together.

Pretty in Pink Bath Set

Designed by Diana Foster

Light and soft washcloths are the order of the day for delicate baby skin, and this cotton set fills the bill. You may want to knit a set for yourself, too.

FINISHED MEASUREMENTS
Wash cloth: 10"/25.5 cm diameter
Soap sack: 4 x 6"/10 x 15 cm

YARN
Unger Gloria, 100% cotton, 185 yds (169 m)/1.75 oz (50 g), Color 4307 Pink

NEEDLES
US 3 (3.25 mm) circular needle 40"/100 cm long, two US 3 (3.25 mm) circular needles 24"/60 cm long, or set of four US 3 (3.25 mm) double-point needles, and set of five US 1 (2.25 mm) double-point needles for I-cord *or size needed to obtain correct gauge*

GAUGE
24 stitches and 40 rounds = 4"/10 cm in stockinette stitch on larger needle

OTHER SUPPLIES
8 stitch markers, yarn needle

KNITTING THE WASHCLOTH

Note: Choose appropriate needle type for Magic Loop, two circulars, or double-point knitting.

- Cast on 8 stitches, pm, and join into a round, being careful not to twist the stitches.

- **Round 1:** Knit.

- **Round 2:** *Kfb; repeat from * to end of round. *You now have* 16 stitches.

- **Round 3:** *Yo, k2, pm; repeat from * to end of round.

- **Round 4:** Knit.

- **Round 5:** *Yo, knit to marker; repeat from * to end of round.

- **Round 6:** Knit.

- Repeat Rounds 5 and 6 until you have 18 stitches between each marker, ending with Round 6.

The Lace Pattern

- **Round 1:** *Yo, k8, yo, k2tog, k8; repeat from * to end of round. *You now have* 19 stitches between each marker.

- **Round 2:** Knit.

- **Round 3:** *Yo, k8, yo, k2tog, yo, k2tog, k7; repeat from * to end of round. *You now have* 20 stitches between each marker.

- **Round 4:** Knit.

- **Round 5:** *Yo, k10, yo, k2tog, k8; repeat from * to end of round. *You now have* 21 stitches between each marker.

- **Rounds 6, 8, and 10:** Knit.

- **Rounds 7, 9, and 11:** *Yo, knit to marker; repeat from * to end of round. You will have 24 stitches between each marker at the end of Round 11.

- **Round 12:** Knit.

Working the Picot Bind Off

- K2, bind off 1, slip stitch from right needle to left needle, cast on 2 stitches using the cable cast on method (see page 276); *bind off 5 stitches, place last stitch from right needle to left needle; repeat from * around, bind off last stitch.

- Weave in ends. Block.

KNITTING THE SOAP SACK

- Cast on 8 stitches, pm, and join into a round, being careful not to twist the stitches.

- **Round 1:** Knit.

- **Round 2:** *Kfb; repeat from * to end of round. *You now have* 16 stitches.

- **Round 3:** K1, *pm, yo, k2; repeat from * to last stitch, k1. *You now have* 24 stitches.

- **Round 4:** Knit.

- **Round 5:** K1, sm, *yo, knit to next marker; repeat from * to end of round. *You now have* 32 stitches.

- **Rounds 6–9:** Repeat Rows 4 and 5 two more times. *You now have* 6 stitches between the markers, 48 stitches total.

- **Round 10:** Knit.

- **Round 11:** Purl.

- **Round 12:** K1, *yo, k2tog, k4; repeat from * to end of round.

- **Round 13:** Knit.

- **Rounds 14–45:** Repeat Rounds 12 and 13 sixteen more times.

- **Rounds 46 and 47:** K1, *p1, k5; repeat from * to last 4 stitches, k4.

- **Round 48:** K1, *yo, k2tog, k4; repeat from * to last 3 stitches, k3.

- **Rounds 49 and 50:** Repeat Rows 46 and 47.

Working the Picot Bind Off

- Work the picot bind off as for wash cloth, but in last set bind off 6 stitches instead of 5. Weave in ends.

FINISHING

- With smaller needle, make a 2-stitch I-cord (see page 277) 14"/35.5 cm long. Weave cord through last set of yarnovers.

Bath Toy Hammock

Designed by Kathy Sasser

With this fun and easily knitted hammock, bath toy storage is no longer a problem. Worked on a large needle, the net-like fabric will stretch to accommodate lots of toys.

255

FINISHED MEASUREMENTS

Approximately 30"/76 cm circumference, 9"/23 cm deep

YARN

Lily Sugar 'n Cream, 100% cotton, 710 yds (650 m)/14 oz (400 g), Pale Yellow (4)

NEEDLES

US 8 (5 mm) straight needles and US 11 (8 mm) circular needle 16"/40 cm long *or size needed to obtain correct gauge*

GAUGE

10½ stitches and 16 rows = 4"/10 cm in pattern (gauge is not crucial)

OTHER SUPPLIES

Stitch marker, yarn needle, 2 large suction hooks

Pattern Essentials

NET LACE
(multiple of 6 stitches)

Round 1: *K3, yo, k3tog, yo; repeat from * to end of round.

Round 2: Knit.

Round 3: *Yo, k3tog, yo, k3; repeat from * to end of round.

Round 4: Knit.

Repeat Rounds 1–4 for pattern.

KNITTING THE HAMMOCK

- With large circular needle, cast on 78 stitches. Place marker and join into a round, being careful not to twist the stitches.

- Purl 3 rounds.

- Work Rounds 1 through 4 of Net Lace pattern 9 times.

- Next Round: *K2tog; repeat from * to end of round. *You now have 39 stitches.*

- Cut yarn leaving a 12"/30.5 cm tail. Thread tail through remaining stitches, pull up snug, and fasten off.

The Handles (make 2)

- With smaller straight needles, cast on 20 stitches. Bind off.

FINISHING

- Fold cast-on edge in half and mark the fold. Sew ends of handles ½"/13 mm to each side of mark.

- Weave in ends.

- Apply suction cup hooks to tub area and suspend hammock from hooks.

Net Lace

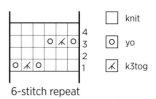

	knit
O	yo
⅄	k3tog

6-stitch repeat

Best Friend Hot Water Bottle Cover

Designed by Kendra Nitta

Use this cuddly cover on a hot water bottle to warm up the crib or to help calm an earache. It's also good for holding ice packs to soothe bumps and bruises. Worked in the round on two circular needles, the pattern easily adapts to a taller or wider bottle.

....
FINISHED MEASUREMENTS
To fit a 16-oz hot water bottle: 6"/15 cm wide and 11"/28 cm long
....
YARN
Knit Picks Galileo, 50% merino wool, 50% bamboo, 131 yds (120 m)/ 1.75 oz (50 g), Color 5183 Pearl 🧶
....
NEEDLES
Two US 4 (3.5 mm) circular needles 24"/60 cm long *or size needed to obtain correct gauge*
....
GAUGE
22 stitches and 32 rounds = 4"/10 cm in stockinette stitch
....
OTHER SUPPLIES
Stitch markers, yarn needle, small bits of contrasting yarn (optional)

KNITTING THE COVER

Note: The project uses two circular needles throughout to make it easier to differentiate between the front and the back and to try the piece on your hot water bottle as you go.

The Body

- Using Judy's Magic Cast On (see page 278), cast on 64 stitches, 32 on each needle.

- Round 1: On needle 1, *p3, (k2, p4) to last 5 stitches, k2, p3; on needle 2, repeat from *.

- Round 2: On needle 1, *kfb, p2, knit the knits and purl the purls to last 2 stitches, kfb, p1; on needle 2, repeat from *. *You now have* 68 stitches.

- **Round 3:** On needle 1, *p1, (k2, p4) to last 3 stitches, k2, p1; on needle 2, repeat from *.

- **Round 4:** On needle 1, *kfb, (k2, p4) to last 3 stitches, k1, kfb, p1; on needle 2, repeat from *. *You now have 72 stitches.*

- **Rounds 5–7:** On needle 1, *p2, (k2, p4) to last 4 stitches, k2, p2; on needle 2, repeat from *.

- **Rounds 8–12:** On needle 1, *k1, p4, (k2, p4) to last stitch, k1; on needle 2, repeat from *.

The Front Motif

- **Rounds 1–5:** On needle 1, p2, k2, work Rows 1–5 of chart, k2, p2; on needle 2, p2, (k2, p4) to last 4 stitches, k2, p2.

- **Rounds 6–10:** On needle 1, k1, p3, work chart as established, p3, k1; on needle 2, k1, p4, (k2, p4) to last stitch, k1.

- **Rounds 11–15:** Repeat Rounds 1–5, working chart as established.

- **Rounds 16–20:** Repeat Rounds 6–10, working chart as established.

- **Rounds 21–25:** Repeat Rounds 1–5, working chart as established.

- **Rounds 26–30:** Repeat Rounds 6–10, working chart as established.

- **Rounds 31–35:** Repeat Rounds 1–5, working chart as established.

- **Rounds 36–40:** *K1, p4, (k2, p4) to last stitch, k1; on needle 2, repeat from *.

- **Rounds 41–45:** *P2, (k2, p4) to last 4 stitches, k2, p2; on needle 2, repeat from *.

Shaping the Top

- **Round 1:** On needle 1, *p3, p2tog, (k2, p4) to last 7 stitches, k2, p2tog tbl, p3; on needle 2, repeat from *. *You now have 68 stitches.*

- **Round 2:** On needle 1, *p4, (k2, p4) to end of needle; on needle 2, repeat from *.

- **Round 3:** On needle 1, *p2, p2tog, (k2, p4) to last 6 stitches, k2, p2tog tbl, p2; on needle 2, repeat from *. *You now have 64 stitches.*

- **Round 4:** On needle 1, *p3, (k2, p4) to last 5 stitches, k2, p3; on needle 2, repeat from *.

- **Round 5:** On needle 1, *p1, p2tog, (k2, p4) to last 5 stitches, k2, p2tog tbl, p1; on needle 2, repeat from *. *You now have 60 stitches.*

- **Round 6:** On needle 1, *p2tog, (k2, p2) to last 2 stitches, p2tog tbl; on needle 2, repeat from *. *You now have 56 stitches.*

- Try the piece on the water bottle. If it does not fit over the widest part of the bottle, undo the last two rounds so you have 64 stitches.

The Ribbing

- Transfer the first stitch from needle 1 to needle 2.

- **Next Round:** On needle 1, (k2, p2) to last stitch, p1, p1 from needle 2; on needle 2, (k2, p2) to end of round.

- Continue in k2, p2 rib as established for 4½"/11.5 cm or desired length. Bind off using Jeny's Surprisingly Stretchy Bind Off (see page 277).

FINISHING

- Weave in ends. Gently block piece around hot water bottle, folding the cuff down at the top. Optional: Use contrasting yarn and duplicate stitch (see page 276) to add a nose and collar.

Best Friend

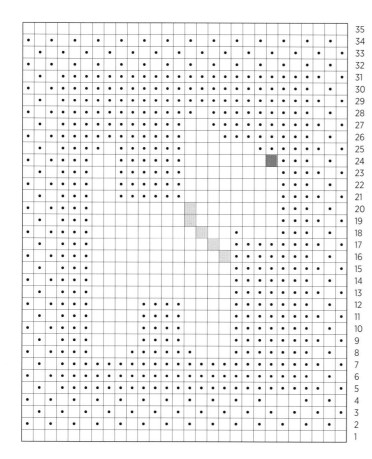

□	knit
•	purl
▨ ▨	duplicate st

Little Sweetheart Sleeping Sack

Designed by Mone Dräger

Keep baby warm and secure in a lovely and snuggly sleeping sack. This one features a row of hearts up the center front.

SIZE AND FINISHED MEASUREMENTS
To fit 0–3 months: 15½"/39.5 cm long, 17"/43 cm circumference

YARN
Malabrigo Worsted, 100% merino wool, 210 yds (192 m)/3.5 oz (100 g), Color 11 Apple Green (4)

NEEDLES
US 7 (4.5 mm) circular needle 16"/40 cm long and two US 7 (4.5 mm) double-point needles for cast on *or size needed to obtain correct gauge*

GAUGE
20 stitches and 30 rounds = 4"/10 cm in stockinette stitch

OTHER SUPPLIES
3 stitch markers, yarn needle

KNITTING THE SACK

- Using the figure-8 cast on method (see page 277), cast on 46 stitches. With circular needle, knit 23 stitches from first needle then 23 stitches from second needle as follows.

- **Set-Up Round:** K3, pm, k20, pm, k23 tbl, pm.

- **Round 1:** K1, M1R, knit to marker, work row 1 of Little Sweetheart chart across next 17 stitches, knit to one stitch before marker, M1L, k2, M1R, knit to one stitch before marker, M1L, k1. *You now have 50 stitches.*

- **Round 2:** Knit to marker, work chart as established, knit to end of round.

- **Round 3:** (K1, M1R) twice, knit to marker, work chart as established, knit to 2 stitches before marker, (M1L, k1) twice, (k1, M1R) twice, knit to two stitches before marker, (M1L, k1) twice. *You now have 58 stitches.*

- **Round 4:** Repeat Round 2.

- **Round 5:** K1, M1R, knit to marker, work chart as established, knit to one stitch before marker, M1L, k2, M1R, knit to one stitch before marker, M1L, k1. *You now have 62 stitches.*

- **Round 6:** Repeat Round 2.

- **Round 7:** K1, M1R, k2, M1R, knit to marker, work chart as established, knit to three stitches before marker, (M1L, k2) two times, M1R, k2, M1R, knit to three stitches before marker, M1L, k2, M1L, K1. *You now have 70 stitches.*

- **Rounds 8 and 9:** Repeat Round 2.

- **Round 10:** Repeat Round 5. *You now have 74 stitches.*

- **Rounds 11 and 12:** Repeat Round 2.

- **Round 13:** Repeat Round 7. *You now have 82 stitches.*

- **Rounds 14–16:** Repeat Round 2 working Rows 14–16 of chart.

- **Round 17:** Repeat Round 5. *You now have 86 stitches.*

- Continue even in pattern as established until Little Sweetheart chart Rows 1 through 26 have been worked four times total.

The Ribbing

- **Set-Up Round:** P1, (k2, p1, p2tog) twice, k2, work Row 1 of chart, (k2, p1, p2tog) twice, (k2, p2) four times, (k2, p1, p2tog) three times, (k2, p2) three times, k2, p1.

- **Next round:** P1, (k2, p2) twice, k2, work chart Row 2, (k2, p2) to last 3 stitches, k2, p1.

- Continue in pattern as established until Chart Rows 1 through 13 have been worked.

FINISHING

- Knit two rounds. Bind off loosely. Weave in ends and block slightly.

Little Sweetheart

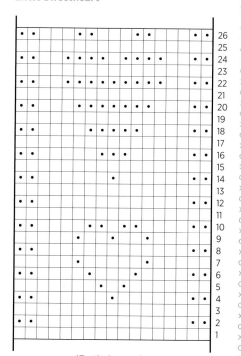

17-stitch panel

☐ knit

• purl

Full of Love Sleep Sack

Designed by Kelli Kemery

Starting at the top, this sleep sack is knit back and forth and then joined and finished in the round. The long button band allows for easy accessibility, and the drawstring bottom makes diaper changing easy.

SIZE AND FINISHED MEASUREMENTS
To fit 0–3 months: 15"/38 cm chest circumference, 17"/43 cm long

YARN
Madelinetosh Tosh DK, 100% superwash merino wool, 225 yds (205 m)/3.5 oz (100 g), Amber Trinket (3)

NEEDLES
US 6 (4 mm) circular needle 16"/40 cm long and one US 6 (4 mm) double-point needle *or size needed to obtain correct gauge*

GAUGE
22 stitches and 28 rows = 4"/10 cm in stockinette stitch

OTHER SUPPLIES
Cable needle, yarn needle, seven ¾"/ 19 mm buttons, sewing needle and coordinating thread

SPECIAL ABBREVIATIONS

2/2 LC
   Slip 2 stitches to cable needle and hold in front, knit 2 from left needle, knit 2 from cable needle

2/2 RC
   Slip 2 stitches to cable needle and hold in back, knit 2 from left needle, knit 2 from cable needle

2/1 RPC
   Slip 1 stitch to cable needle and hold in back, knit 2 from left needle, purl 1 from cable needle

2/1 LPC
   Slip 2 stitches to cable needle and hold in front, purl 1 from left needle, knit 2 from cable needle

KNITTING THE YOKE

- Cast on 68 stitches using the long-tail cast on method (see page 279).

- Row 1 (WS): K6, pm, k17, pm, k14, pm, k17, pm, k14.

- Row 2: (Knit to 1 stitch before marker, kfb, sm, kfb) 4 times, knit to end of row. *You now have* 76 stitches.

- Row 3: Knit.

- Row 4: (Knit to 1 stitch before marker, kfb, sm, kfb) 4 times, knit to last 6 stitches, k2tog, yo (buttonhole made), k4. *You now have* 84 stitches.

- Row 5 and all odd-numbered rows: Knit.

- Rows 6-13: Repeat Rows 2 and 3 four times. *You now have* 116 stitches.

- Row 14: Repeat Row 4 (buttonhole made). *You now have* 124 stitches.

Note: As you work down the body, place a buttonhole in this manner every 10th row.

- Row 15: Knit.

- Row 16: Repeat Row 2. *You now have* 132 stitches.

SEPARATING FOR THE ARMHOLES

- Row 1 (WS): Removing markers as you come to them, *knit to one stitch before marker, kfb, bind off next 33 stitches, kfb; repeat from * for second shoulder, knit to end of row. *You now have* 70 stitches; 15 left front stitches, 32 back stitches, 23 right front stitches.

- Row 2: Knit left front stitches, cast on 10 stitches for the underarm, knit back stitches, cast on 10 stitches for underarm, knit right front stitches. *You now have* 90 stitches.

Cable Panel

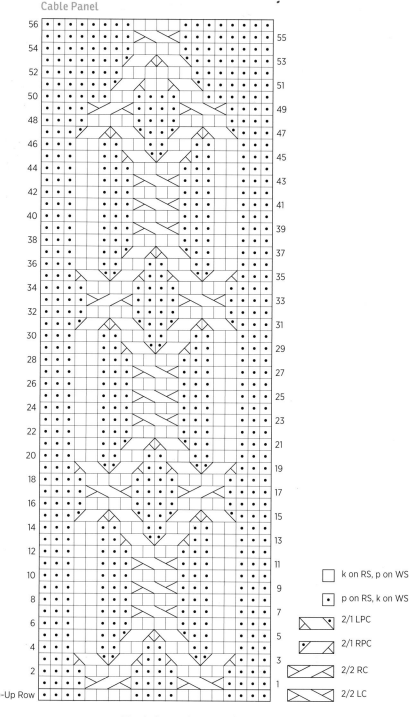

20-stitch panel

Legend:
- ☐ k on RS, p on WS
- ⊡ p on RS, k on WS
- 2/1 LPC
- 2/1 RPC
- 2/2 RC
- 2/2 LC

KNITTING THE BODY

- **Row 1 (WS):** K6, work set-up row of Cable Panel chart across next 20 stitches, pm, purl to last 6 stitches, k6.

- **Row 2:** Knit to marker, work Row 1 of cable chart, k6.

- Keeping first and last 6 stitches in garter stitch and continuing to work chart and buttonholes as established, work even until Row 56 of the chart is complete.

Joining for Knitting in the Round

- **Round 1 (RS):** Place the last 6 stitches of the row (buttonhole band) onto a double-point needle and hold in front of the first 6 stitches (button band). Place marker to indicate beginning of round, knit the first stitch on the double-point needle together with the first stitch on the left needle to join bands, continue to join each of the remaining 5 pairs of stitches; knit to end of round. *You now have* 84 stitches.

- Continue knitting in the round until your work measures 12"/30.5 cm from the underarm.

- Work k2, p2 ribbing for 1½"/4 cm.

- **Eyelet Round:** *K2, yo, p2tog; repeat from * to end of round.

- Work k2, p2 ribbing for 3 more rounds. Bind off in pattern.

FINISHING

- Knit 4-stitch I-cord (see page 277) for 26"/66 cm. Thread I-cord through eyelets and tie into a bow. Weave in ends, block, and enjoy!

Car Seat-Friendly Baby Sack

Designed by Judith Durant

Here's a quick and easy way to bundle up baby for a car trip in the dead of winter — simply slip this over clothing, including shoes. The split for legs makes it possible to buckle baby up in the car seat.

SIZE AND FINISHED MEASUREMENTS
To fit 0–3 months: 25"/63.5 cm circumference, 22"/56 cm tall, including hood

YARN
Lion Brand Fishermen's Wool, 100% wool, 465 yds (425 m)/8 oz (227 g), Color 098 Natural (4)

NEEDLES
US 9 (5.5 mm) circular needle 29"/74 cm long and US 7 (4.5 mm) circular needle 16"/40 cm long *or size needed to obtain correct gauge*

GAUGE
18 stitches and 30 rows = 4"/10 cm in pattern stitch on larger needle

OTHER SUPPLIES
Stitch markers, stitch holders or scrap yarn, yarn needle, five ⅝"/15 mm buttons, sewing needle and coordinating thread

SPECIAL ABBREVIATIONS
k2sps
    K2tog, slip resulting stitch back to left needle, lift second stitch on left needle over slipped stitch, slip remaining stitch to right needle.
p2sps
    P2tog, slip resulting stitch back to left needle, lift second stitch on left needle over slipped stitch, slip remaining stitch to right needle.
sk2p
    Slip 1, k2tog, pass the slipped stitch over the k2tog.
sp2p
    Slip 1, p2tog, pass the slipped stitch over the p2tog.

Pattern Essentials

MOSS STITCH
(multiple of 4 stitches plus 2)

Row 1: *K2, p2; repeat from * to last 2 stitches, k2.

Row 2: *P2, k2; repeat from * to last 2 stitches, p2.

Row 3: K1, p1, *k2, p2; repeat from * to last 4 stitches, k2, p1, k1.

Row 4: P1, k1, *p2, k2; repeat from * to last 4 stitches, p2, k1, p1.

Repeat Rows 1–4 for pattern.

KNITTING THE "LEGS"

• Cast on 58 stitches. Work in Moss Stitch until piece measures 6¼"/16 cm, ending with Row 2 or 4 of pattern. Cut yarn and place stitches on holder. Repeat for second "leg" but leave stitches on needle.

JOINING THE TWO HALVES

• With RS facing, place held stitches on circular needle to the left of the current stitches. Work stitches of first half in pattern as established to the last stitch. Slip last stitch of first half and first stitch of second half to right needle. Pass last stitch of first half over first stitch of second half; slip the resulting stitch from right needle to left needle; pass second stitch on left needle over first stitch and off the needle — 2 stitches decreased. Continue in pattern as established to end of row. *You now have* 114 stitches. Place markers in the first and last stitches of this row.

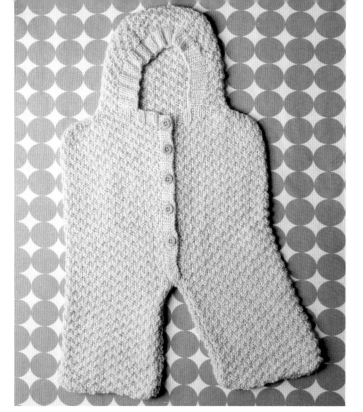

• Continuing in pattern as established, work 29, pm, work 56, pm, work 29. Continue in pattern as established until piece measures 15"/38 cm, ending with Row 4 of Moss Stitch.

SHAPING THE SHOULDERS

• Row 1: *Work to 4 stitches before marker, sk2p, k1, sm, k1, k2sps; repeat from * once, work in pattern to end of row. *You now have* 106 stitches.

• Row 2: *Work to 4 stitches before marker, sp2p, p1, sm, p1, p2sps; repeat from * once, work in pattern to end of row. *You now have* 98 stitches.

• Repeat Rows 1 and 2 twice more, ending with Row 2 of Moss Stitch. *You now have* 66 stitches and piece measures 16"/40.5 cm.

KNITTING THE HOOD

• Next Row: (K2, p2) twice, k2, pm; work in Moss Stitch as established over 46 stitches, pm; (k2, p2) twice, k2.

- This row establishes k2/p2 rib on first and last 10 stitches, and a continuation of Moss Stitch over remaining 46 stitches. Work in pattern as established for 3 more rows.
- **Next Row:** Bind off 10 stitches in pattern; work Moss Stitch over 46 stitches; with separate 10"/25.5 cm length of yarn, bind off remaining 10 stitches in pattern.
- Turn work and, with attached yarn, begin Moss Stitch, establishing stockinette stitch edge stitches, and continue for 5"/12.5 cm.
- Bind off 14 stitches at the beginning of the next two rows. Working remaining 18 stitches only, continue in pattern as established until piece measures 3"/7.5 cm from bound-off rows or is equal to the width of the bound-off sides. Bind off. Sew the top of the hood to the side panels.

The Hood Band

- With RS facing, beginning at lower right edge of hood, and using smaller needle, pick up and knit 24 stitches to first seam; pick up and knit 16 stitches along top; pick up and knit 24 stitches to lower left edge. *You now have* 64 stitches.
- **Row 1 (WS):** P3, *k2, p2; repeat from * to last 5 stitches, k2, p3.
- **Row 2:** K3, *p2, k2; repeat from * to last 5 stitches, p2, k3.
- Repeat Rows 1 and 2 three more times.
- Bind off in pattern with larger needle. Sew beginning and ending band edges to 5 bound-off front edge stitches.

KNITTING THE FRONT BANDS

- With RS facing, smaller needle, and beginning at left neck edge, pick up and knit 43 stitches to marker.
- **Row 1 (WS):** *P2, k2; repeat from * to last 3 stitches, p3.
- **Row 2:** K3, *p2, k2; repeat from * to end of row.
- **Row 3:** Repeat Row 1.
- Bind off in pattern with larger needle.

- With RS facing, smaller needle, and beginning at marker on right front edge, pick up and knit 43 stitches to neck edge.
- **Row 1 (WS):** P3, *k2, p2; repeat from * to end of row.
- **Row 2 (Buttonhole Row):** K2, p2, *k2, p2, k1, yo, p2tog, p1; repeat from * 3 more times, k2, p2, yo, k2tog, k1.
- **Row 3:** Repeat Row 1.
- **Row 4:** *K2, p2; repeat from * to last 3 stitches, k3.
- Bind off in pattern with larger needle.

FINISHING

- Weave in all ends. Fold sides to center front and sew "legs" together along bottom and through crotch. Lap buttonhole band over button band and sew together at bottom. Sew buttons securely with needle and thread opposite buttonholes.

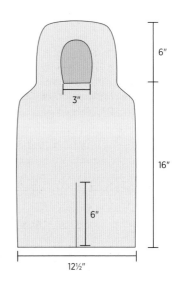

Mom's Stress Reducer

Designed by Judith Durant

Rice fills this handy little pillow that can be used hot or cold to ease sore muscles or soothe a headache. While the little one sleeps, remove this from the freezer or zap it for a minute or more in the microwave, place where needed, and relax.

Pattern Essentials

LITTLE BIRDS
(multiple of 14 + 8 stitches)

Row 1 (WS): Purl.

Row 2: Knit.

Row 3: Purl.

Row 4: K10, slip 2 wyib, *k12, slip 2 wyib; repeat from * to last 10 stitches, k10.

Row 5: P10, slip 2 wyif, *p12, slip 2 wyif; repeat from * to last 10 stitches, p10.

Row 6: *K8, slip 2 wyib, drop 1st slipped stitch from previous row to front, slip same 2 stitches back to left needle, pick up dropped stitch and knit it, k2, drop slipped stitch from left needle, k2, pick up dropped stitch and knit it; repeat from * to end of row.

Row 7: Purl.

Row 8: Knit.

Row 9: Purl.

Row 10: K3, slip 2 wyib, *k12, slip 2 wyib; repeat from * to last 3 stitches, k3.

Row 11: P3, slip 2 wyif, *p12, slip 2 wyif; repeat from * to last 3 stitches, p3.

Row 12: K1, repeat from * of Row 6 to last stitch, k1.

Repeat Rows 1–12 for pattern.

FINISHED MEASUREMENTS
Approximately 10"/25.5 cm wide and 5"/12.5 cm tall

YARN
Kollage 1/2 N 1/2, 50% milk/50% wool, 174 yds (159 m)/1.75 oz (50 g), Eggplant (3)

NEEDLES
US 3 (3.25 mm) straight needles *or size needed to obtain correct gauge*

GAUGE
30 stitches and 43 rows = 4"/10 cm in pattern, blocked

Note: Gauge is not crucial, just be sure your stitches are small enough to hold the rice. Needle size used on sample is smaller than manufacturer's recommended needle size.

OTHER SUPPLIES
Crochet hook for cast on, yarn needle, scrap yarn for cast on and stitch holder, white rice

KNITTING THE PILLOW

- Cast on 78 stitches using a provisional cast on method (see page 281) and leaving a 30"/76 cm tail for seaming. Work Rows 1 through 12 of the Little Birds pattern 9 times. Place stitches on scrap yarn to hold. Cut yarn, leaving a 12"/30.5 cm tail for seaming. Block piece to approximately 10½ x 10½"/26.5 x 26.5 cm.

FINISHING

- Place held stitches onto a needle. Undo provisional cast on and place stitches onto second needle. Join the ends with Kitchener stitch (see page 278). Sew one short end. Weave in ends. Fill the pillow with rice as desired (sample uses 2 cups). Sew remaining edge.

Little Birds Pattern

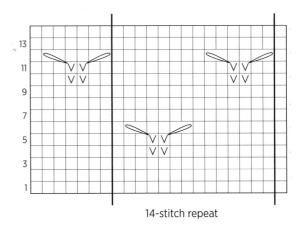

14-stitch repeat

☐ knit on RS, purl on WS

▣ purl on RS, knit on WS

V Slip 1 wyib on RS, slip 1 wyif on WS

sl 2 wyib, drop slipped st to front, sl same 2 sts to needle, k2, knit dropped st

drop 1 slipped st to front, k2, knit dropped st

appendix

About the Designers

Grace Akhrem

Since 2006, Grace has been publishing patterns and teaching advanced knitting classes across the country. In addition to having her own line of patterns, she has been published in several books and magazines. You can find Grace's full pattern store on Ravelry (*www.ravelry.com/stores/grace-akhrem-2*).

Robin Allen

Knitwear designer Robin Allen (atexasgirl on Ravelry) lives in a little red cabin in the Texas Hill Country. She loves cables, stranded colorwork, and designs that look more challenging than they are to knit. See what she's up to at: *http://atexasgirlknits.wordpress.com*.

Julie L. Anderson

Julie is a self-taught knitter and from the start she was creating things on her own and could often be found knitting toys for children. This soon became her passion. She strives to design toys with a whimsical feel that children will love. She likes to incorporate different textures into her designs. Visit her online at *www.the-byrds-nest.com*.

Kirsten Avent

Kirsten is a stay-at-home mom to four young children and a college student. In her down time she loves to create new knitting patterns.

Tonia Barry

In addition to writing patterns for Tonia Barry Designs (available on Ravelry), Tonia is a member of the design team at Classic Elite Yarns. She blogs about her knitting endeavors at *http://toniabarrydesigns.wordpress.com*. Tonia has designs in several knitting publications, including Lorelei and Goose Rocks, available at *www.twistcollective.com*. She lives in New Hampshire with her husband, two teenage daughters, and a beagle.

Joan Beebe

Joan enjoys fiddling, dabbling, and puttering with yarn from her home in North Carolina. She is a long-time knitter and crocheter and has recently added weaving to her list of fiber addictions. You can find her on Ravelry, Facebook, and Twitter as SSKnits, and on Instagram as SSKnitsJoan.

Uyvonne Bigham

Uyvonne is a professional knitwear designer. She is currently a professor at the Fashion Institute of Technology (FIT) in New York City, where she teaches textile and surface design and fashion design. She has been published in *Vogue Knitting*, *Knitters*, *Family Circle Knitting,* and numerous books and periodicals in the United States. She currently resides at her estate in Bucks County, Pennsylvania.

Susan Boye

Sue has been knitting for more than 30 years and designing for more than 24. She has sold her patterns through retail outlets and online. Sue has designed and knit numerous commissioned works. She resides with her family in the greater Toronto area.

Janice Bye

Janice has a bachelor of mathematics degree and is a Canadian master knitter who believes there is always something new to learn. She loves a challenge and can always be found with many knitting and quilting projects in progress. She finds the rhythm of knitting and the interaction of color and texture to be relaxing and magical.

Vicki K. Byram

Vicki's been knitting for more than 60 years. She co-owned The Yarn Dome with her mother, Maxine Katzenberger, for many years, and then Red Oak Designs with her sister, Karla K. Brown. She's now retired with 10 grandchildren who always need new sweaters, socks, or hats. She designs with beautiful yarns made by her dear friend, Ellen, from Ellen's ½ Pint Farm, LLC.

Cathy Campbell

Cathy officially began her yarn career at Crystal Palace Yarns/Straw into Gold in 1999. She has designed for both O-Wool and Crystal Palace Yarns, and her designs have appeared in previous One-Skein Wonders books, on Ravelry, and on the show *Knitty Gritty*. She currently is promotions manager at Crystal Palace and lives in northern California with her husband, Gerry.

Lisa Chemery

Lisa is the designer behind Frogginette Knitting Patterns. Originally from France, Lisa currently lives in Germany with her husband and two young children. She started designing knitwear in 2008, with a particular love for children's knits with a European flair. You can find her and her Frogginette Knitting Patterns on Ravelry as frogginette.

Alice Curtis

Alice has had a life-long love of knitting, crocheting, and sewing, and teaching these skills to others gives her great happiness and satisfaction. She also enjoys gardening, raising chickens, and playing with her granddaughter. Her most recent accomplishment has been returning to school as a mature student to earn her business degree.

Kathleen Day

When Kathleen isn't knitting, she stays out of trouble by being a wife, mother, grandmother, friend, nurse, author/illustrator, and sock knitter. She lives in sunny California with her husband and dog, close to her children and grandchildren.

Tamara Del Sonno

Tamara has knit and crocheted since childhood and started designing for her Barbies. The loves of her life are: her beautiful growing family, her fabulous knitting buddies, and lots of yarn. Her Clickity Sticks designs can be found on Ravelry and Craftsy, or you can email her at: ClickitySticks@aol.com.

Mone Dräger

Mone lives in a small village in Germany and loves to craft and be creative. She enjoys playing around with colors and stitch patterns and has a special fancy for accessories and quick and easy knits. Find out more about her crafting adventures at *http://monemade.com*.

Judith Durant

Judith has been up to yarny things for more than 50 years. She is editor of the One-Skein Wonders series and author of several other books about knitting, including *Knit One, Bead Too* and *Increase, Decrease*. Judith is on the Web at *www.judithdurant.com*.

Ann Faith

Ann settled on knitting as her preferred needle art after cycling through the usual suspects: embroidery, quilting, and counted cross stitch, plus a brief fling with crochet. After receiving a certificate in hand knitting design from the Rhode Island School of Design in 2014, she now focuses on creating patterns for babies and children.

Diana Foster

Diana is owner of and designer for Lowellmountain Wools, LLC, a farm shop in the Northeast Kingdom of Vermont that has sheep and offers knitting classes. She is a member of the Knitting Guild Association and knitting instructor at The Old Stone House Museum in Brownington, Vermont. Visit her at *www.designs bydianafoster.com*.

Gail Gelin

Gail lives in New Hampshire with her husband, Stan, and Australian shepherd, Zephyr. She has been knitting for 48 years and continues to learn new skills to improve her craft and she passes that knowledge on to her students.

Sarah Gomez

Sarah is a young Christian knitting designer living near Pittsburg, Pennsylvania. Her previous designs have been published in *Enchanted Knits* and *Jane Austen Knits*, special issue magazines from Interweave Press. More of her designs can be found at her Website, *www.alittlebit toknit.com*, or on Ravelry, where she goes by aLittleBittoKnit.

Anita Grahn

Anita lives in the countryside outside Uppsala, Sweden, where she recently left the bioscience industry. She now works full time writing, knitting patterns, and holding classes and workshops. And doesn't regret it! If you want to see more of her work, check out *www.anitayarn.com*, or like AnitaYarn on Facebook for the latest news.

Sarah Grieve

Sarah has loved to knit since she was a child, and she also loves to design. She is continually inspired by nature and always trying something new. Her designs can be found in various magazines and on her website at *www.asarahgrieve production.com*

Ellen Harvey

A lifelong knitter, Ellen's designs have appeared in various magazines, calendars, and books, including *Lace One-Skein Wonders*. A CYCA certified knitting instructor, Ellen teaches in various settings in Connecticut and New York. When not knitting, she can be found in the library, working as a reference librarian.

Debbie Haymark

Debbie and Joe Haymark reside with their adorable Boston terrier, Bella, just north of Houston, Texas. They own a yarn shop, iPurl, located in The Woodlands, Texas. Debbie has been a knitter and crocheter for more than 40 years. In addition to being "hands on" at iPurl, they enjoy baseball, movies, antiquing, and gardening.

Rachel Henry

Rachel began designing in 2009 after a lifetime of knitting for pleasure. She is a "Fiber Factor" alum, and her patterns can be found through Ravelry, A Hundred Ravens, Classic Elite Yarns, Knitty.com, and Skacel. Rachel enjoys the little details of knitting — she adores unusual construction and novel stitch patterns. Read more at her blog: *http://remilyknits.com*.

Deborah Hess

Deborah is a teacher, but the craft (and art) of knitting continues to teach her. It has long been a source of pleasure, a springboard for problem-solving, and a refuge. She loves and gives thanks to Netta Drummond, who taught her how to knit — and much more than that — when she was just a child.

Gina House

Gina is an archer, hula hooper, and photographer, as well as the author of both *Dreamscape* and *Wonderlace* knitting books. She loves to design unique knitwear accessories with luxurious yarns. Her SleepyEyes app is free on iTunes and includes free patterns to download, patterns to purchase, and knitting tools. You can visit Gina on Facebook (SleepyEyesKnits) and on her website, *http://ginahouse.net*.

Kelli Kemery

Kelli is a mom to four little ones and learned to knit specifically to be able to make clothes for them. It wasn't long before she realized her love of designing. Now, when she is not chasing down kids or working her day job, she is creating. You can find more of her work at *www.fiber-love.com*.

Brigitte Lang

Brigitte learned to knit at age five, but didn't start writing and publishing patterns until 2000. She opened Rainbow Yarn & Fibres in Germantown, Tennessee, in 2004 and has taught countless people how to knit since. Visit her when you are next in town.

Lindsay Lewchuk

Knit Eco Chic, Lindsay's knitting pattern design company, specializes in the highest quality hand knits and knitting patterns featuring organic, natural, socially responsible, and alternative fiber yarns for the modern age. Knit Eco Chic embodies three foundational philosophies: 1. Use of eco yarns; 2. Knits that fit curves; 3. Unique and intricate patterns.

Reyna Thera Lorele

Reyna's knit and crochet patterns are featured in her Etsy shop, www.etsy.com/shop/yiyodesigns. She blogs about her fiber adventures at *www.yarn inyarnout.blogspot.co*m. She is an award-winning author of both fiction and nonfiction.

Noël Margaret

Noël is inspired by the natural world and her knitting and illustration work is dominantly animal-based. She also enjoys sharing her passion for knitting with her community and reaching further audiences through Ravelry and social media. Learn more about Noël Margaret by visiting her website, *www.noelmargaret.com.*

Karen Marlatt

Karen first picked up knitting needles in 2006 and considers it her daily meditation in a hectic house full of boys. Karen's designs are inspired by textures in nature, colors that create a mood, and finding practical ways to blanket everyday items with yarn. Find her on Ravelry as kdmcreative.

Doreen L. Marquart

When she was nine Doreen taught herself to knit and she has been knitting ever since. In 1993 she opened Needles 'n Pins Yarn Shoppe, which is now the largest shop in the Delavan, Wisconsin, area devoted exclusively to the needs of knitters and crocheters. In addition to numerous individual patterns, she has published six books, including *Easy Knits for Baby* and *Pick a Stitch, Build a Blanket*. Visit her online at *www.needlesnpins yarnshoppe.com* or on Ravelry.

Jessica Miller

Jessica is a portrait and landscape painter who has been making things as long as she can remember. She fell in love with knitting 15 years ago and has never looked back. Jessica lives in the Hudson River Valley with her family, Tarzan the cat, and way too many sweaters. Her paintings can be found at *http://jessicamillerpaintings.blogspot.com.*

Melissa Morgan-Oakes

Author of the best-selling *2-at-a-Time Socks* and *Toe-Up 2-at-a-Time Socks*, Melissa lives an eclectic lifestyle in a small Western Massachusetts home. She shares her life with her family of humans, chickens, and a dog named Yoshi.

Terry Liann Morris

Terry, also known as The Sailing Knitter, knits and designs patterns while living full time aboard her sailboat. At every port she seeks out other knitters to play with yarn together and to share her experiences, skills, and love for the craft.

Ranée Mueller

Ranée, a homemaker and mother, has been knitting since 1987. She has been designing as Arabian Knits Designs since 2004. Her designs can be found on Nimblestix and Ravelry. She shares her love of knitting, cooking, crocheting, and faith at *http://arabianknits.blogspot.com,* where she probably writes a little too much about her husband and children.

Angela Myers

Angela currently lives in northern California. She has been knitting since her Grandma taught her at age 10. She can be found on Ravelry as AMyers.

Liz Nields

Liz is a recently retired freelance designer living in the quiet community of Carlisle, Massachusetts. These days she spends her time tending orchids, gardens, and grandchildren.

Kendra Nitta

Kendra's handknit designs have appeared in several One-Skein Wonders books, as well as numerous other publications. She also designs modern quilts and sewing projects. Follow along on Twitter @missknitta and online at *www.miss knitta.com.*

Marina Orry

Marina is a French designer and knitting and crochet technical translator living in Italy. She's the author of the book *Tricot, Premières leçons* (France), published in 2012 and now in its 3rd printing. She works regularly with yarn companies and indie designers, and dreams about creating her own brand of hand-dyed yarns. She blogs at *http://melusinetricote.com.*

Izumi Ouchi

Izumi is a Japanese designer, teacher, and author of a toe-up socks book in Japan. She likes to explore Ipponbari technique and machine knitting. For more information visit her online at *http://izumiknittingdesign.jimdo.com.*

Brenda Patipa

Brenda has designed patterns for *Knitty*, *Knitter's Magazine*, *Knitscene*, *Twist Collective*, and *Lace One-Skein Wonders*. You can find her and her designs on Ravelry as BeeeepatipaKnits.

Caroline Perisho

Caroline, a former yarn store owner, found teaching inmates in her state's correctional facility for women to be her humblest knitting experience. Caroline designs patterns for several yarn and pattern companies and for her adorable pug, Ellie. This is her third book appearance in the delightful One-Skein Wonders series.

Margaret Radcliffe

Margaret is the author of the best-selling *Knitting Answer Book*, *Circular Knitting Workshop*, *The Knowledgeable Knitter*, and *The Essential Guide to Color Knitting Techniques*. She is an inveterate teacher of both knitting technique and design. You can find more about her writing, teaching, and designs at *www.maggiesrags.com*.

Jenise Reid

Jenise designs full time, mostly self-publishing, delighting in the process and end result. Her current passion is working with fine-weight yarns. She loves to hang out in her group on Ravelry, which is more fun than work!

Ruth Roland

Ruth has designed for yarn companies and online publications such as *Knitty*. Her patterns have a rhythm of interest and ease. Find her online at *http://kangathknits.weebly.com*, on Ravelry as kangath, or on Twitter @kangathknits.

Barbara Rottman

Barbara has been knitting since childhood and has explored all forms of knitting in an attempt to "master it all." Thankfully, there is no end in sight, and her endless curiosity is matched by the abundant possibilities of fiber and patterning.

Yumiko Sakurai

Yumiko has been designing since 2009. Her works appear in *Knitty*, *Interweave Knits*, and *Lace One-Skein Wonders*. She lives in Atlanta with her beautiful family. She loves photography, reading, and playing music. Please see more of her works at *www.harumidoridesigns.com*.

Kathy Sasser

Kathy is a certified Master Knitter, former yarn shop owner, and freelance knitwear designer. Her work has been published in numerous books and magazines and can also be seen on Ravelry, Craftsy, and Etsy.

Faith Schmidt

Faith designs under the name DistractedKnits for a very good reason. With nine children in the house, there's always something going on! This has led her to design patterns that are interesting to knit, but are also easy to memorize and "read," in case of one of those all-too-frequent interruptions. Faith can be found on Ravelry as DistractedKnits.

Pam Sluter

Pam is a knitting designer and teacher living in Rhode Island. She can be found on Ravelry as pamslu and on the web at *www.pamsluter designs.com*.

Anna Smegal

Anna learned the basics of knitting from her sister and then taught herself everything else from books. She teaches knitting classes in her community, enters projects at fairs, and never finishes knit gifts on time. Find Anna at *www.aersknits .wordpress.com* or on Ravlery as aersknits.

Jenny Snedeker

Jenny was taught to knit as a teenager and over the years has developed her knitting skills and taught herself design. Having worked exclusively with children's designs since 2009, she now enjoys designing for teens and adults. Because of a love of all things lacy, her main focus is on simple garments with a distinct feminine style.

Marcia J. Sommerkamp

Marcia has been working full time and commuting three hours daily, leaving little time for designing. But she did manage to keep Butterfly Hill in Waterford, Virginia, stocked with original pieces and to sell items in the Baker Block Museum's gift shop in Baker, Florida, and also online in the Facebook shop Camo Heaven and Friends — all while raising five rescue kittens!

Carol J. Sorsdahl

Carol learned to knit in the early 70s. She also enjoys quilting, reading, and playing music for church. Carol sold her baby's and children's sweaters for many years. Carol is published in *Machine Knitters Source*, *Woman's Day Quick and Easy Knitting and Crocheting*, *Creative Knitting*, *Cozy Winter Knits*, *Luxury Yarn One-Skein Wonders*, *Sock Yarn One-Skein Wonders*, and *Lace One-Skein Wonders*.

Stana D. Sortor

Stana's grandmother taught her how to knit and crochet when she was a little girl. Ever since then she's taken her projects everywhere. Of course she has experienced some sidesteps on her knitting path, like trying to be an artist, photographer, or writer, but she always returned to her favorite activity. Find Stana on her blog, Stana's Critters Etc., at *http://stana-critters-etc.blogspot.com*.

Myrna A. I. Stahman

Myrna, designer, author, and publisher of *Stahman's Shawls and Scarves: Faroese-Shaped Shawls from the Neck Down and Seamen's Scarves*, enjoys exploring the many facets of lace knitting and introducing others to those explorations through her teaching and publishing endeavors. Her explorations in circular flat lace knitting is the subject of her upcoming book.

Gwen Steege

A confirmed fiber fanatic since childhood, Gwen edits books on crochet, knitting, spinning, weaving, and dyeing, and has contributed designs to several books in the One-Skein Wonders series. She shares her passion for fiber in her book, *The Knitter's Life List* (Storey, 2011). She lives in Williamstown, Massachusetts.

Julia Swart

Julia has been knitting for more than 20 years and designing for five. She began designing for her children, but her designs have evolved to span many categories. Julia aspires to make simple stitches look complex and to make functional items fun.

Evelyn Uyemura

Evelyn began knitting in 2006, when her daughter left for college, and hasn't stopped since. When she's not knitting, she teaches English and ESL at a community college. She lives in southern California, but luckily has family in Chicago and her home-state of Maine, who love warm woolies.

René E. Wells

René's Grandma Kay taught her the joy of fiber when René was seven years old. Now she herself is a granny teaching private and small group classes. She is a member of TNNA, TKGA, and is published in *Luxury Yarn One-Skein Wonders*, *Sock Yarn One-Skein Wonders*, and *Crochet One-Skein Wonders*.

Kim Whelan

Kim lives in Berkley, Michigan, and is a married mother of three adult children. When not at work, she spends her time designing knitwear, planning knitting projects, talking about knitting, hanging out on Ravelry, and actually, maybe, knitting.

Lynn M. Wilson

Lynn is a designer, knitting instructor, and dedicated knitter. Her designs have been featured in many knitting books and magazines. She also designs for yarn companies and has her own collection of Lynn Wilson Designs knitting patterns. For more information, visit her website at *www.lwilsondesigns.com*.

Andrea Wong

Andrea was raised in South America. For 12 years Andrea has taught thousands of knitters to use the Portuguese style of knitting, either personally or through her publications. Andrea's experience allows her to transmit in-depth knowledge of this style into clear, concise instructions, making the technique attainable for any knitter who is interested in learning this effective method.

Glossary

Backward loop cast on. Hold the end of the yarn and a knitting needle in your right hand. Hold the working yarn in your left hand. Bring your left thumb over the top, down behind, and up in front of the yarn, creating a loop. Insert needle into loop on thumb as if to knit and slide loop onto needle. You may also use the backward loop cast on to add stitches to the end of a row of knitting or to increase stitches mid-row.

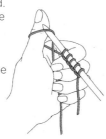

Cable cast on (knitwise). Make a slipknot and place it on your left-hand needle. *Note:* If you're casting on to add to already existing stitches, begin at Step 3.

1. Knit a stitch into the slip knot, leaving the slip knot on the needle.

2. Place the new stitch onto the left-hand needle by inserting the left-hand needle into the front of the new stitch.

3. Place the right-hand needle between the two stitches on the left-hand needle.

4. Knit a new stitch between the two stitches, pull it long, and place it on the left-hand needle.

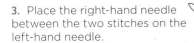

Continue in this manner, knitting between the last two stitches on the first needle, until you have the required number of stitches.

Cable cast-on (purlwise). Work as for cable cast on (knitwise) but purl the stitches instead of knitting them.

Chain (crochet). Begin with a slip knot on the hook. Wrap yarn over the hook and pull the loop through the slip knot. Yarn over hook, and pull loop through loop on hook to make second chain. Repeat for the required number of chain stitches.

Circular cast on (cast on and divide). Using double-point needles, cast on the desired number of stitches and slip half of the stitches to a second needle. Join into a round and knit the stitches evenly onto three or four needles.

Circular cast on (crochet). This cast on can be used for both crocheted and knitted items.

1. Leaving a 4"/10 cm tail, wrap the ball of yarn twice loosely around your thumb. Remove the loop from your thumb and work single crochet into the loop for the desired number of stitches.

2. Distribute the stitches evenly onto three or four double-point needles (figure 1).

3. Pull up on the tail to snug the stitches into a tight ring (figure 2).

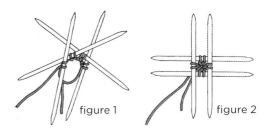

figure 1   figure 2

Duplicate stitch.

1. Thread contrasting yarn onto yarn needle. Bring yarn from back to front at the base of the stitch to be covered, below the V.

2. Pass the needle from right to left under both loops of the stitch in the row above the stitch to be covered and pull the yarn through.

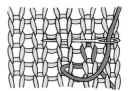

3. Bring the yarn from front to back through the original exit point.

4. Bring the yarn from back to front at the base of the next stitch to be covered and repeat Steps 2 and 3.

Figure-8 cast on.

1. Hold two double-point needles parallel. Leaving about a 4"/10 cm tail, and holding the tail against the needles with your left hand, *bring the yarn over the top needle from front to back, then bring the yarn between the needles and under the bottom needle from front to back. Repeat from * until you have the desired number of stitches, with the same number on each needle.

2. With a third needle, knit the stitches from the top needle. Turn the work 180 degrees and, with another needle, knit the stitches from the bottom needle.

French Knot. With yarn threaded on a yarn needle, bring yarn from wrong side to right side where you want your knot to be. With the tip of the needle close to where the yarn exits the fabric, wrap the yarn around the needle twice (figure 1).

Hold the yarn so the wrap stays on the needle and insert the needle close to where it originally exited but not in the exact same spot. Pull yarn through to the wrong side to make the knot (figure 2).

figure 1   figure 2

Garter stitch. When knitting back and forth in rows, knit all rows. When knitting circularly, knit 1 row, purl 1 row.

I-cord. Use two double-point needles to make I-cord. Cast on the required number of stitches. *Knit all stitches. Without turning work, slide the stitches to the other end of the needle. Pull the working yarn across the back. Repeat from * until cord is desired length. Bind off.

I-cord bind off. At the beginning of the bind-off row and using the knitted cast on (see page 279), cast on required number of stitches onto the left needle (the needle that is holding the edge stitches). *Knit to last cast-on stitch, ssk; without turning, slip all worked stitches to left needle; repeat from * until all edge stitches have been bound off. Bind off the I-cord stitches. If binding off a circular piece, cut the yarn, leaving a 6"/15 cm tail and use the tail to seam the two ends of the I-cord bind off together.

Jeny's Surprisingly Stretchy Bind Off.

1. Yarn over top of right-hand needle from back to front to back.

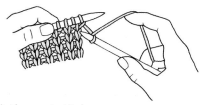

2. Knit the next stitch.

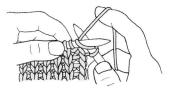

3. Pass the yarnover over the knit stitch.

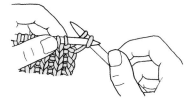

*Repeat Steps 1 through 3, then pass the pass the right stitch over the left stitch and off the right-hand needle. Repeat from * until all stitches are bound off, cutting the yarn and pulling it through the last stitch.

Judy's Magic Cast On.

1. Hold two double-point needles or two circular needles together with your right hand, tips pointing left.

2. Loop the yarn around the top needle, with the tail sandwiched between the top needle and the bottom needle. The tail should hang down between the needles and should be long enough to make the number of stitches you are casting on (figure 1).

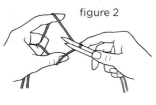

figure 1

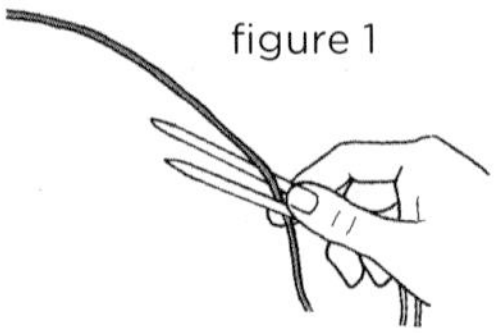

3. With your left hand, pick up the yarns in the slingshot position, with the tail over your index finger and the working yarn over your thumb. The yarn tail should be positioned to the right of the working yarn underneath the needle. This twists the yarns and creates a loop on the top needle that counts as the first stitch (figure 2).

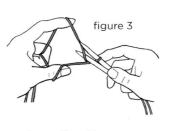

figure 2

4. While holding the first stitch in place with your right index finger, rotate the pair of needles up to the 10 o'clock position and wrap the yarn on your finger around the bottom needle, as if making a yarn-over. Gently tighten the loop (figure 3).

figure 3

5. Rotate the pair of needles down to the 8 o'clock position and wrap the yarn on your thumb around the top needle as if making a yarnover (figure 4). Gently tighten the loop.

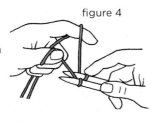

figure 4

6. Repeat steps 4 and 5 to cast on the desired number of stitches. Alternate between top and bottom needles, with thumb yarn wrapping around the top needle and finger yarn wrapping around the bottom needle. End with step 4.

7. Rotate the pair of needles 180 degrees so that the needle tips are facing left; the bottom needle has become the top needle and the yarn ends on the right. Drop the tail and bring the working yarn up behind the top needle ready to knit. Make sure the tail lies under the working yarn, between the working yarn and the needle. This twists the yarns so you can knit the first stitch (figure 5). Figure 5 shows the correct yarn orientation on the wrong side.

figure 5

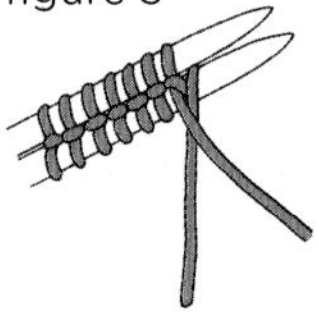

Knit the stitches on the top needle. The first stitch may become a little loose; just pull on the tail to tighten it.

8. Rotate needles 180 degrees. Knit the stitches on the top needle (the second half of the first round). See figure 6.

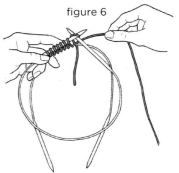

figure 6

Kitchener stitch. This grafting technique is used to join two sets of live stitches invisibly. It is most often used for sock toes but can be used to join shoulder seams or two halves of a scarf. These instructions are for joining stockinette stitches.

1. Place the two sets of live stitches to be bound off on separate needles. Hold the needles parallel in your left hand with wrong sides of the knitted fabric together. Thread yarn tail onto a yarn needle and set up by passing through the first stitch on the front needle as if to purl and leaving it on the needle, then pass through the first stitch on the back needle as if to knit and leave it on the needle.

2. Insert the yarn needle into the first stitch on the front needle as if to knit, and slip the stitch off the needle. Then insert the yarn needle into the next stitch on the front needle as if to purl, and leave the stitch on the needle.

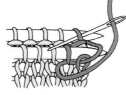

3. Insert the yarn needle into the first stitch on the back needle as if to purl, and slip the stitch off the needle.

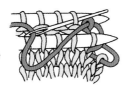

4. Insert the yarn needle into the next stitch on the back needle as if to knit, and leave the stitch on the needle.

Repeat steps 2–4 until all stitches have been joined.

Knit the knits and purl the purls. This means to work the stitches as they appear on the needle. If the next stitch is a knit stitch, that is, with a smooth V below the loop, knit the stitch. If the next stitch is a purl stitch with a bump below the loop, purl the stitch.

Knitted-on cast on. Make a slipknot and place it on your left-hand needle.

1. Knit a stitch into the slipknot, leaving the slipknit on the needle.

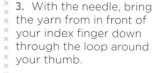

2. Place the new stitch onto the left-hand needle by inserting the left-hand needle into the front of the new stitch.

3. Tighten the stitch and continue until you have the required number of stitches.

Knitwise. When a pattern says "slip the next stitch knitwise," insert your needle into the next stitch on the left-hand needle from front to back as if you were going to knit it, then slip it to the right-hand needle without knitting it.

Long-tail cast on. Leaving a tail long enough to cast on the desired number of stitches (a generous guess would be 1"/2.5 cm per stitch), make a slip knot and place it on the needle.

1. Wrap one of the tails around your thumb and the other around your index finger. Hold the tails with your other three fingers.

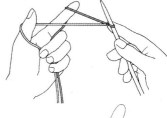

2. Insert the needle into the loop around your thumb from front to back and over the yarn around your index finger.

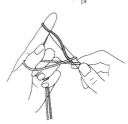

3. With the needle, bring the yarn from in front of your index finger down through the loop around your thumb.

4. Drop the loop off your thumb, tighten the stitch, and form a new loop around your thumb.

M1 (make 1) increase. This increase is worked into the strand between the current stitch and the next one. Work in pattern to where you want to increase, lift the strand between the two needles, place the lifted strand on the left-hand needle as shown below, then knit or purl the stitch as shown on the next page.

M1L (left slant, knit). Insert the left-hand needle from front to back, knit through the back.

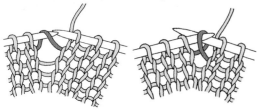

M1R (right slant, knit). Insert the left-hand needle from back to front, knit through the front.

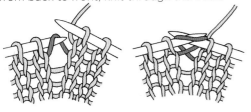

M1LP (left slant, purl). Insert the left-hand needle from front to back, purl through the back.

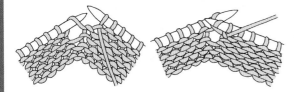

M1RP (right slant, purl). Insert the left-hand needle from back to front, purl through the front.

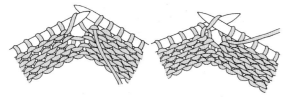

Magic loop. Using a circular needle at least 32"/80 cm long, cast on the required number of stitches and slide them onto the cable. Pull a loop of cable out between the two center cast-on stitches. Keep pulling the cable out between the stitches

until the stitches are moved onto the needle tips, half the stitches on each tip.

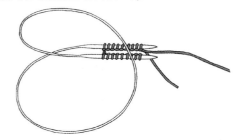

Hold the needle tips parallel and make sure the working yarn is on the back needle tip — if it's not on the back needle, slide the stitches back to the cable and start again, making sure the yarn ends up on the back needle tip. Now slide the stitches on the back needle tip down onto the cable and use the back needle tip as your working (right-hand) needle to knit the stitches from the other (left-hand) needle tip.

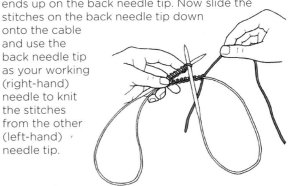

You've just knit half the round. Turn the work and hold the needles with both tips facing to the right and slide the unknit stitches onto the free needle tip and then slide the stitches that you just knit onto the cable. Now use the free needle tip as your right-hand needle to knit the second half of the round. Continue in this manner, rearranging the stitches after completing each half-round.

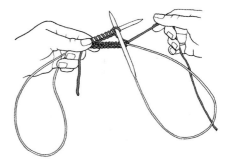

Mattress stitch. For a half-stitch seam allowance, work through the horizontal bar at the base of the stitches in every other row (figure 1).

For a full-stitch seam allowance, work through two horizontal bars on either side of the stitches (figure 2).

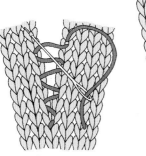 

figure 1   figure 2

One-row buttonhole. Yarnover, slip 1 purlwise with yarn in front, *slip 1 purlwise with yarn in back, pass rightmost slipped stitch over next slipped stitch as if to bind off; repeat from * until desired number of stitches have been bound off. Slip remaining stitch on right-hand needle back to left-hand needle; turn. Using the cable method, cast on the number of stitches bound off plus 1; turn. Slip 1 purlwise, pass 2nd stitch on right-hand needle over stitch just slipped.

Pick up and knit. With right side facing, insert the needle under both strands of the edge stitch, then wrap the yarn around the needle and knit the picked-up stitch.

Picot bind off. Using the cable method, *cast on 2 stitches; bind off 4 stitches; slip 1 from right needle back to left; repeat from * until all stitches have been bound off.

Provisional cast on (crochet chain).

1. Make a crochet chain with scrap yarn that is at least 6 chains longer than the number of stitches to be cast on.

2. Cast on by knitting with the project yarn into the back loops of the chain.

3. To remove the scrap yarn when you've finished the knitting, pull out the crocheted chain and carefully place the live stitches on a needle.

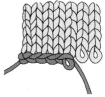

Provisional cast on (crochet over needle).

1. Make a slip knot and place it on a crochet hook. Hold your knitting needle on top of a long strand of yarn.

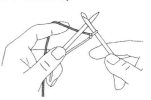

2. * With the crochet hook, draw the yarn over the needle and through the loop on the hook. To cast on another stitch, bring yarn behind knitting needle into position as for step 1, and repeat from *. *Note:* If you find it awkward to cast on the first couple of stitches, work a few crochet chain stitches before casting onto the needle so you have something to hold on to.

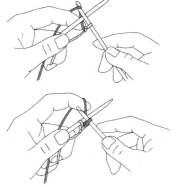

3. When the last stitch has been cast on, work 2 or 3 extra crochet chain stitches without taking the yarn around the knitting needle, then cut the yarn, leaving a 10"/25.5 cm tail, draw the tail through the last loop on the hook, and pull the tail to close the loop loosely — just enough so the tail can't escape. To remove the scrap yarn when you've finished the knitting, pull the tail out of the last loop and gently tug on it to "unzip" the chain and carefully place the live stitches on a needle, holder, or separate length of scrap yarn as they are released.

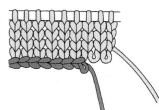

Purlwise. When a pattern says "slip the next stitch purlwise," insert your right-hand needle into the next stitch from back to front as if you were going to purl it, then slip it to the right-hand needle without purling it.

Satin stitch. With yarn threaded on a yarn needle, bring yarn from wrong side to right side at one edge of the shape you are stitching. Insert needle from front to back at opposite edge of the shape, then bring it from back to front along the design edge directly next to where the yarn originally exited. Continue in this manner until shape is covered with thread.

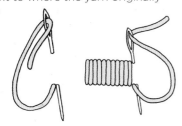

Single crochet. Insert hook into next stitch, wrap yarn over hook, and draw the loop through the stitch. You now have 2 loops on the hook. Yarn over hook and draw loop through both loops on hook.

Slip stitch (crochet). Insert hook into stitch or space indicated, yarn over and pull through all loops on hook.

Stockinette stitch. When knitting back and forth in rows, knit the right-side rows, purl the wrong-side rows. When knitting circularly, knit all rounds.

Tassel.

1. Cut a piece of cardboard about 4"/10 cm wide and a little longer than you want your tassel to be. Wrap the yarn lengthwise around the cardboard to desired thickness of tassel. Cut the yarn even with the bottom edge of the cardboard.

2. Cut a piece of yarn 24"/61 cm long. Fold the piece in half, insert it between the cardboard and the wrapped yarn, and slide it up to the top edge of the cardboard. With the edges even, tie the piece tightly around the wrapped yarn.

3. Cut through the wrapped yarn opposite the tie.

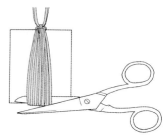

4. Cut a 12"/30.5 cm length of yarn and wrap it tightly around the tassel two or three times, about 1"/2.5 cm from the top. Tie it securely. Using a yarn needle, pull the ends through to the inside of the tassel so they hang down inside. Shake out the tassel and trim any uneven ends.

Three-needle bind off. This technique is used to join two sets of live stitches.

1. Place the two sets of stitches to be bound off on separate needles. Hold the needles parallel in your left hand with right sides of the knitted fabric touching.

2. Insert the tip of a third needle into the first stitch on both needles and knit these 2 stitches together.

3. Repeat step 2. *You now have* 2 stitches on the right-hand needle. With one of the needles in your left hand, lift the first stitch on the right-hand needle over the second and off the needle as for a regular bind off. Repeat until all stitches are bound off.

Whipstitch. Holding the two pieces to be joined together, insert needle from back to front through one stitch on each piece; repeat until the pieces are joined.

WT (wrap and turn). Work number of stitches specified. Bring yarn forward and slip next stitch purlwise. Bring yarn back and return stitch to left needle. Turn the work.

Page numbers in *italic* indicate illustrations.

Welcome to the World of One-Skein Wonders

Judith Durant's best-selling One-Skein Wonders books each come with 101 unique projects for using those spare skeins — or giving you a reason to buy more! From scarves and shawls to home dec accessories and outfits for baby, there are so many fabulous projects in each book, you'll want to own them all!

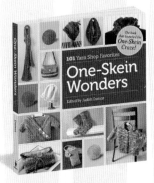

One-Skein Wonders
240 pages. Paper.
ISBN 978-1-58017-645-3.

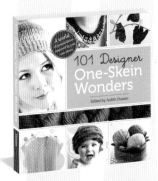

101 Designer One-Skein Wonders
256 pages. Paper.
ISBN 978-1-58017-688-0.

Sock Yarn One-Skein Wonders
288 pages. Paper.
ISBN 978-1-60342-579-7.

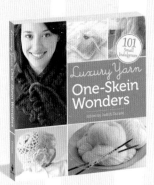

Luxury Yarn-One-Skein Wonders
272 pages. Paper.
ISBN 978-1-60342-079-2.

Lace One-Skein Wonders
304 pages. Paper.
ISBN 978-1-61212-058-4.

Crochet One-Skein Wonders
288 pages. Paper.
ISBN 978-1-61212-042-3.

These and other books from Storey Publishing are available
wherever quality books are sold or by calling 1-800-441-5700.
Visit us at www.storey.com or sign up for our newsletter
at *www.storey.com/signup*.